John Tilden Prince

Courses and Methods

A Handbook for Teachers of Primary, Grammar and Ungraded Schools

John Tilden Prince

Courses and Methods
A Handbook for Teachers of Primary, Grammar and Ungraded Schools

ISBN/EAN: 9783337779573

Printed in Europe, USA, Canada, Australia, Japan

Cover: Foto ©Thomas Meinert / pixelio.de

More available books at **www.hansebooks.com**

COURSES AND METHODS.

A HANDBOOK FOR TEACHERS

OF

PRIMARY, GRAMMAR, AND UNGRADED
SCHOOLS.

BY

JOHN T. PRINCE,

AGENT OF MASSACHUSETTS BOARD OF EDUCATION; FORMERLY
SUPERINTENDENT OF THE PUBLIC SCHOOLS OF
WALTHAM AND WATERTOWN, MASS.

————o○°♀°○o————

BOSTON:

GINN & COMPANY, PUBLISHERS.

1886.

PREFACE.

THIS book is not intended to be an exhaustive or philosophical treatise upon Education; nor does the author claim for the ideas advanced in it much that is new or original. It is written in response to a frequently expressed desire in various quarters for a brief plan of studies that may be pursued in elementary schools, and for a simple and direct statement of good methods of organization, teaching, and discipline. While the hints and suggestions are directed mainly to untrained and inexperienced teachers, it is hoped that they may commend themselves to the judgment of the best teachers, as being based upon correct principles of teaching.

A Course of Studies may be so general as to be of little direct use, or so definite as to apply to few schools. It has been the aim in preparing the courses here presented to avoid both extremes, with the understanding that they may be modified to suit existing conditions. The best Course that can be made is simply a guide for the teacher in pointing out what subjects are to be taught, the order in which subjects and parts of subjects are to be presented, and the approximate amount to be done in a given time. The best use of such a Course will be determined not so much by the rigidity with which it is followed as by the way it is interpreted and applied to the wants of the pupils. In other words, the subjects of study are of less consequence than the way in which they are taught. It is for this reason that comparatively little space has been given to the course or plan of studies and much to methods of teaching.

Nearly all of the topical outlines presented in Part II. have been tried in the schoolroom and found to be practical and helpful. A few of them were taken in the first instance from professional books and periodicals, with no thought of republication, and therefore their authorship was not preserved. So far as the authors are known, due credit has been given.

It should be said that while the suggestions given in Parts II. and III. are meant to apply to any Course of studies, the Course as here outlined should not be used alone. The bare outline of subjects as given in Part I. would be likely to be misunderstood and misapplied without the explanations given in Part II.

Teachers of each grade should familiarize themselves with the requirements and methods of all other grades, so as to know what has been, or what should have been, previously done, and also to know the kind of work for which they are to prepare their pupils.

J. T. P.

WALTHAM, MASS.,
  Nov. 1, 1886.

CONTENTS.

——◆——

I. COURSES OF STUDY.

II. METHODS OF TEACHING.

III. ORGANIZATION, MORAL TRAINING, AND GOVERNMENT.

1. ORGANIZATION.

Part I.

COURSE OF STUDIES FOR GRADED SCHOOLS.

————∘o˙ჟ˚o∘————

THE following course includes a plan of work for nine years, divided into periods of five months each. The work of the ninth year may, if it is desired, be incorporated into one of the courses of the high school, making the grammar school course complete at the close of the eighth year.

In addition to the subjects named, instruction in the following subjects is given throughout the entire course.

DRAWING, SINGING, MEMORY LESSONS, GENERAL INFORMATION LESSONS, PHYSIOLOGY AND HYGIENE.

For plan of work in these subjects, see Part II., where specific directions in reference to methods of teaching will be found. Attention is also given to MORALS AND MANNERS and to PHYSICAL CULTURE. For details in these important departments, see pages 321 and 283.

FIRST YEAR. FIRST HALF.

OBSERVATION LESSONS.

Color. — Differences and resemblances.
Form. — Differences and resemblances.
Size and Weight. — Relative.
Place. — Opposites; as, over, under; above, below; behind, before.
Qualities. — Most prominent; as, rough, smooth, hard, soft, heavy, light.
Plants. — Common flowers observed and compared.
Human Body. — Parts of body and movements.

LANGUAGE.

Talking. — Facts and stories in connection with observation and reading lessons.
Reading. — Words and sentences from blackboard, chart, and first pages of two First readers.
Writing. — Words and sentences from blackboard and from cards. Practice upon letter i with and without copy.

ARITHMETIC.

Develop numbers from 1 to 5. Count objects to 10.

FIRST YEAR. SECOND HALF.

OBSERVATION LESSONS.

Color. — Red, orange, yellow, green, blue, violet, gray, brown.

Form. — Spherical, cubical, and cylindrical bodies; points, lines, angles; moulding and drawing.

Size and Weight. — Relative.

Place. — Objects arranged from dictation; position, direction. Plan-drawing begun.

Human Body. — Parts of body and movements.

Plants. — Flower, leaf, stem; common plants observed and named.

Animals. — Most familiar animals compared.

LANGUAGE.

Reading. — Sentences from blackboard, chart, and several First readers.

Spelling. — Words from readers.

Talking and Writing. — Statements and stories in connection with reading and observation lessons. Copying from blackboard and from cards. Practice upon letters *i, u, w.*

ARITHMETIC.

Develop numbers to 10 by objects. Express by words and figures all combinations to 6 at sight. Counting objects to 50.

SECOND YEAR. FIRST HALF.

OBSERVATION LESSONS.

Color. — Shades and tints of common colors.

Form. — Surface, edge, corner, triangle. Design with splints, colored paper, etc.

Place. — Relative distance; also inch, foot, yard. Plans: top of desk, floor of schoolroom.

Qualities. — Tough, brittle, elastic, fragrant, opaque, transparent, porous, fluid, solid. Parts of objects; form of parts; uses.

Plants. — Parts of plant: root, stem, leaf, bud, flower. Names of common plants.

Human Body. — Organs of senses.

LANGUAGE.

Reading. — Easier pieces of two Second readers. Easy sight-reading from several First readers daily.

Spelling. — Words from readers. Oral and written.

Composition. — Oral and written statements and stories in connection with reading and observation lessons. Teach use of capitals, period, and question-mark.

Writing. — Copying from blackboard and cards. Writing from dictation. Practice upon letters

m,   *n,*   *x,*   *v.*

ARITHMETIC.

Combination with objects to 15; without objects to 10. Teach halves and fourths. Original problems with objects. Counting to 100. Expression by words and figures. Signs $+$, $-$, $\times$, $\div$ used.

SECOND YEAR. SECOND HALF.

OBSERVATION LESSONS.

Color. — Hues, tints, shades.

Form. — Prism, pyramid, cone, square, oblong; designs with splints, colored paper, etc.

Weight and Measure. — Pound, ounce, peck, gallon, quart, pint, gill.

Place. — Points of compass. Plan-drawing of school-room and yard.

Plants. — Parts and shape of leaf: blade, veins, margin; parts of flowers: petals, stamens, pistils; names of common plants and trees.

Animals. — Common birds and fowls. External parts observed and compared.

LANGUAGE.

Reading. — Second readers completed. Sight-reading from several First readers daily.

Spelling. — Words from readers. Oral and written.

Composition. — Punctuation and capital letters. Letter-writing. Stories from pictures. Statements and stories in connection with observation and reading lessons.

Writing. — Copying from card or blackboard. Writing from dictation. Copy-book practice. Special practice upon

o, e, c, t, h, k, l, b.

ARITHMETIC.

Operations to 25. Building of tables; teach thirds and sixths. Original problems, with and without objects.

Dozen, score, quire. Coins of United States. Writing of numbers to 100. Roman notation to XX.

THIRD YEAR. FIRST HALF.

OBSERVATION LESSONS.

Plants. — Growth from seed to fruit traced.

Color. — Complementary colors. Harmony of colors. Arrangement in designs.

Form. — Spheroid, circle, ellipse, oval. Invention and design.

Place. — Simple plans drawn to scale.

Human Body. — Parts of body. Movements. Uses of parts. Health of parts.

Home Geography. — Observation of neighborhood. Plans drawn and moulded. Land surface. Water surface. Give geographical names.

LANGUAGE.

Reading. — Easier pieces of two Third readers. Sight-reading daily from several Second readers.

Spelling. — Writing of words and sentences selected from the readers.

Composition. — Statements and stories in connection with observation and reading lessons. Letter-writing.

Writing. — Copying from blackboard, cards, and readers. Writing from dictation. Practice upon

a, d, A, N, M, T, F.

Copy-book practice.

ARITHMETIC.

Operations to 50, in addition, subtraction, multiplication, and division. Teach eighths. Reading and writing of numbers to 1000. Roman notation to L. Building of tables, including common weights and measures. Original problems involved in common transactions and making change.

THIRD YEAR. SECOND HALF.

OBSERVATION LESSONS.

Color. — Continuation of work of First Half. Review.

Form. — Systematic review of entire work.

Human Body. — Continuation of work of First Half.

Animals. — Common birds and insects. Parts and habits observed and compared.

Home Geography. — Teach geographical ideas based upon observation, using geographical language: bodies of land; bodies of water; projections of land and water; climate (weather); soil; productions; drawing and moulding of neighborhood and town.

LANGUAGE.

Reading. — Selection from two Third readers. Easy sight-reading daily.

Spelling. — Writing of words and sentences dictated from readers and from other sources.

Composition. — Statements and stories in connection with observation and reading lessons, and pictures. Letter-writing.

Writing. — Copying and writing from dictation. Copy-book practice.

Practice upon

q, z, j, y, g, A, A, P, B, R.

ARITHMETIC.

Operations to 144, in addition, subtraction, multiplication, and division. Ninths, twelfths. Reading and writing of numbers to 100,000. Roman notation to M. Original problems involved in doing errands at a store. Rapid and accurate adding of columns of two figures.

———◆———

FOURTH YEAR. FIRST HALF.

OBSERVATION LESSONS.

Plants. — Name and description of parts of a plant, of a leaf, of a flower.

Animals. — Sponge and coral examined. Star-fish and sea-urchin examined and compared.

LANGUAGE.

Reading. — Prescribed reader for study. Easy sight-reading daily.

Spelling. — Writing of words and sentences from spelling-book and from other sources.

Composition. — Statements in connection with observation lessons. Abstracts from memory. Stories from pictures. Letter-writing.

Writing. — Copying and writing from dictation. Copy-book practice.

Single-letter practice upon

$\mathscr{S}, \quad \mathscr{L}, \quad \mathscr{h}, \quad \mathscr{f}, \quad \iota, \quad \jmath, \quad \mathscr{G}, \quad \mathscr{Q}, \quad \mathscr{J}.$

ARITHMETIC.

Operations to 10,000, in addition and subtraction. Tenths and hundredths written decimally. Oral exercises daily, involving yards, feet, inches, gallons, quarts, pints.

GEOGRAPHY.

Preparatory work reviewed and continued. People (races, occupations, settlements, government, religion, states of society). Study of maps of known places (scale, natural features, etc.).

———◆———

FOURTH YEAR. SECOND HALF.

OBSERVATION LESSONS.

Plants. — Work of First Half continued.

Animals. — Oyster, clam, and snail examined and compared. Lobster and crab examined and compared.

LANGUAGE.

Reading. — Prescribed reader for study. Easy sight-reading daily.

Spelling. — Writing of words and sentences from spelling-book and from other sources.

Composition. — Same as First Half.
Writing. — Copying and writing from dictation. Copy-book practice.
Single-letter practice upon

O, L, E, L, U, V,
W, X, Y, Z, Q.

ARITHMETIC.

Operations to 10,000, in multiplication and division. Writing and reading whole numbers. Teach by objects to add and subtract easy fractions in halves, fourths, and eighths. Notation in United States money.

Oral exercises daily, involving yards, feet, inches, gallons, quarts, pints, bushels, pecks, dozen, quire.

GEOGRAPHY.

Earth as a whole: form and motions of the earth; hemispheres; bodies of land; bodies of water; climate; productions; commerce.

FIFTH YEAR. FIRST HALF.

OBSERVATION LESSONS.

Plants. — History of plant life. Embryo, growth, bud.
Animals. — Spider, daddy-long-legs; grasshopper, dragon-fly; squash-bug, beetle; examined and compared.

LANGUAGE.

Reading. — Prescribed reader for study. Easy sight-reading daily.

Spelling. — Writing of words and sentences from spelling-book and from other sources.

Composition. — Statements and compositions in connection with the observation, reading and information lessons. Abstracts from memory. Dictation exercises. Stories from pictures. Letter-writing.

Writing. — Copying and writing from dictation. Copy-book practice.

ARITHMETIC.

Operations in whole numbers to millions, involving common weights and measures. Addition and subtraction of fractions, both common and decimal, to twelfths and thousandths. Oral exercises, abstract and concrete.

GEOGRAPHY.

Study of North and South America by topics. Map-drawing by tracing.

FIFTH YEAR. SECOND HALF.

OBSERVATION LESSONS.

Plants. — History of plant life. Flowers, fruit, seeds.

Animals. — Flies, butterflies, and moths; ants, wasps, and bees; examined and compared.

LANGUAGE.

Reading. — Prescribed reader for study. Easy sight-reading daily.

Spelling. — Writing of words and sentences from spelling-book and from other sources.

Composition. — Work of First Half continued.

Writing. — Copying and writing from dictation. Copy-book practice.

ARITHMETIC.

Multiplication and division of fractions, both common and decimal, to twelfths and thousandths. Operations involving use of United States money and common weights and measures.

Oral exercises with abstract and concrete numbers.

GEOGRAPHY.

Study of Europe, Asia, Africa, and Australia by topics.

Map-drawing by tracing.

———◆———

SIXTH YEAR. FIRST HALF.

OBSERVATION LESSONS.

Plants. — Differences in stems, roots, leaves.

Minerals. — Common minerals compared and named. Compared with reference to hardness, color, form, structure, lustre.

LANGUAGE.

Reading. — Prescribed reader for study. Easy sight-reading daily.

Spelling. — Writing of words and sentences from spelling-book and from other sources.

Composition. — Statements and compositions in connection with the observation, reading, and information lessons. Abstracts from memory. Dictation exercises. Stories from pictures. Letter-writing.

Writing. — Copy-book practice.

ARITHMETIC.

Factors and multiples. Addition and subtraction of common and decimal fractions. Oral exercises involving common weights and measures.

GEOGRAPHY.

Study of countries and sections by topics: United States, Mexico, West Indies, British America, Brazil. Map-drawing.

Earth as a whole: mathematical and physical features.

———◆———

SIXTH YEAR. SECOND HALF.

OBSERVATION LESSONS.

Plants. — Differences in flowers, fruits, and seeds.

Minerals. — Work of First Half continued.

LANGUAGE.

Reading. — Prescribed reader for study. Easy sight-reading daily.

Spelling. — Writing of words and sentences from spelling-book and from other sources.

Composition. — Work of First Half continued.

Writing. — Copy-book practice.

ARITHMETIC.

Multiplication and division of fractions, common and decimal.

Oral exercises involving common weights and measures.

GEOGRAPHY.

Study of countries and sections by topics: British Empire, France, Germany, Russian Empire; also State and section in which pupils live. Map-drawing.

Mathematical and physical features of the earth as a whole.

———◆———

SEVENTH YEAR. FIRST HALF.

OBSERVATION LESSONS.

Plants. — Differences in habits. Many kinds of shrubs and trees compared and named.

Animals. — Marked and essential characteristics of fishes; frogs and toads; reptiles; birds; mammals. As many of each examined as practicable.

LANGUAGE.

Reading. — Prescribed reader for study. Easy sight-reading daily.

Spelling. — Writing of words and sentences from spelling-book and from other sources.

Composition. — Original compositions. Abstracts from memory. Paraphrasing. Letter-writing. Correction of false syntax. Business forms.

Writing. — Copy-book practice.

ARITHMETIC.

Compound numbers, including all practical operations in long, square, and cubic measures, avoirdupois weight.

GEOGRAPHY.

Important features of the countries of Asia and Africa. Mathematical and physical features of the earth as a whole.

SEVENTH YEAR. SECOND HALF.

OBSERVATION LESSONS.

Plants. — Composition and uses of different parts of plants.

Animals. — Varieties of mammals, as flesh-eaters, gnawers, cud-chewers, etc.; also of birds, as climbers, birds of prey, swimmers, etc.; described and compared.

LANGUAGE.

Reading. — Prescribed reader for study. Easy sight-reading daily.

Spelling. — Writing of words and sentences from spelling-book and from other sources.

Composition. — Work of First Half continued.

ARITHMETIC.

Compound numbers, including metric system and all practical operations in all the weights and measures. Percentage. Simple interest.

GEOGRAPHY.

Important features of sections of Africa, Australia, Islands of Pacific. Also State and section in which pupils live. Mathematical and physical features of the earth as a whole.

EIGHTH YEAR. FIRST HALF.

OBSERVATION LESSONS.

Plants. — Forest trees named and compared with reference to size, stem, bark, leaves, fruit, wood.

Minerals. — Teach to distinguish quartz, mica, feldspar, granite, galena, pyrite, halite.

LANGUAGE.

Reading. — Prescribed reader for study. Easy sight-reading daily.

Spelling. — Writing of words from spelling-book and from other sources.

Composition. — Exercises three times a week upon work indicated for the seventh year.

Grammar. — Sentence, subject, and predicate. Parts of speech.

Writing. — Copy-book practice.

ARITHMETIC.

Percentage, including commission and brokerage, insurance, taxes, duties. Oral exercises daily.

GEOGRAPHY.

Three exercises a week upon countries and sections of Western Hemisphere by topics.

HISTORY.

Connected reading of American history up to the time of the Revolutionary War. Recitation by topics.

EIGHTH YEAR. SECOND HALF.

OBSERVATION LESSONS.

Plants. — Work of First Half continued. Grains recognized; parts compared.

Minerals. — Teach to distinguish fluorite, corundum, magnetite, asbestos, hornblende, garnet, tourmaline, talc, serpentine, gypsum, calcite.

LANGUAGE.

Reading. — Prescribed reader for study. Easy sight-reading daily.

Spelling. — Writing of words from spelling-book and from other sources.

Composition. — Work of First Half continued.

Grammar. — Adjective, objective, and adverbial elements; kinds and properties of noun, pronoun, verb, adjective, adverb, preposition, conjunction.

Writing. — Copy-book practice.

ARITHMETIC.

Interest, problems in interest, discount, notes, partial payments, banking. Oral exercises daily.

GEOGRAPHY.

Three exercises a week upon countries and sections of Eastern Hemisphere by topics.

HISTORY.

Connected reading of American history from the beginning of the Revolutionary War up to the present time. Recitation by topics.

NINTH YEAR. FIRST HALF.

OBSERVATION LESSONS.

Physics. — Teach matter, body, substance, extension, volume, impenetrability, mobility, divisibility, porosity, compressibility, density, expansibility, elasticity, resistance (inertia, friction), velocity, momentum, energy, effect of several forces acting together, cohesion, adhesion.

Astronomy. — Form and motions of the earth.

Sun : Effects, composition, comparative size, spots, eclipses.

Moon : Light, phases, eclipses.

LANGUAGE.

Reading. — English history and works of standard authors.

Spelling. — Written reviews twice a week.

Composition. — Exercises twice a week upon work indicated for Seventh Year. Essays monthly.

Grammar. — Analysis continued; words, phrases, clauses, complex and compound sentences; rules of construction taught and applied in parsing and in correction of sentences.

ARITHMETIC.

Ratio and proportion, square and cube root, and their application in mensuration of land, lumber, etc. Oral exercises daily.

BOOK-KEEPING.

Simple forms of accounts.

GEOGRAPHY.

General review once a week by topics.

HISTORY.

Work of Eighth Year reviewed.

NINTH YEAR. SECOND HALF.

OBSERVATION LESSONS.

Physics. — Application, by experiments, of facts learned during First Half, as balance, steelyard, pop-gun, lifting-pump, forcing-pump, barometer.

Astronomy. — *Planets:* Appearance, movements, names, relative size, length of year, moons and rings, phases, conjunction.

Fixed Stars : Appearance, distance, stars of first magnitude observed and named, constellations observed and named.

LANGUAGE.

Reading. — Work of First Half continued.

Spelling. — Work of First Half continued.

Composition. — Work of First Half continued.

Grammar. — Parsing and analysis ; constant application of rules of syntax in writing and correcting.

ARITHMETIC.

General review, involving definitions, formulas, and principles. Practical business problems and short processes. Oral exercises daily.

BOOK-KEEPING.

Simple forms of accounts.

GEOGRAPHY.

General review once a week by topics.

HISTORY.

General topical review by subjects.

COURSE OF STUDIES FOR UNGRADED SCHOOLS.

———oo̤o̤oo———

INTRODUCTORY NOTE.

THE subjects to be taught are arranged in three groups, each group covering the work of three years. The work as here laid down is not intended to mean that the school should be divided into three classes and that each class should take the subjects indicated. The outline is given in three groups so as to indicate in a general way what ground should be gone over in a given time. For hints upon classification, see Classification and Teaching of Ungraded Schools, page 309.

———◆———

FIRST PERIOD (THREE YEARS).

Reading and Spelling.

Reading from blackboard, chart, and several First and Second readers. At end of Period to be able to read at sight and with good expression any ordinary Second reader. Vocal drill. Use of words in original sentences. Oral and written spelling of all common words of readers.

Writing.

Short, easy words in the beginning, and sentences as soon as possible. Use ruled or spaced lines. During first half of Period, provide copies; during last half, let the pupils write without copies. Practise with and without copy upon the following letters in the order given : —

i, u, w, n, m, x, v, o, e, c, t, a,

d, l, b, h, k, A, N, M, T, F,

g, j, y, q, z, H, K, P, B, R.

Arithmetic.

Accurate and rapid combinations and separations up to 100, carrying on the four fundamental rules together. Use objects up to 20. Children to make their own tables. Common store problems to be practised upon, using ordinary weights and measures. Teach halves, fourths, eighths, also pointing off for dollars, cents, and mills.

Language.

Daily practice in one or more of the following exercises : copying sentences from cards or blackboard; talking and writing after information and object lessons; oral and written abstracts after reading; writing gems from memory; literal descriptions of, and imaginary stories from, pictures; writing of letters.

Observation Lessons.

At least one lesson of fifteen minutes daily upon some one of the following subjects: form, distance, direction, color, human body, plants, animals, rocks.

Home geography and plan-drawing.

Miscellaneous.

Drawing of leaves and other objects. Copying from drawing-cards.

Singing by rote simple songs.

Memorizing gems, from five to ten lines weekly.

Information lessons.

SECOND PERIOD (THREE YEARS).

Reading.

Several third and fourth readers. Frequent practice in sight-reading. Vocal drill. New words in original sentences.

Spelling.

Chiefly written. Half of the time from spelling-book, other half from readers, geographies, written papers, etc.

Writing.

Practice upon single letters continued in following order: —

p, f, i, s, S, L, G, I, J, V,

Q, G, V, U, Y, W, O, C, E, D.

Three copy-books with pen and ink. Penmanship to be considered in language and other written exercises.

Arithmetic.

Four fundamental rules to 1000, and afterwards to higher numbers; also tenths, hundredths, and thousandths. Applications in United States money, weights, and measures. Fractions, such as are involved in ordinary business, adding, subtracting, multiplying, and dividing. Daily exercises in mental problems. Short processes in practical problems.

Geography.

Home geography reviewed. Plan-drawing of neighborhood. General study of earth and continents from globe. United States, British Empire, France, Russia, Germany, Spain, Mexico, New England States, Massachusetts. Study and recite by topics. Map-drawing. Voyages and travels.

Language.

Same kind of exercises as given in First Period, only more complex. Correction of false syntax.

Observation Lessons.

From May to November: natural history, plants, trees, flowers. From November to May: rocks and animals; common phenomena: dew, rain, snow, etc.

Miscellaneous.

In DRAWING, SINGING, MEMORY LESSONS, INFORMATION LESSONS, MORALS, and MANNERS, select from outlines given in graded course.

Reading.

Several advanced Fourth and Fifth readers or their equivalent. Easy sight-reading of histories and geographical readers. Vocal drill. Use of new and difficult words in sentences. Definitions and synonyms. Use of dictionary in defining and pronouncing.

Spelling.

Writing of words and sentences from spelling-book. Half the time should be given to words selected from the reader, written examinations and other papers.

Writing.

Three copy-books. Blank books for practice and for copying topics and pieces of poetry. All written work to be carefully written.

Arithmetic.

Fractions, common and decimal. Weights and measures. Mensuration. Percentage, including interest, insurance, profit and loss, discount and all ordinary business problems. Mental work daily, with explanations. Book-keeping in simple forms of accounts.

Language and Grammar.

Language work of previous Periods continued. Part of the time during latter half of Period to be given to the study of grammar and analysis. Correction of false syntax, with rules for correction. Composition-writing.

Observation Lessons.

Lessons of Second Period continued, one hour a week. Also elementary lessons in physics.

Geography.

Effects of motions of the earth. Latitude, longitude, climate, zones, winds (kinds and cause). Formation of land surface. Topical study and map-drawing of countries not previously studied. Latter part of period given to reviews. Books of travel to be read.

History.

Easy books of history and biography to be read at sight and talked about. Topical study with regular text-book during latter part of period.

Miscellaneous.

In DRAWING, SINGING, MEMORY LESSONS, PHYSIOL- OGY and HYGIENE, and INFORMATION LESSONS, select from work given in Part II.

PART II.

METHODS OF TEACHING.

----◦○⦂●⦂○◦----

IMPORTANCE OF METHOD.

THE importance of method in all kinds of skilled work has always and everywhere been recognized. The artist and the skilled artisan know that patient study and labor are necessary to the best success, and they are willing to spend years in acquiring their art. On the other hand, there are some kinds of work, like shovelling sand or turning a grindstone, which place method in a relatively subordinate position. On which side shall we place teaching — on the side of skilled or unskilled work? Is teaching an art which requires thought, purpose, and method, or does it belong to that other kind of work which requires little or no method?

In determining the place and character of teaching, we should not regard instruction as the whole of education, nor should we be misled by the practice of some teachers whose teaching consists of assigning and hearing lessons from a book. We should think of the teacher not simply as a purveyor of facts, but as a moulder of the human mind. If we think of him in this way, his work is exalted in our estimation and

placed where it should be — alongside of that other
work whose object is the cure of disease and the promotion of bodily health. ‹ Thus the work of the teacher,
like that of the physician, becomes a profession in which
there are clearly defined methods based upon laws and
principles.

But why, it may be asked, should there be any more
care and solicitude in feeding and training the mind
than in feeding and training the body? For very obvious
reasons. In the first place, however important it is to
have a sound body, it is still more important to have a
sound mind. Moreover, it is far easier to keep the body
in health and vigor than to build up the mind com-
pletely, and to keep it in a condition to do all that it is
capable of doing. While the laws of both body and
mind are fixed and constant in their operation, the laws
of the mind are more obscure and more difficult to understand than are those of the body. Unlike the body,
the mind does not hang out its danger-signals of aches
and distortions when food of an improper kind is given
or when there is improper training. It is for this reason,
and also because they are hidden from sight, that weakness and deformity of the mind are not guarded against
as are weakness and deformity of the body, although the
former are quite as common as the latter and far
more deplorable. Repugnance to study, want of application, idleness, defective observation and memory, unre-
liable judgment and reasoning, and moral turpitude, all
may result, in part at least, from wrong methods or no
methods of teaching and affect the whole future life of
the boy or girl. The best safeguard against these de-
fects is a good school, taught by a teacher who un-

derstands and perseveringly follows right methods of
teaching. How shall we determine what methods are
right and what methods are wrong?

———◆———

OBJECTS OF EDUCATION.

To know the means of doing anything, it is all important that we should have a clear idea of what we
desire to accomplish. One of the chief causes of defective methods of teaching is want of purpose on the
part of teachers. Without purpose there can be no
definite plan, and without plan there will be mistakes
and wasted energy. Our first question should be, there-
✓ fore, What is the end or use of education? "To prepare us for complete living," Spencer says, "is the
function of education." No one is likely to find fault
with such a statement, especially if the highest and
best service to others is regarded as an essential element of complete living. Assuming this to be the end
of education, let us see what objects of school education are to be sought by the teacher.

⟍ The conditions of the highest and best service to
others are a sound body and a well-informed mind.
Bodily health should be promoted both directly and
indirectly in the school. Physical exercises of the right
kind and amount should be practised. habits of regularity should be formed, and the business of the school
should be so regulated as to prevent over-work and
over-worry on the part of the pupils. Moreover, thorough instruction should be given in physiology and
hygiene, that the pupils may know the importance of

keeping the body in health and that they may know
how it can be done.

The second condition of the highest and best service to others, is a well-informed mind. What is
meant by a " well-informed mind"? If it is simply
a mind possessed of knowledge or facts, there would
be little need of carrying school studies beyond the
rudiments, for books and lectures could do the rest.
Or, if it were thought best to carry on such an education in the schools, books could be placed before the
children to be memorized and recited, — a practice which
can hardly be called teaching, although it passes for
such in some schools at the present day. The possession of facts, even though they are gained in this way,
may be useful, but unless more has been done for the
child than this, or rather unless he has done more for
himself than this, he cannot be said to be properly educated. The life which awaits him as a worker in some
useful occupation, as a citizen and as a man, needs a
well-developed mind, which he does not possess. His
active powers, both of intellect and will, have not been
strengthened by exercise. He has not formed the habit
of concentration or prolonged attention; his powers of
observation and of reasoning are defective; what he
has acquired does not lie in his mind in an orderly way
so as to be ready for use; and most of all, his moral
nature has not been so trained as to enable him to control his acts, both in refraining from evil and in doing
good to others.

1.   The first object of education, so far as the mind
is concerned, is knowledge. What is knowledge? If a
rubber ball is placed before a child, certain ideas are

formed in his mind, in agreement or disagreement with ideas previously formed. Ideas of color, form, hardness, etc., are thus formed; and if names are applied to them, he says that the ball is white, round, and hard. This constitutes his knowledge of the ball. If the child had never seen a ball, or if he had never seen anything white or felt anything round or hard, no ideas of whiteness or roundness or hardness could have been formed in his mind by simply telling him that the ball was white and round and hard.

Words, then, are not knowledge, nor do they convey knowledge of material things to any one, unless the words are associated with ideas that have been previously formed by the aid of the senses. The same principle is true of acts of the mind, which we may also call objects of thought. If, for example, we say "we form judgments," no idea of that act would be formed by any one who has not observed such an act in himself. In seeking knowledge, therefore, and in instructing others, we must not make the mistake of supposing that knowledge can be gained from words only or that memorizing the product of other people's thinking is thinking itself. To lead pupils to think for themselves and to acquire knowledge, objects of thought should be so presented as to lead them to know the objects themselves by recognizing their resemblances and differences and by perceiving the relations which their parts have to one another.

2. The amount of knowledge which the young graduate of the school or college has is very small. He may be able to tell much of what others know, and this may be of use to him, but what he really has as the

result of his own thinking, or what he has that will stay by him for any length of time, is comparatively little. What he most relies upon for assistance in the duties of life is his well trained powers of mind. If his memory only is trained, he has but little to aid him; but if his powers of observation, attention, judgment, and reasoning have been strengthened by orderly exercise, he has in his developed powers constant assistance in whatever he undertakes. Indeed, the difference between an educated and an uneducated person is seen more in the difference of mental development than in the difference of amount of knowledge possessed.

3. But the powers of the mind to be developed include the sensibilities and will as well as the powers of the intellect. The usefulness of a man, for which his early education prepares him, depends quite as much upon his desires and purposes as upon the thought employed in carrying them into effect. It is important, therefore, that there be a harmonious development of *all* the powers of the child if he is to be truly educated.

To attain these objects of education, the wise teacher acquaints himself with the principles of mental growth and development which have been deduced from much observation and experience, and which will serve as a guide for him in his difficult work.

A few general principles of teaching are here given in the hope that they may suggest to young teachers the importance of having a well defined purpose in all their methods. They may also serve to explain the reason for some of the methods recommended in the following pages.

GENERAL PRINCIPLES.

1. Education aims to develop all the powers of the child,— physical, intellectual, moral, and spiritual.

Complete living calls for all the assistance which every power of mind and body is capable of giving. The efficiency of each power depends upon the development of all, because they are closely connected and dependent upon one another. The activity of willing depends upon feeling, and feeling depends upon knowing. Moreover, the developed mind needs the developed body through which to act.

2. The powers of mind and body are strengthened and developed by exercise.

Weakness is the result of inaction,— a fact no less true of the mind than of the body. Teachers do not recognize this important principle when they do for their pupils what the pupils can do for themselves. Telling is not teaching, and helping a pupil over every obstacle is no kindness to him. Self-development and self-instruction are the ends of teaching which is to lead the pupil to gain new knowledge through his own efforts. It is by these efforts that his faculties become strong and ready to act in any emergency.

The cultivation of each faculty of the mind strengthens that faculty and all the rest, and the neglect of any faculty tends to lessen the efficiency of all. Some exercise of the feelings and will is necessary to thought, while excessive indulgence of the feelings prevents clear and effective thinking.

3. Exercise of the mental faculties should be judicious and harmonious.

The subjects and methods of teaching should be progressive, and always adapted to the strength and capacity of the learner. Too much exercise may be as harmful as too little, and a wrong kind of development may do incalculable injury by neglecting some faculties which need to be exercised, and by exercising other faculties which are not ready for action. Again, modes of mental action differ greatly, and different treatment is needed for the proper development of each faculty.

4. The natural development and capabilities of the mind are the guides to teaching.

The teacher does not develop the minds of his pupils, nor does he determine the order of their development. Nature is the real educator, of whom he is only an assistant, and to whom, in general and in particular, he constantly looks for guidance. By observation and study, the teacher becomes acquainted with the laws of mental growth and development, and is governed by them in choosing objects of knowledge, and in presenting these to his pupils.

5. The mental powers are most vigorous when they are exercised voluntarily.

As a rule, we can do those things best which we most desire to do, and we generally desire to do that which is most pleasing to us. The degree of effort exerted is also measured by our willingness to do certain work, or to accomplish certain results. If this is true, it is plainly the duty of teachers to conduct their teaching in such a way as to make study pleasurable and voluntary. The work done by pupils need not necessarily be easy to be pleasurable. It is a mistake to suppose that children enjoy any work because it is easy. Food and physical exercise are pleasurable to the healthy body, but they are no more so than truth and mental exercise are to the healthy mind, provided the truth and exercise be of the right kind. Want of interest in school and aversion to study are frequently due to the fact that wrong subjects are taught or that a wrong kind of mental exercise is demanded.

Sometimes teachers believe it to be necessary to give to pupils extra inducements to study or to attend to the work in hand, such as fear of punishment, loss of privilege, hope of reward, desire for a high rank or mark. Pupils may be made to work harder for a time under such stimulants, but like artificial stimulants of the body, their effects are temporary and harmful. There is in the right kind of mental exercise a positive enjoyment which acts as an incentive to increased effort. It may be impossible with many requirements and a large number of pupils, to reach all in the right way; but a constant effort should be made by the teacher to make the work of every pupil voluntary and pleasurable.

6. All mental acts depend for their efficiency upon the power of attention, which should be assiduously cultivated from the beginning.

The great value of attention and concentration of mind is unquestioned by any one. The difference between a disciplined and an undisciplined mind is shown by the difference in the degree of attention of which it is capable. Some even go so far as to say that to learn to give attention is all there is of education.

To cultivate the power of attention, the teacher should see that the mind of the pupil is not bent upon one subject too long; that there are few diverting influences, at least until the habit of voluntary attention is fixed; that the objects of attention are suited to the capabilities of the pupil; and that the illustrations, anecdotes, and information are such as will arouse interest or an expectant curiosity, and not divert the attention from the subject in hand.

7. Education consists largely in the formation of habits.

The importance of forming correct habits in childhood cannot be overestimated; indeed, the principal work of all who have the care of the young is in this direction. A young person who enters upon the duties of life with correct habits of thought and action can be said to be well educated. Among the best habits to be formed in school are those of industry, attention, observation, correct judgment, desiring to do good to others, doing good to others.

These and all habits are formed by many repetitions of the same act, until there are both inclination to act and facility in acting. The best way, therefore, to form good habits or to correct bad ones, is to lead the child to do what we desire him to do, in such a way as to give him pleasure, and with such frequency as to render the act easy to him.

8. The perceptive powers should be most exercised in child-hood.

Although the powers of the mind are in a greater or less degree active in all periods of life, it is a matter of common observation, that during childhood the observing powers are more active and the reflective powers less active than at a later period. Facts and phenomena of the external world are to be known primarily through the senses. Objects or representations of objects should be constantly presented, so as to affect the mind and to lead it to know new truth. Resemblances and contrasts should be observed, and the judgments formed should be correctly expressed.

9. Following the order of natural development, memory and imagination should be cultivated during the entire course.

The qualities of a good memory are, retentiveness, by which ideas are retained in the mind; and readiness, by which the ideas are reproduced when needed. These qualities may be gained by (1) observing distinctly, attentively, and accurately, and (2) repeating the judgments formed in the order of observation and with the strictest accuracy. Memory depends upon association of ideas and attention. Thoughts of visible things are held more strongly than those of other things. Models, diagrams, and illustrations are therefore helpful. The principal laws of association are, resemblance; contiguity in time or place; cause and effect. The last-named law is very important, and should be emphasized in the higher grades.

The power of imagination needs most careful guidance so that the images formed may be pure and refined. For the purpose of having good materials to draw from, the child should come in constant contact with objects of beauty, beautiful pictures, refined conduct, and poetical language. The imagination may be exercised by practice in writing and drawing, in observing beautiful objects and pictures, and in listening to or reading good imaginative stories or poems. Simple imagination, or the power of combining thoughts of parts of different wholes so as to make a new whole, may be exercised in the primary school. Invention seeks to discover new truths, and should be exercised in the higher grades.

10. Elementary instruction should proceed from the known to the unknown.

Very much is involved in this generally accepted but much abused principle. In the primary school, or while the perceptive faculties are most active, the child's knowledge is gained through the senses, passing from the whole to its parts or properties, from ideas to words, and from thoughts to sentences. Later, the child's knowledge of individual objects is extended to a class, facts are formulated into principles, and causes are inferred from known effects. To follow this order fully will take much time and patience, and more will *seem* to be accomplished sometimes by following a reverse order or by leaving out the first steps; as very much more would seem to be accomplished by putting all of a given amount of effort into a building and neglecting the unseen foundation.

11. General forms of truth are derived from particulars.

Rules, definitions, and principles should not be given pupils to be memorized without first being taught in accordance with the principle that generals are derived from particulars. The definition of a noun, for example, would be taught by presenting many nouns in sentences and by having the pupils discover one or more common characteristics of the given nouns. The statement formed by the pupils may then be corrected in respect to form of expression and memorized.

Rules of arithmetic should be taught by having pupils discover the steps of a given process, and subsequently give a general statement containing the steps taken in their proper order. Rules of grammar are general principles which are derived from the observation of many examples.

12. A proper cultivation of the feelings tends to promote happiness, to stimulate thought, and to provide good motives of action.

The conduct of little children is guided more by feeling than by an intellectual perception of right. Cultivation of the feelings consists of (1) repressing those emotions which are injurious, as anger, hatred, envy, vanity, pride, and all forms of excitement which hinder clear thinking and rational willing; and (2) stimulating the higher emotions, as love of the beautiful, reverence, pity, respect, sympathy, and love of home, companions, and study. The higher feelings are promoted more by association and the influence of example than by direct instruction.

Among the motives to be encouraged in school in

the order of merit from lower to higher are, obedience to authority, respect for the opinions of schoolmates, respect for the opinions of the teacher, a sense of right and duty, and a desire to serve others for their sake.

13. Self-control belongs primarily to the will, but is applied to the thoughts, feelings, and actions.

There are all stages of self-control, depending upon the motive involved, from that which has in it the gratification of sense to that in which the welfare and happiness of others are involved. The faults of the will which sometimes result from improper training are indolence, irresolution, impulsiveness, and obstinacy. With as few rewards and punishments as possible, by gradually widening the circle of the child's freedom, and by constantly appealing to his honor and self-respect, the wise teacher leads his pupils to control themselves in forming habits of choosing wisely, firmly, and quickly between two courses of action, of persevering in whatever is undertaken, and of treating others as they themselves would be treated.

———◆———

GENERAL SUGGESTIONS.

Graded and Ungraded Schools.

In order to avoid the danger of misdirected effort, it is always well for teachers to know the advantages and disadvantages of the circumstances in which they find themselves placed. There is no question that the graded school, all things considered, has a great advantage over the ungraded school; and yet there are some dangers of the graded system which teachers should understand and carefully avoid. There is danger, unless care is taken, of turning pupils out after the same pattern, of repressing their originality and individuality, and of abusing competition. It is impossible, of course, to consider the needs and characteristics of each pupil of a large school, and yet it is not necessary, even in a large school, to oblige every pupil to do the same work in the same way as every other pupil; neither is it necessary or wise to stimulate the exertions of pupils by marking and ranking. The school exists for the pupil, and not the pupil for the school. System and order are good, but they should always have in view the common good, and interfere with the individual rights of pupils as little as possible. Some pupils are physically strong, some are weak; the intellects of some pupils are bright, of others dull; some pupils have much outside work to do, others have none. It is necessary, so far as possible, to fit the requirements of the school to these various conditions. There is little danger of pupils taking advantage of a difference of requirements or privileges, provided the teacher is uniformly just in his dealings with them, and provided the teaching is what it should be.

There is another danger in graded schools scarcely less imminent than those which have been named, and that is the danger of not allowing time and opportunity for uninterrupted study and independent thinking. A large class of forty or fifty pupils often spends five-sixths of the school time in recitation, and the little time left for study is frequently interrupted by explanations from the teacher; so that the pupils get scarcely more than a few minutes at a time for uninterrupted and independent study. The remedy in part lies in a division of the class into two sections in some of the studies, so as to allow one section to study while the other is reciting.

The disadvantages of ungraded schools are too apparent to need mention here. The danger is, however, that the disadvantages will be unduly magnified in the minds of teachers of those schools. It is not to be expected that the pupils of ungraded schools can be as carefully trained, or that they can have the same incentives to study as pupils of graded schools, and yet it is wrong to assume that good principles of teaching cannot be applied in ungraded schools, and that the pupils of such schools must necessarily have little interest in their studies. The want of time so often spoken of as an excuse for poor teaching or no teaching, is obviated to some extent by care in classification, and by allowing the older pupils to recite but two or three times a week in some studies. These and other points will be spoken of more at length under the head of Classification.

Purpose and Plan.

The teacher who wishes to succeed, and who does not wish to waste his strength, must have a purpose in all that he does, and a distinct and definite plan of action, both in general and in particular. Preparation for all recitations that need it should be made in providing means of teaching and illustration, in laying out the next day's lessons, and in giving supplementary information.

The Recitation.

The uses of the recitation are various, depending upon the subject and the age of the pupils. The principal uses are (1) to discipline the mind, (2) to encourage right methods of study, (3) to awaken interest in the subject, (4) to impart information. It is evident that these objects, or any one of them, cannot be gained to the fullest extent by a simple examination of pupils to ascertain what they have learned, especially if the examination is conducted by the question and answer method, and seeks to bring out only what the pupils have learned from a text-book. Neither are the best objects of the recitation gained by what may be called the "pouring in" or lecture method. Examination and talking are useful as a means of encouraging study and of giving information; but something more is needed to gain the most important objects of the recitation.

Teaching. — The active faculties of pupils should be exercised, and true ideas of the different subjects should be awakened. These ends can only be accomplished by teaching, and by teaching is meant the presenting of objects as the occasions of thought and of knowledge. Every new subject, and every new phase of a subject, should be taught by leading the pupils to think, and to discover the facts for themselves. It takes much time and patience to teach in this way, and there is often great temptation for a teacher to tell the facts instead, or to present the words of the book to be learned. The teaching of a subject may occupy an entire recitation, as when a difficult subject is taken up; or it may be interspersed with other parts of the recitation, as when some part of a lesson is not quite clear to the pupils; or it may be done at the close of a regular recitation in preparation of a new lesson which is given out for study.

Drill. — When the knowledge of a fact or principle is gained, it is necessary to fix it in the mind by much repetition. This is called drill, and may occur both in study and in recitation. Care should be taken in drilling, as in teaching, that all the pupils are actively thinking of the subject in hand, and that there is no obscurity of mind or dependence upon others. Answering in concert, therefore, is to be largely avoided. Prompt and complete answers to all questions should be given by individual pupils, the teacher seeing to it that the pupils, and not he, do most of the talking. By constant change of method, by arousing the curiosity of the pupils, and by skilful questioning, the attention of every pupil is secured.

Supplementary Information. — In some studies — as reading, geography, and history — the giving of information in addition to what is found in the regular textbook should be encouraged. The information may be gathered from people and books away from the school, and from reference-books in the school or public library. The teacher should also be ready to give additional information and to answer questions. Some of the questions may have to " lie upon the table," to be answered by teacher or pupils at a subsequent time.

Topical Study and Recitation. — Instead of the question and answer method quite generally pursued in the schools, carefully prepared topics should be used. There are many reasons why this form of recitation is to be preferred. In the first place, it is more likely to gain the interest and thoughtful attention of pupils than the question and answer method, and it enables them to express their ideas in entire and connected sentences. If the topics are carefully arranged, the facts learned follow one another in the order of their dependence. and are so connected as to enable the pupil to remember them.

The character of the recitation in any branch determines the character of the pupils' study. If original thought and independent expression are encouraged in the recitation, the pupils' study will be likely to be thoughtful. For this reason also the topical method is to be preferred.

Topical study will be found especially useful for reviews. Frequently the pupils themselves will be able to prepare the topics, but the teacher should see to it that they are arranged in such a way as to give a good general view of the subject and to assist the memory. Teachers who have not been trained in preparing topics, would do well to consult the best text-books, in which good outlines will be found.

Attention. — The best uses of the recitation will not be gained unless the close attention of every pupil is secured. As soon as the slightest inattention is observed, the teacher, by skilful questions and illustrations, should bring back the wandering thought to the subject in hand. Nor should the teacher be deceived by an attentive manner on the part of pupils. An earnest gaze does not always betoken interest in, or attention to, what is said. Members of the class should be ready to ask questions or to add thoughts of their own as soon as a

topic is recited. In all teaching exercises and explanations, the teacher should occasionally question individual pupils to test their knowledge of what is taught or
explained, and to secure attention.

Economy of Time.

The large number of pupils in some schools and the
number of recitations to be heard make it a matter of
great importance to employ the time of the school to
the best possible advantage. This will depend chiefly
upon the selection and distribution of subjects to be
taught, — including both course of studies and daily
programme, — the classification of the school, and the
wisdom of the teacher in directing the study and recitation of the pupils. To direct wisely the work of the
school, the teacher should prepare beforehand, as far as
possible, for the busy work of young children and for the
recitation of all classes, especially the plans and illustrations for teaching. He should discourage too frequent
calls upon his time to give special assistance to pupils
between and during recitations, should not repeat the
answers of pupils given in reply to questions, should
not, as a rule, call for voluntary answers to questions by
the raising of hands, should follow as closely as possible
a prescribed order of recitations, should discourage
desultory and irrelevant conversation during any exercise, and should begin and close a session and pass from
one recitation to another promptly, without unnecessary formalities.

Examinations.

In addition to the examinations which are given
daily, and which are largely oral, there should be given

occasionally short written examinations, the principal objects of which are (1) to indicate to the teacher how much of what has been taught is retained and what needs to be reviewed, and (2) to give pupils practice in making clear, concise, and correct statements of what they know. These examinations may be given at regular intervals or at the close of a general subject, and the questions should be made out by the teacher.

Examinations by the supervisor are given to indicate to the teacher the kind of work which is expected to be done, and to show to the supervisor whether the teaching and instruction have been of the right kind.

READING.

To read is to form in the mind ideas and thoughts by means of the written or printed signs representing them, and to read aloud is to express orally those ideas and thoughts so as to be *heard*, *understood*, and *felt*. In reading, as in talking, there is an association of ideas with their proper signs, and in both acts, when the signs are perceived, the ideas represented by them are formed. The process of learning to read, therefore, is not unlike that of learning to talk, and the ways of teaching a child to read are in many respects like the ways by which he was taught to talk.

First Steps. — As soon as the child enters school, he should be led to express his thoughts freely and naturally. The time of two or three reading recitations may be profitably spent in making him feel "at home" in the schoolroom. The freedom he acquires in talking will be of great assistance to the teacher in every way. Beginning by the natural method already suggested, the teacher first leads the child to think by presenting some object or picture. It may be the picture of a man. The child recognizes it, and says, in reply to the teacher's question, "Man." The word is then written upon the board, and named by the children. In the same way a dozen simple words are taught first by occasioning the idea, and then having the children give its oral sign or name. When these words can be named at sight, let the sentences be taught in a similar manner, thus: —

Teacher. "What is that?" (*Pointing to a hat.*)
Pupils. "That is a hat."

T. "I will write what you have said." (*Writing.*)
" What am I writing?"
P. " That is a hat."
T. " Now read this story on the board."
P. "That is a hat."

Other sentences, as, " This is a ——," "I see a ——,"
" Oh! see a ——," " Here is a ——," " There is a ——,"
" I have a ——," " You have a ——," should be taught
in the same way, using words which have been taught
and other words to the number of fifty or sixty. The
words and sentences should be carefully written upon
the board many times before the children, who should
be led to read with as good expression as they talk.
Talking by the children serves a double object. It not
only serves as a model for their reading, but also tends
to increase their interest in and attention to the reading lesson. Care should be taken, however, that the
talk be not aimless, and that the interest of the children
be not taken away from the subject in hand in their
eagerness to tell what they know.

Do not point, or have the children point, at each word
separately, but have them read the sentence exactly as
they would speak it. If they do not do this at first,
ask them a question the answer of which will be in
the words of the sentence required to be read. For
example, if the sentence is, " The dog is on the mat,"
and they pause after " is " or " on," ask where the dog
is, so as to bring out the reply, " The dog is on the mat."
Then ask them to read the story as they told it to you.

Much depends, in these first steps, upon the teacher's
ability to keep the attention of the children, and to have
each child follow every part of every exercise. This is a

difficult matter, especially with a large class. But with a dozen pupils or fewer it can be done, if the teacher is alert in the use of those expedients which primary teachers come to know. When the interest flags, question those who are least attentive, arouse their curiosity by writing a new story on the board, praise each honest effort, and appeal to the pride of each one to do as well as some other one has done. Do not keep the children too long in recitation, and constantly vary the exercise, so that it may not become monotonous or tiresome.

If any of the words of a new sentence are unknown to the pupils, teach those words upon the board before the reading of the sentence is attempted. After the words are known, and recognized on the board or in the book, ask the pupils to read the sentence silently first, and then orally. If any pupil still falters, tell him he is not ready to read it aloud, and that he must read the story or sentence over again to himself.

The first fifty words taught should represent ideas already familiar to the children; that is, they should be words which are in their spoken vocabulary. In selecting the words to be read first, reference also should be had to phonic resemblance, so that when the time for analysis comes, the words known can be arranged in groups, as *man, fan, cat, rat.* It will generally be a safe rule to teach from the board or chart all of the words and sentences on the first four pages of the primer which is to be first placed into the hands of the children.

When the book is taken, as it may be, in two or three months after the children enter school, there will be little difficulty in reading the first few pages, if the words and sentences on those pages are thoroughly taught from the board. But when the book is taken, do not give up the board and chart work. Every new lesson will have to be taught from the board first, and frequent reviews will have to be made in the same way so that the words may not be forgotten. Soon after the book is taken, analysis of words by sound should be begun, first by pronouncing the words very slowly, as *m-a-n*, then more slowly, until the sounds of the word are separated and their signs are recognized. After this practice has continued for some time, new words will be recognized at sight by unconsciously putting the known signs into new combinations. For instance, if the words *man, mat, cat, rat,* are analyzed, and the signs of each word are readily recognized, the children will know the words *can* and *ran* without being told them. Slow progress must be expected at this stage, and great patience must be exercised until the children are able to analyze without help all the words they have learned. Phonic drill may be given for the purpose also of securing clearer enunciation.

Analysis by letter need receive no special attention. The spelling of words will be learned by degrees after the first half-year, and before the close of the first year the pupils will be able to spell orally the words they read, without much time being spent in teaching them the names of the letters. In oral spelling during the first and second years it would be well to have the pupils "spell by sound" first, then by letter, and lastly give the name of the silent letter or letters.

Transition. — To pass from script to print will not be found difficult if care is taken not to present new or unfamiliar words in the new form. If the learner has begun in script, the transition will of course be made when the book is taken. If it is found at all difficult for him to read the printed words readily, let the two forms, script and print, be placed together upon the board and read. After two or three lessons of this kind there will be no difficulty. After the book is taken, let the reading of both forms go on together throughout the course.

SILENT READING.

Much of the reading we do after we leave school is done silently. We should therefore encourage the pupils to read silently in the best way. There may be a regular exercise for the purpose in which pupils are given a piece to read silently. It is also done in a regular reading recitation when members of the class read silently while one of the class reads orally. The main object to be secured in these exercises is to get the pupils to think of what they are reading. This is done by questioning with the view of having them reproduce the thought in their own words. Put into the hands of the pupils a piece which they have not seen before, and give them time to read it over carefully once. Then have them lay the piece aside and talk or write about what they have read. Such exercises will cultivate the power of attention and lead the pupils to gather quickly the thoughts expressed on the printed page. Exercise in silent reading is also had in preparing the regular reading lesson.

ORAL READING.

Objects. — From our definition we learn that the object of oral reading is " to be heard, understood, and felt." The good teacher of reading keeps this object in mind in all of his teaching, and makes his pupils feel that when they read anything, it is for the purpose of making others understand and feel what is read. But they cannot do this without themselves understanding and feeling what they read. In other words, the reader should not direct the words he utters to the page of the book, but to a listening audience. There should be a constant effort on the reader's part to enter into the feelings and thought of the author. If there is a description of natural scenery to be read, the reader should as far as possible form the mental picture of the described scene. If there is a conversation between two people to be read, the states and thoughts of the speakers should be shared by the reader. If from the beginning the pupil is constantly taught to feel and think while he reads, the chief obstacle to good-reading will be overcome.

If, now, we analyze the general purpose of reading, to ascertain what particular ends are to be sought in teaching reading, we may find three principal ends, or objects; viz., (1) naturalness of expression, (2) correct pronunciation, (3) fluency.

Naturalness of Expression. — To read naturally is to read as one should talk, for the reason that in both acts there is an effort on the part of the speaker to be understood and felt. In reading, as in talking, the thought precedes the expression, and if the thought of the writer is readily understood by the reader, and the words are quickly recognized, there ought to be as little difficulty in reading naturally as there is in talking naturally. How shall we lead the pupil, first, to think the thoughts expressed in print or script, and, secondly, to express those thoughts to others so as to be understood and felt? The conditions mentioned under the general head of "Object of Oral Reading" should be always observed. Lead the pupil to think and feel what he reads by constant questioning. Question him before he begins to read a given lesson. Question him after he has read a paragraph or a sentence, or whenever you think his mind is wandering from the subject. Let the questions be such as will encourage him to enter into the feelings and thoughts of the writer, and to become interested in what is to follow. Sometimes the questions may be such as will oblige the pupil to answer in his own words, and sometimes they may be such as will allow the answer to be in the words of the book, to serve as a model for expression in reading.

But to know the thought expressed in any sentence, the pupil must know what each word means. Difficult and unfamiliar words, therefore, should be taught before the pupil reads either silently or orally. It is true that the meaning of words is known, especially nice shades of meaning, by observing their use in spoken and written language; but in forming habits of correct expression, it is well to know the use of all the words which are to be read. Pupils who are allowed to halt before every unknown or difficult word, waiting to spell out or to be told the word, cannot give much attention to the thought to be expressed. Difficult words of a new lesson should be taught at the close of every lesson, objectively or by familiar illustrations. The following words, from a single page of a third reader, could be taught in this way: *distant, stretched, engineer, whistled, notice, gladness.* After these words have been taught, they may be used in sentences by both teacher and pupils, and written upon the board for special study. In preparing the next day's lesson, the pupils will write out sentences of their own, putting in the words which have been taught, and other difficult words.

Correct Pronunciation. — Words may be very *naturally* read, but if they are not correctly pronounced, they may not be understood, or the attention of the hearers may be diverted from the thought of the author to the blunders of the reader. It is necessary, therefore, to teach the pupils the correct pronunciation of words.

Correct pronunciation is gained by imitation, by correction, and from the dictionary. Children of all ages learn to pronounce by imitation, and sometimes a bad example is more powerful than that which is set before them in the schoolroom. Constant correction in all of the oral exercises of the school, supplemented by special lessons in connection with the reading lessons, may do much to counteract the influence of careless or ignorant companions outside of school hours. The difficult words of every new lesson should be pronounced by the teacher if the pupils are young. Older pupils should learn to use the dictionary for correct pronunciation.

Pronunciation matches, by "pronouncing down," or by choosing sides, may help to create an interest in the subject. and encourage study. Difficult words or words most frequently mispronounced may be placed upon the blackboard from time to time and practised upon. The following list is given as an example : —

Lenient, tiny, exhaust, finance, contents, carbine, débris, depot, jugular, lien, squalor, mitten, often, naïve, beneath, oaths, truths, sacrilegious, bronchitis, nape, extant, isolated, suite, coadjutor, comely, deficit, exhausted, matinée, gondola, cognomen, tirade, epicurean, vagaries, precedence, complaisant, decade, lyceum, notable, heinous.

Clear Enunciation. — One may read naturally and pronounce the words correctly and still fail to give that clearness and distinctness of utterance which are necessary to make the expression agreeable to the ear. In other words, we cannot always take the enunciation of words spoken in conversation as a standard for reading. Sounds of words are frequently run into each other or omitted altogether. Wrong and impure tones are used, or the tones are uttered in a drawling manner. To correct these common faults of speech, and the not uncommon dialects, both foreign and native, which are heard in many schools, vocal exercises should be given daily, either in connection with the reading lesson or as a general exercise. Purity of tone and distinctness of articulation are the two objects to be sought in these exercises. Arrange carefully a few short exercises which have in view one or the other of these objects, and encourage the pupils to practise upon them out of school. Correct, by individual and concert practice, impurities of tone, such as the nasal, guttural, and pectoral quality. The broad vowel sounds, either alone or in words, should be practised upon to secure pure tones. In such exercises see that the jaw is used freely, and that a free action of the vocal organs is not hindered by a poor position of the body.

To secure distinct articulation, have the pupils practise upon those exercises which will give an easy action of the lips, tongue, and palate. Careful analysis of words by sound will be found to be useful in securing distinct articulation. Exercises like the following may be used for a similar purpose. Other exercises will be found in the various school readers.

1. Pronounce clearly, moving the jaw freely, the following : —

ah	ē	oo	aw
ō	ā	ī	oy	ow

Pronounce the same with the sound of *k ;* as, *kah, kē,* etc.

2. Pronounce vowel sounds : —

ā, ä, â, ă; ē, ĕ; ī, ĭ; ō, ô, ŏ; ū, ŭ, û; oi, ou.

Pronounce the same with the sound of *k : kā, kä,* etc.

3. Practise upon the following until the action of the organs of speech is accurate and energetic. Do not use much breath in the exercise, and let the touch of the tongue, lips, and palate be of the shortest possible duration.

t	p	k	d	b	g
at	ap	ak	ad	ab	ag

et, etc.
it, etc.

4. Repeat at first slowly and then rapidly : —

He talks in earnest.

On either side is an ocean.

She sought shelter. Shelter sought she.

The railroad ran directly across the rapid river.

With a thick thimble, Theresa Thornton thrusts thirty-three threads through the thick cloth.

Skilful pilots gain their reputation from storms and tempests.

Round the rough rock the ragged rascal ran.

Shoes and socks shock Susan.

Pronounce distinctly : —

Help[p], elf[f], else[s], felt[s], child, milk, lamp, tent, dance, ink, sharp, task, health, Welsh, Welch, nymph, dreampt, ninth, strength, depth, steps, apt, fifth, fifes, left, broths, wasp, post, looks, act, alps, gulped, gulfs, twelfth, lamps, stamped, triumphs, tempts, tenths, against, prints, lengths, ringst, harps, warped, serfs, earths, first, droopst, adepts, fifths, laughst, rafts, lookst, facts, asps, posts, desks, satst, patched, lookst, acts, helpst, twelfths, mid'st, halt'st, filched, limp'st, attemp'st, want'st, flinched, precincts, thinkst, sixths, texts.

The quality of tone and articulation often depends upon the control or management of the breath. For this purpose breathing exercises such as are given elsewhere,[1] will be found helpful, especially to older pupils.

Fluency. — By fluency is meant the ability to recognize quickly and to pronounce readily the words as they are seen in reading. This can be gained only by constant and long-continued practice in easy reading at sight.

Sight-Reading. — In addition to the regular reading lesson, which may be short, there should be frequent practice in reading at sight by pupils of all grades. Four or five pages may be read daily at sight in almost every grade ; but care should be taken that the reading of this kind be sufficiently simple for the pupils. The regular reading lesson may be quite difficult, that is, it may contain several new and difficult words which should be taught in the way indicated above ; but in the sight-reading there should be few words not previously known, the object being to accustom the pupils to recognize the words quickly as they

[1] p. 284.

come to them. The sight-reading should not be "studied" or read silently beforehand unless it is too difficult to be read easily at sight. If there are some words which the pupils have not met before, they should be taught before the reading begins; and if the reader still finds difficulty in reading the sentence or paragraph, it may be read silently before it is read orally.

To encourage thought in reading, it is always well to follow the reading by questioning. Let the questions be such, however, as will oblige the pupils to give long answers and to give them in their own words. In the lower classes, well-graded reading-books will be found best for sight-reading, although there are some simply written books of other kinds admirably fitted for the purpose. In the higher classes, voyages, books of travel, histories, and biographies will be found useful not only for sight-reading, but also for the purpose of interesting pupils in geography and history. Occasionally it may be found well to allow the pupils to select pieces 'or stories to be read to the entire school. Such practice will give them confidence and help them to feel that their object in reading orally is to interest others.

Regular Reading Lessons. — Important as sight-reading is for securing the principal objects of oral reading, the use of the regular reading lesson should not be lost sight of. Unlike reading to be read at sight, the books for assigned lessons should be somewhat difficult for the pupils. The advantages of having regular reading lessons a little in advance of the pupil's comprehension are, (1) new words are added to the pupils' vocabulary, (2) the thought of the pupils is raised to a higher plane. If all that the pupils read is so simple as to be wholly within their comprehension, they are not likely to learn many words new to them, and the thought expressed is so simple as to call for little mental exertion. It is a mistake to suppose that children like that only which is simple and easy. It is true that, by want of proper exercise, their minds may become incapable of much effort; but with careful training children may read understandingly and come to like the best of our English classics, both in prose and poetry. It will be found well in reading such literature to encourage the pupils to give their idea of the meaning of a figure of speech or of a difficult phrase or sentence, and gradually, by judicious assistance, lead them to discover its full meaning and force. Such exercise will be found as interesting as guessing a puzzle or working out a problem in arithmetic. Occasionally, after a chapter or poem has been read, the pupils will find it profitable and agreeable to write an abstract of it in their own words.

Preparation of Lesson. — It cannot be expected that very young children will "study" a reading lesson to any extent. The most that they can do is to practise in copying the words and sentences of their lessons from the blackboard. Neither can older pupils prepare a reading lesson in the right way unless they are shown how to prepare it, or unless the recitation leads them to do it. The character of the recitation in every branch of study determines the character of the study. This is especially true in reading. Just before the reading lesson begins, some or all of the class should be called upon to give the substance of the lesson in their own words. This exercise, if rightly conducted, furnishes practice in oral expression, and at the same time encourages pupils to find out the story or the thought of the author before they come into the class. Again, at the close of the recitation, the teacher should teach the most difficult words of the next lesson, and if his pupils be young, ask them to bring into the class written sentences of their own construction containing the words thus taught. By this practice, the pupils will become more familiar with the difficult words of the lesson and at the same time add to their vocabulary. The sentences should be glanced at or looked over by the teacher, to see that no mistakes are made in the use of words. and to encourage pupils to write the sentences.

To induce the older pupils to consult the reference-books of the school library, inquiry should be made in recitation for facts connected with any name or place mentioned in the text, and for synonyms, derivation, and definition of words.

The greatest value of questioning as an incentive to study will not be seen if it is done wholly by the teacher. After a paragraph or sentence has been read, the pupils themselves should be encouraged to question the reader in regard to its general meaning or concerning any part of it. Thus there may be called for the definitions and synonyms of difficult words, explanation of figures, location of places, facts about persons and past events mentioned in the text, and such other information as the ingenuity and previous study of the questioners will suggest. Pupils in preparing for questioning will be likely to be more particular and earnest than in preparing simply to answer questions of the teacher. Moreover, questioning by the pupils greatly adds to the interest of a reading exercise.

Principles. — The pupils up to the age of twelve or fourteen years are learning to think as they read, and to acquire the art of reading so as to be understood and felt. Up to this time nothing has been said of pitch, emphasis, or any of the principles which underlie good reading. When the art has been acquired to a tolerable degree of proficiency, the older pupils may begin to learn principles which may aid them in understanding and reading difficult or obscure passages. Instead, however, of presenting the rules and principles ready made, they should be taught as in other departments of study. For example, if it is desired to teach *emphasis*, let the pupils read the following sentence with the desire to tell *how* the horse trots: "The black horse trots rapidly." Again, ask the pupils to read the same sentence so as to tell which horse trots rapidly. A few questions will bring out the idea that certain words were uttered with more force than others, or in a different way. They may be told that such words were emphasized, and be asked to emphasize other words. When they have well in mind the idea of emphasis, lead them to discover the principle of correct emphasis. For example, place upon the blackboard a number of sentences like the following: "John is here," "Thomas is here," "We are all here," and ask the pupils to read them naturally. After they find that "Thomas" and "all" are emphasized, lead them to see that those words express new ideas, or ideas not previously expressed. After a sufficient number of examples of this kind have been read, they will give a rule of their own making: "Words expressing new ideas are emphasized." In the same way develop the rule that "Words expressing important ideas are emphasized," and also the rule that "Words expressing contrasted ideas are emphasized." By combination, the general rule is formed: "Words expressing new, important, and contrasted ideas are emphasized."

The next point to bring out may be the kinds of emphasis and the various terms used to express them. The pupils, by reading understandingly and feelingly several sentences like the following, will see that some words are emphasized by using more force, some by making a pause after the words, some by raising or dropping the voice, and some by prolonging the words : —

> I assure you that the charge is *false.*
> The boy! oh, where was he?
> One´ if by land´, and two´ if by sea´.
> The day is c-o-l-d and d-a-r-k and d-r-e-a-r-y.

After sufficient practice of this kind, the names of the kinds of emphasis may be given: (1) stress, (2) pause, (3) inflection, (4) time.

It will be interesting and useful for the pupils to apply the knowledge of emphasis which they have gained to passages in their reading lessons. Take, for example, the lines, —

> " Scarcely a man is now alive
> Who remembers that famous day and year."

Nine out of ten pupils would at first emphasize the words "day" and "year." Application of their rule of emphasis will teach them that "remembers" is the word to be emphasized.

Pupils in the higher grades are much inclined to emphasize too many words — so many as to destroy the effect of emphasis where it belongs. To prevent this fault, application of the rule of emphasis should be constantly made, and the reader should be asked why a particular emphasis is made. If, for example, a pupil reads the sentence, "Put a ring on his hand and shoes on his feet," and emphasizes, as he is likely to, *ring*, *hand*, *shoes*, and *feet*, the application of the rule will lead him in a second reading not to emphasize *hand* and *feet* as if they expressed important ideas.

The same course should be pursued in teaching other facts, relating to quality of voice, movement, pitch, force, and inflection. The teacher should first gather such facts as may be thought useful, from reading or other books, and then teach the facts by first presenting the examples and leading the pupils to deduce the facts or principles from the examples given.

Cultivation of Taste. — It is the privilege as well as the duty of the teacher to do much toward elevating the reading tastes of the young. In no way can the extensive reading of the worthless and demoralizing literature which now fills the shops be more effectually checked than by creating a desire and demand for something better. Good methods of teaching will do much in this direction; for the pupil in being led to think as he reads, finds positive pleasure in reading thoughtful books, and having learned to read such books easily at sight, he is no longer attracted solely by the excitement of the narrative, or by the simplicity of the language, but is willing and glad to read the best books within his reach. Moreover, the constant use of good supplementary reading in school has given him a taste for good reading and a distaste for what is worthless and bad.

In addition to the direct influence which is exerted in the reading classes, the teacher should direct the outside reading of the pupils by suggesting good books in all departments. Every high and grammar school should have a carefully selected library from which books can be taken home by the pupils. If there is no library connected with the school, the teacher should suggest to the pupils what books of the public or circulating library will be best for them to read. The geography, history, observation, and information lessons will afford a good opportunity for the teacher to suggest books or periodicals from which the pupils may learn other interesting facts in connection with the subjects studied.

Frequently, or as often as once a week, time should be taken to talk with the pupils about what they have read out of school, occasionally calling for an abstract or synopsis of a book when completed, and their opinion of it.

WRITING.

THE art of writing legibly should be acquired as early in the school life of the child as possible; first, because it is a direct assistance to the other work of the school, and secondly, on account of the shortness of time during which many children attend school.

Appliances. — During the first year there should be provided ruled slates, and sharpened- slate-pencils at least four inches in length. The lines for the small letters may be one-fourth of an inch apart, and even wider for work of the first few weeks. After the first year, paper and lead-pencils should be provided in addition to the slates and slate-pencils. The spaced lines may be, during the second year, three-sixteenths of an inch apart for the small letters. The proper height of capitals and tall letters should also be indicated in the ruling. During the next two years, or as long as spaced lines are thought to be necessary, the lines for the small letters may be a little more than one-eighth of an inch apart. Copy-books of a suitable kind should also be provided as early as the second year, and pen and ink at the beginning of the third year in school. Blackboard and crayons will be found indispensable by the teacher, and writing-charts and card-board copies will be of great assistance.

Grading. — In graded schools all the teaching exercises in writing should be given to the entire school, and much of the practice should be carried on together. Special assistance, however, will have to be given to a few of the poorer writers during the lesson. Opportunity should be given these pupils to take extra time for practice upon a lesson, and they should be advised to practise out of school hours.

It may be found advantageous in writing, as in drawing, to divide the ungraded school into two sections both for teaching and for practice. At least two uniform lessons a week should be given each section. At other times the pupils might go on in their copy-book, independent of each other; but at no time should undue haste or scribbling be allowed.

Objects and Means. — Legibility first and rapidity afterwards are the ends to be reached in writing, and they are reached only by constant practice either in imitating good models or in following rules which have been taught.

Words and Sentences. — The first copies for imitation may be the words and sentences which have been taught and placed upon the board in the reading exercise. The earlier efforts of the children in writing will be very crude, and it may take many trials before any appreciable progress is made; but with the help of the teacher in making the copy upon the slate and in guiding the hands of the children, it will be found that easy words like *man, on,* and *cat* will soon be made so as to be recognized. It will be well to encourage the children at first by giving for copies words which they can write the best, leaving the more difficult words until they have a good command of the hand.

The copies upon the blackboard and slate should be made in the presence of the children, that they may know how the letters are formed. In order to have the form of the letters clear and distinct, the copies should be written at first in a large hand, and the writing of the children should also be large, as indicated by a wide ruling. Time may be saved by placing cardboard copies before the children instead of writing copies upon the board or slate; but this should be done only after the words have been written in the children's presence.

After the first year the children may be able to write without a copy, and yet the work of imitation must go on until all of the letters are accurately formed. Much depends upon the teacher's ability to write well before his pupils. While it is true that a poor writer may, by substituting the copies of others, lead his pupils to write well, it should be understood that a teacher who can present the proper form for imitation has a great advantage over one who cannot write well, or who has to write his copies out of sight of the children.

Single Letters. — While the copying of words and sentences is required in the lower grades, drill upon single letters should also be carried on in regular order, as indicated in the "Course of Studies." The aim in these exercises is accuracy. No new letter should be taken up until the preceding letters are made with almost perfect accuracy. For example, the children are given *i* to write during the first half-year. Let them practise upon it a little every day until there can be no improvement, and then they may take the next letter, *u*. This practice will lead them into that control which is necessary to the good writer, and will give a good foundation for subsequent work.

Position. — During the first two years, or while the

children are confined to the use of the pencil in writing, due attention is given to position; but as we do not wish to make the difficulties too great in the beginning, we seek more to secure perfect forms than perfect movements. As soon as the pen is taken, however, special attention should be given to (1) position of the body, (2) position of the paper or book, (3) position and movement of the hand and arm.

Different positions are recommended by different teachers, and doubtless each has its advantages. The following positions are suggested as having few objections and as being useful for the purpose designed.

It should be said, however, that, whether these or other positions are taken, there should be uniformity throughout the course.

The face nearly front, the left side of the body being slightly turned toward the desk; the left hand above or on the upper part of the paper or copy-book, and the body slightly bent; the paper or copy-book in an oblique position so as to allow room for the right forearm to rest upon the desk; the pen and holder held between the thumb and first two fingers so as to allow the freest movement of the fingers, the holder resting upon the forefinger between the first and second joints and pointing nearly over the right shoulder; the wrist slightly raised from the desk, the third and fourth fingers resting lightly upon the paper. These, or some other equally good positions, should be taught at the beginning of the third year or when the pen is first taken, and the pupils should be constantly corrected until a correct habit is established. Some teachers find the tracing-book helpful during the first few weeks of pen-and-ink practice, or while the pupils are learning a good position and movement of the hand.

Movements. — Movement practice should be begun as soon as the pen is taken, and continued until there is a free and easy movement of the fingers and arm. In the early practice, the movements should be made with a pencil or a dry pen. First show by example what the arm movement is, and have the pupils practise on slides, with the fingers fixed and in a good position. The slides may be made by the direction " forward — back," given slowly. After some facility is gained in this simple arm movement explain as before, by example, the finger movement, and have the pupils practise it, first by bending and straightening the fingers without touching pencil or pen to paper. Then with the dry pen upon paper, combine the slide and the simple up-and-down finger movement in the following exercise : —

Give slowly the direction " slide — down," by which the movement is guided, and after some practice let the same exercise be written with ink.

To secure accuracy of finger and arm movements, practice in parallel lines, both curved and straight, in all directions, will be found useful. These and other exercises for securing freedom and accuracy of movement may be found in the copy-books, and should be practised daily for the first two or three years after ink is taken, or until the pupils can write easily with the combined arm and finger movement. As soon as the

pen is taken, and in all subsequent writing, care should
be taken to have the pupils hold the pen very lightly in
the hand, so as to make smooth and light lines. A
firmer grasp may be allowed for pupils who have an
unsteady hand, but even these should be encouraged to
hold the pen lightly as soon as they are able to write
rapidly.

Copy-Book. — In addition to practice in writing from
copies made by the teacher, and in connection with the
language lessons, there should be throughout a greater
part of the course, copy-book practice at least three
times a week. The copy should be taught from the
blackboard before practice is begun, each principle or
letter being made carefully, and the correct and incorrect forms being pointed out. Every pupil should be
provided with paper or blank-book for practice, and
when a fair degree of accuracy is attained, the letter,
word, or sentence may be written in the copy-book. In
using the copy-book, lead the pupils to imitate the copy
and not their own writing. To encourage thoughtful-
ness and care in imitating the copy, it may be well to
have all the pupils write the same line at the same time,
and when the line is written, to compare each letter
they have made with the copy. Sometimes interest is
increased by criticising each other's writing, marking
slightly with lead-pencil the errors.

Special and separate attention should be given to the
shape, size, slant, distance apart, and shade of letters.
The first four points should be attended to from the
first. The shading should receive no attention until
the pupils are able to form the letters and join them
together with almost perfect accuracy. Generally it

takes two years of practice with pen and ink before the
pupils are ready to give attention to shading.

The rule in regard to the relative height of letters
may be understood and followed by pupils as early as
the second year in school. During the first four years
the pupils may have the aid of spaced lines to guide
them in making letters of proper and uniform height.
This assistance should be gradually removed until
equally good work is done without the lines.

The slant should be about fifty-two degrees. For
board and slate work, the proper slant may be ascertained by drawing a parallelogram, thus, —

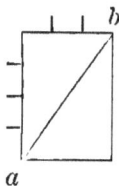

four parts high, three parts wide. The diagonal ab
will be nearly the proper slant.

The proper distancing of letters and the proper shading can be gained only by imitation and practice. Indeed, this is true of all good writing. Practice in
imitation of good models for accuracy, and afterwards
practice for rapidity, should be encouraged both in and
out of school. For "home study," practice in writing
is especially useful, as no possible harm can be done by
injudicious assistance.

Pupils should not be allowed to repeat their faults
until they become a habit. To avoid this they should
be led to observe closely correct forms and to detect
any faulty line which may be made. First present a

correct form of the letter upon the board and call attention to the position or direction of its parts. Then ask
one or more of the pupils to make the same letter upon
the board for the inspection and criticism of the rest.
In this way they will be prepared to criticise and correct their own writing in the copy-books.

Rate. — In all the writing of the first few years, let
slowness be encouraged. The child who can write
slowly, can be taught to write well, and only when he
can form every letter accurately without a copy, should
rapidity be encouraged or allowed. For this reason
every written exercise, whether it be in spelling, language, copy-book, or examination, should be an exercise
in penmanship. No careless writing should be allowed
to remain upon the slate, and all carelessly written exercises upon paper should be destroyed and rewritten.
By the fifth or sixth year in school, the pupils, if they
have been properly taught in the lower grades, should
be prepared to quicken their movements in writing.
Practice in rapidity may be had first upon single letters
and words, and afterwards upon sentences, until by the
eighth year the pupils will be able not only to write
well but with a good degree of rapidity.

It is expected that book-keeping, and the writing of
compositions and examination-papers, will afford sufficient practice for writing in the ninth year.

SPELLING.

Objects. — In teaching spelling we have to lead the pupils to arrange in proper order the letters of a word. In addition to this, other forms of expression should be taught incidentally, as use of capital letters, punctuation, possessive forms, common contractions and abbreviations, division into syllables, pronunciation and diacritical marks.

The correct form of words is learned by observation and practice. Accurate habits of observation should be encouraged as early as possible, and opportunity given for much practice in writing. In the first year there should be daily practice in copying words and sentences from the board and from cards. In the second year, and afterwards, there may be some practice in copying from the reader. Instead of allowing pupils to copy by writing only a letter or two after each inspection of the copy, lead them to get an accurate picture of one or more words before writing. Write a word or sentence upon the board, ask the children to look at it carefully, then to write it without looking at the copy, and lastly to see if their word or sentence is written correctly, and, if not, to erase and rewrite it. Lead them to do the same in copying from books.

Study. — Pupils should be taught early in the course how to study a spelling lesson. It will be well to have the spelling lesson copied plainly upon the board by the teacher, and when the time for studying the lesson comes, to have the pupils copy the words upon their slates, as has been described. Whenever a mistake has been made, instead of having them erase and correct a part of the word, have them erase the entire word and rewrite it. Some practice of this kind under the teacher's direction will lead the pupils to form in the mind correct pictures of the words at a single glance, and enable them to study profitably alone. For the younger pupils, draw a line through the silent letters, and encourage them to do the same in copying and in writing from dictation. This will lead them to notice the silent letters.

Recitation. — The spelling lesson may be recited orally or in writing. For obvious reasons, the writing of words is far more useful than spelling orally by letter. As soon as the pupils can write without copy, or after the first year, the words and sentences of the spelling lesson should be written from dictation, in books provided for the purpose. In the latter part of the first year, spelling "by sound" and by letter should be practised. In the second and third years there may be some oral spelling ; but generally with the exception of spelling reviews and recreations, the lessons should be written.

During the first three years the school readers may be used as text-books for spelling. Afterwards regular spelling text-books should be used, time being allowed for practice upon words from other sources. Sometimes the spelling lesson may consist of the words misspelled in the written examination papers and compositions; sometimes the technical words of other lessons may be given, or the difficult words of two or more paragraphs of the reader, or a review of the difficult common words, such as the following : —

Knife, money, shoes, ladies, which, whose, where, there, their, piece, would, watch-chain, lead-pencil, window-curtain, yours, comb, crayon, door-key, floor, believe, guess, through, threw, dropped, walked, laughed, aunt, father, ought, ache, dozen, fruit, Wednesday, beautiful, flowers, sugar, color, collar, brother's, baby's, whole, pair, eight, half, twelve, tough, button, caught, neighbor, minute.

These are among the words which children should write correctly in sentences before they leave the primary school; but it will be found that not all grammar school pupils will be able to write even half of them correctly, without being reviewed.

The words and sentences should be generally dictated by the teacher, and, if possible, but once. In this way the power of attention is cultivated, and time is saved. In giving out words to spell it is well sometimes for the teacher or the pupils to give a sentence containing each word or, in the higher grades, to give synonyms or definitions. Sometimes it may be well for the pupils to give out the words of a lesson from memory; but no word should be spelled whose use or meaning is not understood.

All misspelled words should be rewritten correctly and reviewed frequently. The lessons should be of varied length, depending upon the character of the words. Sometimes a long lesson of easy words or of words spelled alike may be assigned; in which case the hardest words of the lesson only will be given out. In no case should haste or carelessness in writing be allowed.

Derivations, synonyms, and definitions should be learned in connection with the spelling lesson in the higher grades, and may be recited at the time of, or after dictation of the words. In these classes the dictionary should be in constant use by the pupils. Small dictionaries in the desks of older pupils, and one large dictionary for reference, on the teacher's table, will be found necessary for the preparation of reading and spelling lessons.

Homonyms in sentences should be frequently given, and in the higher grades, words derived from the same root should be selected and explained. The force of the various prefixes and suffixes may also be taught in the same way. Syllabication should be taught in connection with the regular spelling lesson, the syllables being separated by short spaces and not by hyphens. In oral spelling the syllables may be indicated by slight pauses, without pronouncing each syllable.

Rules. — It is not well to burden the pupil with many rules for spelling, the exceptions being frequently so numerous as to defeat the end sought. Yet there are some rules which may be profitably learned; as, for example, the rules for joining suffixes to words ending in *y* and *e*, and rules for the formation of the plural of nouns. These, and other rules which have few exceptions, may be of some assistance.

Methods of Examining and Correcting. — In small classes, and with young pupils, the teacher should examine and correct each slate or paper. Pupils may be allowed to correct their own exercises, rewriting the misspelled words upon a separate paper. Or pupils may exchange slates or papers, and examine each other's exercise, the right of appeal being allowed when the exercise is returned. Instead of slate or paper, it would be well to have each pupil provided with a spelling blank-book. From the lists of misspelled words the teacher should occasionally prepare review lessons.

To avoid temptation, which might exist if the papers were examined by the same pupils every day, or if the pupils simply exchanged their papers, it is well to have two or three different directions for passing the papers to be examined. At the proper time the teacher may say, "pass back," "front," "to the left," or "to the right." If the order to "pass front" is given, the pupils in front will immediately stand and pass their books to the pupils in the rear. All the rest will pass their books to the pupils directly in front of them. If the order to "pass back" is given, the pupils in the rear will carry their papers to the front, and all the rest will pass their papers to the pupils behind them.

It is desirable to have the pupils write the lessons with pen and ink, and to mark misspelled words with a lead-pencil. The books should occasionally be collected and passed to the teacher for inspection.

Reviews and Recreations. — Oral review lessons by "spelling down" and choosing sides will be found to be valuable aids. A choice of sides to continue for a month or term has been found to stimulate the efforts of some pupils. When a class becomes indifferent, or consists of many poor spellers, let two of the best spellers choose sides, — the side which misspells the fewest words in the month to have some privilege or mark of honor. If carried on in the right way, great interest will be manifested, the better spellers "spelling" the poorer spellers out of school hours, and the poor spellers making greater effort.

Occasionally the "word game" may be played, in

which words are made up from the letters of a given word. For example, from the word *Congregational* the pupils may be asked first to make as many words as they can beginning with *c*, and using any letters found in the given word. After three or five minutes' trial, the same may be done beginning with *o*, and so on.

LANGUAGE.

THE term *Language* may be used in different ways. As a faculty of the mind, it is the association of ideas with their proper signs. The term is also applied to the expression of ideas and thoughts, generally by words and propositions, spoken or written. By the study of language the power of association is cultivated and the ability is acquired of expressing ideas and thoughts correctly and easily, both in speaking and in writing. In its widest application, language as a branch of study includes reading, writing, spelling, grammar, and expression or composition. As generally used, however, the term is applied to the last-named subject, or that study which has for its object an easy and correct expression of ideas and thoughts. Such a study is elementary in character and precedes the study of grammar, which is scientific.

Objects. — The two chief ends to be sought in elementary language work are correctness and fluency. Correctness of spoken language consists in correct pronunciation, in the use of correct words, both in kind and construction, and in having the words of a sentence follow each other in proper order. Correctness of written language, in addition to the last two features, consists in correct spelling, punctuation, and capitalization.

In securing fluency of expression, it should be the aim of the teacher, first, to see that the pupils have right and useful thoughts to express; secondly, to see that the thoughts are clear and distinct; and thirdly, to see that the expression is direct, simple, free, and natural.

Means. — *Regular Studies.* — All of the objects named cannot be attained by attending to expression merely. Without clear and distinct thoughts of a useful kind, there can be no good expression; and without proper expression, the thoughts are likely to be indistinct and fleeting. It is important, therefore, that language culture should be an essential feature of all the regular studies of the school. Every fact observed and every thought acquired should be expressed in language clear, accurate, and original.

Imitation. — First among the most effective means of acquiring correct expression is imitation of good models. Every one knows by experience and by observation how much good language depends upon early influences. No amount of study in school will entirely overcome a habit of using incorrect language which has been acquired in early life. The importance, therefore, of correct speech in the schoolroom can hardly be overestimated. The teacher should carefully guard himself against the use of language which would not be regarded as a model of excellence for his pupils to imitate.

Correction. — In all the exercises of the school, both teacher and pupils should be ready to correct every incorrect expression which is made. If this is done constantly, and the correct forms are written out and frequently reviewed, much will be done to overcome the influence of poor models in the home and on the street. It is not necessary, nor is it well, to interrupt the thought of a pupil in the midst of a statement by the correction of mistakes. When the pupil has finished what he has to say, mistakes may be pointed out and the proper corrections made.

Copying. — Constantly during the first year, and occasionally afterwards, the copying of sentences and words from accurately written copies should be practised. The copies may be on the blackboard, paper, or cardboard, and should always be most carefully written. No poorly or carelessly written copies should ever be placed before the children, and care should be taken that habits of writing slowly and carefully are formed from the first.

After the first year, or as soon as the child can form letters correctly without a copy, copying from the reading-book may be practised, both for the purpose of learning the use of capital letters, marks of punctuation, etc., and for securing greater familiarity with the words. If the pupils are properly directed, a habit of attention and of picturing in the mind, words and groups of words, is also gained by this exercise. Lead the pupils to look carefully to the words of a phrase or sentence before they write it. After the copy is made, ask them to see whether they have copied the words correctly in all particulars. If any mistake has been made, have them erase what has been written and try again. After a time good habits of attention will be formed, and the copying may be done in study time. Unless care is taken, pupils, even in the higher grades, will be found stopping in the middle of words to look at the copy, thus forming thoughtless and mechanical habits.

Object Lessons. — The first essential for correct expression is the possession of clear ideas, and these are best received through, or by means of observation lessons. Whenever in such lessons an idea or thought is developed, it should find expression first orally and afterwards in writing. After the object lesson is completed, the various statements which the pupil has made should be brought together in proper form. For example, when the shape and color of an envelope have been taught and named, the statement may be, " The shape of this envelope is oblong, and its color is buff." Or when a lesson upon a plant is given, the name and description of the different parts may be made as soon as they are observed. Afterwards these facts should be brought together so as to make a connected statement of what has been learned. If there is not time to do this in the time allotted for the observation lesson, let it be done as a part of the next lesson in language.

Further suggestions will be found in connection with what is said upon observation lessons.

Actions. — One form of object lessons of interest and value to young children, especially for the purpose of expression, is actions. The teacher may do something, as walk across the floor, and then ask his pupils to tell orally in an entire sentence what he did, and afterwards to write the sentence. Thus a simple act, or several acts in succession, may be described, the number and complexity of them depending upon the ability of the pupils. By this means, the spelling of many common, difficult words may be taught, as well as the use of capital letters and marks of punctuation.

The following sentences will suggest to teachers what actions may be described in the various grades : —

John rang the bell.

You walked across the room.

You placed two pencils on the desk.

You picked two petals from the flower.

I heard you stamp your foot twice.

Mary passed her knife to Julia.

Thomas raised the window-sash.

Did you shut the door?

You dropped your handkerchief on the floor.

You put John's hat on the desk.

John and William put their hats on their heads.

William, James, and Sarah went to the teacher's desk.

You threw a ball into the air and caught it when it came down.

Thomas went to the wash-basin, wet his sponge, and returned to his seat.

James went to the teacher's desk, took from it all of the pupils' writing-books, and distributed them to their owners. He then went to his seat and began to study his geography lesson.

Use of Pictures. — Next to the objects themselves, pictures are most valuable in exciting ideas and thoughts, and are therefore useful as a means of language study. They may be used as objects are used when a description of what is seen is called for, or they may be used as a basis for imaginary stories.

In describing the parts of a picture, young children will need special assistance and direction from the teacher. Place a large, interesting picture — not too complex at first — before the class or school, and question somewhat as follows : —

"How many boys are there in the picture?" "What are they doing?" "What animal is following on behind?" "What kind of dog is it?" "What is one of the cows doing?" The answers should be in entire sentences, and should afterwards be written out connectedly under the direction of the teacher. After some practice of this kind the pupils may be able, without much assistance from the teacher, to state in full all they can see in a given picture. Care should be taken that the description does not consist of short statements, poorly arranged or connected together by many " and's." The final description of the picture suggested above might be as follows : —

" I see two boys driving some cows. One of the cows is eating grass by the side of the road, and one is going into a field. A large shepherd dog is running behind the boys."

Another scarcely less valuable use of pictures in teaching language is to suggest imaginary stories to be told by the pupils. The pictures used for young children should be simple and somewhat striking. By presenting a good plan or by asking questions, lead the pupils gradually into good habits of thought and construction. With the picture above indicated the questions might be somewhat as follows: What shall we call the boys? Where do they live? Do both live on the farm? Which one is the visitor from the city? What relation are they to each other? Who came with Charlie to the country? What are they doing? What else do they do on the farm? etc. After questioning, the story may be told orally by one or more of the pupils, and afterwards written out in full. Older pupils may be able to write the story out in full after a given plan, without preliminary questioning or without first telling it orally. The correction and revision of the papers may be made during the time of a regular recitation, or may be given out as a language lesson. Encourage as far as possible independence and originality of expression.

Dictation. — In every grade after the first, exercises in dictation should be given. Avoid the mistake of repeating the phrase or sentence so often as to make the exercise of writing mechanical. The giving out of a short sentence once, with possibly one repetition for younger pupils, should be enough. Long sentences may be repeated two or three times.

The chief value of the dictation exercise lies in the correction of papers by the pupils. Read, letter by letter, the sentences, or place upon the blackboard the correct form, asking them to place a cross above each mistake.

Care should be taken to select sentences for dictation which will involve practice in all marks of punctuation, capital letters, and the spelling of difficult common words. The use and spelling of words pronounced alike but spelled differently may also be taught in this way. The following sentences will indicate the kind of dictation exercises which may be given during the second, third, and fourth years in school : —

The book is very large.
I have two cents in my pocket.
Where is your slate?
There are eight boys in my class.
Which book shall I take?
Mary's doll is very pretty.
The man ate four pieces of bread?
Where did you put my penknife?
Are you sure that you heard me speak?
Many girls wear their hair too short to curl.
I was very weak last week.
Wait a moment, and I will tell you the weight of the sugar.

Col. and Mrs. Smith called to see us last evening.

This is —— day of ——, 188-.

Never separate the letters of a syllable by a hyphen.

There are sixty minutes in an hour, twenty-four hours in a day, seven days in a week, and fifty-two weeks in a year.

"Where did you buy those oranges?" asked William.

"I bought them at Mr. Robinson's grocery store, and I paid two cents apiece for them," replied John.

Oh, what a great piece of maple sugar you have!

I buy all my stationery at Lee and Shepard's.

I have a Worcester's and a Webster's dictionary.

Information Lessons. — It is very important that facts learned in connection with the information lessons be fixed in the mind by talking and writing. Correctness and ease of expression are also gained by such practice, and a good opportunity is afforded to teach a proper combination and arrangement of short statements. After an information lesson has been given, the custom should be to talk and write about what has been learned. The statements may first be given in answer to definite questions, and then they may be combined in proper order and connection; or the lessons may be presented by topics, which can afterwards be brought together in connected statements. One method is best suited to younger pupils, the other to older pupils. Occasionally the description may be given without preliminary questioning or topical arrangement.

Story-Telling and Sight-Reading. — Every teacher of young children should know how to tell stories, partly for the sake of interesting and instructing the children, and partly for the sake of furnishing material for language lessons. A well-told story serves as a model for the pupils, which they will unconsciously imitate. More direct help to a correct and easy expression may be given if, when the story is told, the pupils are asked to reproduce the principal points of it in their own words. Let the story be such as will interest the children, and teach a useful lesson without bringing out the moral too plainly.

If the teacher has not the art of telling stories, he may read from a book such stories as the children have not seen. Better than this, however, is reading at sight by the children. If they know that such reading will be followed by a reproduction of the thought expressed, their interest in and attention to what is read will be increased, and a greater number of ideas will be gained. The same course in respect to talking and writing should be pursued, and the same cautions in respect to combination should be observed, as have been spoken of before. In the lower grades the subject-matter may be brought out by skilful questioning. When this is done, the children should be encouraged to give the story in a connected form, and always in their own language. Unless care is taken, they will seek to remember words only, and give the language of the book. In the higher grades, with little or no questioning the pupils should be able to give the substance of the article read, first orally and then in writing. The written work should be carefully examined, corrected, and rewritten. One of the most common faults is the making of short and disconnected sentences, — a fault which is allowable with beginners, but which should be corrected as soon as possible. Let the sentences be made so as to read smoothly and pleasantly, without many breaks and without the use of too many connectives.

Paraphrasing. — In connection with the reading, the higher-grade pupils may with profit occasionally write out the substance of a difficult piece of prose or poetry. It will not be necessary to rely upon the memory to do this, but, with the book before the pupil, he may freely translate the essay or poem, being more careful to preserve its sense than its letter. Besides directly assisting him in composition, such an exercise will lead him to understand many expressions which he might otherwise pass by.

Letter-Writing. — The writing of letters of one form or another should occupy the attention of all grades of pupils. The proper form of dating, addressing, subscribing, folding, and directing letters should be taught as early as possible, and afterwards attention should be given to the body of the letter. The good letter-writer, like the good talker, has something to say, and says it in a direct and natural way. At first it may be necessary to give to the children some hints of what they should say in a letter. For example, the teacher may say, "Suppose you write a letter inviting your cousin, whom you may call John or Mary, to come to see you for a week during your next vacation. Tell him or her when your vacation is, and then what you could do to entertain yourselves." Similar directions may have to be given to the children in the second or third year in school; but as soon as may be, lead the children to compose their letters without help; encourage in all possible ways originality of thought and naturalness of expression. Imaginary journeys and visits may be described in letters to friends at home, thus bringing in what has been learned in geography and history.

Letters descriptive of familiar scenes may be written to distant friends, and the story of their own experience in vacation time be given in familiar letters to each other. In these and other ways the teacher will encourage the pupils to write good, naturally expressed, and original letters, being careful not to tell too much on the one hand, and not to discourage by too little assistance on the other.

In addition to letters of friendship, pupils in the higher grades should give attention to writing business letters of all kinds. Ask your pupils to write letters applying for board or a situation, or giving an order for goods. Cut out advertisements from the column of " wants," and give one to each pupil to answer in a proper way.

Business Forms and Notices. — Before leaving school, pupils should be able to write in proper form ordinary business papers, such as notes, receipts, orders, bills, and notices of all kinds. Let them practise in writing notices advertising a lecture or a concert, an auction sale, or a private sale of goods of any kind, the loss of a dog or the finding of a pocket-book. For practice in condensation, the writing of telegrams is useful, in which the most is to be said in the fewest words.

The composing of items of news for the newspaper is both interesting and instructive practice. It may do no harm to have the pupils sometimes see the result of their efforts in print. A fire or an accident, or any other event which has occurred in the neighborhood, may be described by the pupils, with the understanding that the best description will be sent to the local newspaper for insertion. They should be taught that a plain, direct statement of facts is to be preferred to the extravagant expressions which are so frequently found in newspapers.

Elliptical Sentences. — The supplying of ellipses is good practice, especially in learning the proper word and correct forms of words to be used. The distinction in the use of such words as *may* and *can, would* and *should, lie* and *lay, sit* and *set, in* and *into, invent* and *discover, between* and *among, beside* and *besides, alone* and *only, remember* and *recollect, ago* and *since, like* and *as,* may be learned in this way. The correct use of the words should first be taught, and afterwards exercises like the following may be given : —

—— I go —— the recitation room to get my book?
—— he lift the stone?
I now —— on the lounge.
Yesterday I —— on the lounge.
I —— the books on the table.
The books —— on the table.
Come and —— by me while I read to you.
—— the pitcher on the table.
He went —— the house.

The same method of teaching the correct *forms* of words may be found useful, as illustrated in the following : —

John and Mary —— in school.
One of the boys —— ill.
They sent Mary and —— to school.
John is taller than ——.
—— do you wish to see?
Who borrowed my pencil? ——.
Which is the —— of the two?
Neither James —— John —— ready to recite —— lesson.
These are ——' bonnets.

Compositions. — In addition to the daily practice in language work, such as has been indicated, the older pupils should be expected as often as once a month to write a composition upon a given subject. Care should be taken to select subjects about which the pupils know something, or which are within their comprehension. Dislike to composition-writing is generally due to the fact that the pupils are called upon to give expression to ideas which do not exist in their minds. The average school boy or girl has very dim ideas, or no ideas at all, of such abstract subjects as hope, beauty, and perseverance, and it is no wonder that discouragement and disgust follow any attempt on their part to write upon them. When we remember that the greatest writers have chosen for their themes the simplest subjects, we can hardly make the mistake of giving too simple topics for our children to write upon.

The following list of subjects will be found suggestive of what may be given to older pupils of the grammar grade : —

My home.
My grandfather's farm.
The town in which I live.
Our school.
Trees.
The coffee plant.
A picnic excursion.
A sleigh-ride.
A visit to the country.
A visit to the city.
A visit to Mammoth Cave.
How I spent my last vacation.
A journey to England.

A letter from Egypt.
Our baby.
George Washington.
Abraham Lincoln.
William E. Gladstone.
Joan of Arc.
The reminiscences of an old tree.
Autobiography of a cent.
History of a loaf of bread.
The old horse's story.
What my dog would say if he could talk.

A tramp's diary. | Good manners.
Six reasons why a boy should not smoke. | "A rolling stone gathers no moss."
How a shoe is made. | "All is not gold that glitters."
How a barrel is made. | Intemperance.
A visit to a paper-mill. | Cruelty to animals.
A visit to a hospital. | A hundred years ago.
A visit to a prison. |

During the latter part of the grammar-school course, pupils should learn to separate their compositions into paragraphs. They may receive some assistance in this direction, by studying carefully the paragraphing of prose in their histories and reading-books.

Outlines. — All original written work should be done according to some definite plan. At first the plan or outline may be provided by the teacher. By degrees, however, the pupils should be led to make their own outlines, which should be submitted to the teacher for approval and correction. For the younger pupils the outlines should be very simple, scarcely more in some cases than two or three questions to be answered in entire sentences; as, for example, in describing an object the teacher may say: What are the parts? What is the shape of each part? What is the use of each part? Or in writing upon any material, as wood or paper, the pupils may answer the questions: Where obtained? How prepared? For what used? Varieties?

In giving an object lesson, the teacher or one of the pupils should write upon the blackboard the principal facts as they are discovered. These statements will constitute material out of which the composition may be written. Frequently it is well for the pupils to analyze a short sketch for the purpose of making an outline.

The following outlines will suggest to teachers what may be given to, and required from pupils as a guide to their writing upon simple subjects: —

Any natural production (as salt) . .
- 1. Qualities.
- 2. Uses.
- 3. Where, when, and how obtained.

Any manufactured article (as glass) .
- 1. Qualities.
- 2. Uses.
- 3. Kinds.
- 4. How made
  - a. Materials.
  - b. Where procured.
  - c. Order of manufacture.

Any animal . . . .
- 1. Size and covering.
- 2. Parts
  - a. Name.
  - b. Description.
  - c. Uses.
- 3. Habits.

Biography . . . .
- 1. Time of birth.
- 2. Circumstances of parents.
- 3. Events of boyhood or girlhood.
- 4. Education.
- 5. Subsequent events in order of occurrence.
- 6. Leading traits of character.

Any plant . . . .
- 1. Name and general appearance.
- 2. Parts:
  - a. Root
  - b. Stem
  - c. Leaves   } Describe each.
  - d. Flowers
  - e. Fruit
- 3. Uses.
- 4. Where found.

Places seen . . {
1. Location.
2. Surroundings.
3. Parts or divisions.
4. What is contained or produced.
5. Objects of interest.
6. Reminiscences.

A journey (real or imaginary) {
1. Time and place of starting.
2. Intended destination.
3. The route taken.
4. Mode of travelling.
5. Description of country.
6. Objects of interest on the way.
7. Description of place visited.
8. Manners and customs of people.
9. Incidents and anecdotes.

It is well sometimes to give in the outlines some topics which will stimulate thought and investigation. Care should be taken that the information furnished be not too extended. The following outline[1] is an example of what may be given to pupils in advanced and grammar grades : —

WINDS.

1. Beneficial on land, as they —
   a. Carry moisture. Where from?
   b. Equalize the temperature. How?
   c. Purify the air. How? Name places benefited.
   d. Carry seed. What kinds? How a benefit?
   e. Pump water and grind flour. How and where?
2. Beneficial on the sea, as they —
   a. Aid in navigation. How?
   b. Produce ocean currents. How? Value of the currents?
3. Injuries on land by —
   a. Hurricanes. Illustrate.
   b. Carrying seed. Illustrate.
   c. Spreading diseases. Explain how.

[1] From *Intelligence*, Chicago.

4. Injuries on the sea by —
   a. Cyclones, etc.
   b. Hindering navigation. How ?

A few pointed, suggestive questions upon a subject when it is assigned, often give direction and method to the work of the pupils; as, —

RAILROADS.

1. When first built and where ?
2. How do they benefit western farmers and eastern manufacturers in our country ?
3. How do they aid the poor ?
4. How do they promote the settlement of new countries ?
5. Do they affect the value of the land ?
6. Illustrate their value in carrying news, merchandise, and people.

Correction of False Syntax. — Mention has been made of the desirability of correcting mistakes as they occur. These mistakes, and others which are most frequently made, should be made a special object of criticism and correction even before the rules of correction are learned. Read the incorrect sentences, or write them upon the blackboard, and ask the pupils what correction should be made. Erase the incorrect form and have the correct form supplied, after which, let the pupils write the corrected sentence in a blank-book. Sometimes the sentence may be written with certain parts omitted, and the pupils be asked to supply the missing parts. Thus the teacher may write, "One of the boys —— here." The pupils are to be led to say whether *is* or *are* is to be used in the sentence, and then they should write the sentence in full as before. Sometimes correct and incorrect sentences may be placed upon the board and the pupils asked to write correctly all the sentences they see. This plan is especially good for examination, when pupils will not be helped by guessing, as they are when something in every sentence is to be corrected. Let the most common errors receive the most attention, and review often enough to have the corrections fixed in the mind.

Do not let the incorrect forms remain upon the board, for fear they will be imitated by children in their writing. Only the correct forms should be written in the blank-book by the pupils, or, if incorrect forms are written, they should be erased or marked with a cross.

Correction of Written Work. — The value of language lessons, so far as accuracy is concerned, depends largely upon the extent and manner of correction. If the incorrect language of pupils is left uncorrected, the errors are impressed upon their minds, and the use of incorrect forms of speech becomes a habit with them. It is advisable, therefore, to allow no language work to be done without correction.

It is well to have each pupil, beyond the first year, provided with a language-exercise book. For the younger pupils, the book may be made by binding together from twelve to twenty leaves of primary ruled paper. Upon the left-hand page the language exercise can be written; and upon the right-hand page the same exercise, after it is corrected, can be rewritten in a correct form.

In dictation and other exercises in which all the pupils are supposed to have the same forms of expression, the proper correction may be made by the pupils themselves as the exercise is repeated by the teacher or

placed upon the blackboard. In other exercises, such
as abstracts, letters, etc., in which the language of each
pupil is different from that of every other one, the correction of errors should be made by the direct assistance
of the teacher. Some corrections may be made at the
time of writing, the teacher passing among the pupils
and pointing out their errors; but most of the errors
will have to be corrected after the papers are collected.
Such corrections should be so made as to have the
pupils ascertain the correct form and rewrite the given
exercise entire. If a slate is used, the sentence containing the error should be erased and rewritten correctly.
If books are used, such as have been suggested, the
errors may be corrected and the exercise be rewritten
on the opposite page.

But it will not be well to have all the corrections
made by the teacher. In the first place, such work, if
done thoroughly, would take up much of the teacher's
time, both in and out of school; and secondly, corrections made by the teacher are not so useful as
those which enable each pupil to see the mistakes of
all the rest and know how they are to be avoided.
This, of course, is most difficult with the younger
pupils, and yet it may be done to some extent even with
them. In correcting mistakes, as in teaching, do not
attempt too much at a time. The time of an entire
recitation may profitably be taken to correct a single
exercise of a few sentences. When a correction is presented to a class, drill upon it as soon as convenient,
so that the mistake may not be made again, or, if it
is made, that it may be corrected by the pupils.

One way of correcting is as follows: Let as many

pupils write their exercises upon the blackboard as can be accommodated there, and call the attention of the entire class to the corrections you make in each, frequently appealing to the class for assistance. One pupil may have punctuated the sentences improperly; another may have failed in the use of capital letters; the sentences of another may be poorly constructed.

When some of the corrections have been made, ask the pupils to re-examine their papers and mark the errors they see. Then after exchanging papers they may correct the mistakes of one another. After all this is done, the teacher, by glancing over the papers, can tell whether they may be copied into the language books as they are, or whether another recitation will be necessary to correct the papers. By this method the teacher's work will be materially lightened, and the pupils will acquire the power of correcting their own and one another's errors.

With older pupils a key for the correction of errors may be used. The following key has been tried with success in some schools: —

W. — Careless writing.
S. — Error in spelling.
P. — Error in punctuation.
C. — Error in capital letter.
Wd. — Error in use of word.
G. — Error of grammar.
V. — Vague; meaning uncertain.
F. — Error in figure.
B. — Borrowed.
Par. — Place of beginning paragraph.
[ ] — Passages within brackets to be recast.
? — To inquire about.
X — Some fault too obvious to require particularizing.

Underline the error, and place the letter indicating correction in the margin.

A simpler form of marking would be to draw an oblique line through an error of spelling, punctuation, or use of capital letter; to underline a word wrongly used, and, if the sentence should need reconstructing, to enclose it in a parenthesis. Anything more than this, to be indicated by writing.

One good method of correcting the compositions of older pupils is to have two or three pupils write their compositions, or a part of them, on the board each morning. During the day the other members of the school may correct what is written, using the signs of a given key. Before the session closes, the teacher, with colored crayon, may go over the work, correcting each error that has been made. The attention of the school should be called to these corrections, and the pupils be asked to copy the signs of correction and rewrite their compositions. The same course may be pursued each day with other compositions. In this way each pupil learns to avoid errors which he and others have made. The pupils also by degrees acquire the ability to correct one another's errors; so that after a time the papers may be distributed among members of the class or school, for correction, subject to final correction by the teacher. The importance of having the pupils rewrite their compositions after correction should not be forgotten.

GRAMMAR.

DURING the first seven years in school the pupil has been learning to express his thoughts with accuracy and facility. In this work he has acquired an art which will be of the greatest practical value to him, and he has also laid the foundation for the study of principles. He may now begin the study of grammar, which treats of the relations and forms of words in sentences. He may also study the elements of logic and rhetoric, which are closely related to grammar, — logic treating of the thought expressed, and rhetoric treating of the manner in which the thoughts are expressed. Analysis of sentences and the choice of words and phrases do not really belong to grammar, which has reference mainly to the construction of sentences. It is important that the teacher should keep in mind these distinctions, though the three subjects may be carried on together.

Outline of Study. — During the last two years of the grammar-school course — if the course is nine years — the study of grammar and analysis may be pursued; but only the simpler facts should be learned in the grammar school, the more abstruse and difficult parts of the subject being left for the high-school course. A book may be used, but it should not be rigidly adhered to either in the order of topics or amount taken. Some things will have to be supplied by the teacher, and in the case of many books much will have to be left out.

The following outline will indicate both the order and amount of work which may be taken in two years: —

1. Sentence : —

Subject, Predicate $\begin{cases} \text{Copula.} \\ \text{Attribute.} \end{cases}$

2. Parts of speech : —
   (1) Noun.
   (2) Pronoun.
   (3) Adjective.
   (4) Verb.
   (5) Adverb.
   (6) Preposition.
   (7) Conjunction.
   (8) Interjection.

3. Sentences : —
   (1) Kinds :
       Declarative, imperative, interrogative, exclamatory.
   (2) Forms :
       Simple, complex, compound.

4. Analysis : —
   (1) Principal elements :
       Subject $\left. \begin{array}{c} \\ \\ \end{array} \right\}$ entire, simple.
       Predicate
   (2) Subordinate elements :   •
       (a) Uses and kinds :
           Objective, adjective, adverbial.
       (b) Form :
           Word, phrase, clause.

5. Nouns : —
   (1) Kinds :
       Common, proper.
       Collective, abstract.
       Simple, derivative, compound.
   (2) Properties :
       Numbers, genders, cases.

6. Pronouns : —
   (1) Kinds :
       Personal, interrogative, relative, adjective.
   (2) Properties :
       Persons, numbers, genders, cases.

7. Adjective:—
   (1) Kinds:
       Descriptive, pronominal, numerals, articles.
   (2) Variations of form:
       Comparison.
8. Verbs: —
   (1) Kinds:
       Regular, irregular.
       Transitive, intransitive.
   (2) Forms:
       Simple, derivative, mode inflections, voices, tense in-
       flections, persons, numbers (conjugation).
9. Adverbs:—
   (1) Kinds:
       (a) Simple (in relation):
           Manner, place, time, degree, cause, etc.
       (b) Conjunctive.
   (2) Properties:
       Comparison.
10. Prepositions.
11. Conjunctions:—
    (1) Kinds:
        Co-ordinate, subordinate.
    (2) Uses.
12. Interjections.

Definitions. — The object of study in grammar is
the sentence, precisely as the mineral is the object of
study in mineralogy or the plant in botany. Beginning
with the sentence, therefore, or with several sentences,
we first lead the pupils to know and define a sentence
and its related parts. Two points are to be observed
in teaching definitions: first, to see that they are constructed by the pupils upon facts which they themselves
have observed; secondly, to secure accuracy of statement. When the definitions have been properly taught,
and when the statements are made by the pupils in

accordance with the facts observed, it may be well to
compare those statements with others which are found
in the text-book, and which may sometimes be substi-
tuted for their own. But even the text-books are not
always correct, as when it is stated that "the subject of
a proposition is that of which something is said" and
that "a noun is a name."

To illustrate how definitions may be made, the following examples are given : —

The pupil is first asked to express a thought about
the book, the crayon, and the schoolhouse. These and
other expressions are placed upon the blackboard, and
the name "sentence" is given to each expression. The
pupils soon see and state that "a combination of words
expressing a thought is a sentence." By observing the
sentences it becomes apparent that there are two distinct parts in every sentence, one part expressing that
of which something is said, and the other part telling
what is said of that expressed by the first part. The
definitions of subject and predicate are accordingly
made from these facts.

Etymology. — The parts of speech and their properties are also learned by observation. Sentences as before are written upon the blackboard, and the attention
of the pupils is directed to those words which name
objects of thought, or things of which we may think.
A noun, then, is seen to be a word which names an
object of thought. By this definition which they have
made the pupils should point out the nouns in many
written and printed sentences until the nouns of any
sentence which they understand are quickly recognized.

From what has been said it will be seen what use

should be made of the book. It may be used by the pupils after the topics have been taught, chiefly for guidance in accuracy of statement and in furnishing suitable sentences for illustration and study.

Much practice will be found necessary before the parts of speech can be readily distinguished and named. It is well for the pupil also to give definitions as he names the parts of speech.

When the parts of speech can be readily distinguished, they may be taken up separately, beginning with the noun. As before, present to the pupils sentences containing nouns having various uses and properties. As these uses and properties are distinguished, they should be classified, named, and defined. The following example will illustrate the method of teaching the kind and properties of all parts of speech. Place several sentences upon the blackboard ; as, —

> The boy lost his knife in Boston.
> John bought an apple for his sister.
> The man's coat was torn.
> William's sister Kate went to the city.
> The girls went to the concert.
> There are seven days in a week.
> The dog is named Donald.

First ask the pupils to select those nouns which name an individual object. The nouns *Boston*, *John*, *William's*, *Kate*, and *Donald* would be selected, to which the name *proper* would be given by the teacher. Proper nouns should then be selected from the reading-books and defined. The other nouns will be seen to be, not the names of individual objects, but the names of classes of objects. These are named and defined as before.

Further classification of the kinds of common nouns, as collective, abstract, and verbal, may be made in the same way, and each kind be defined.

Numbers and genders are easily taught. The pupils' knowledge of language will enable them to distinguish and define these terms at once. Cases are also easily recognized and defined when it is known that there are only two case-forms of nouns, — one used to denote possession, and the other all other relations. The subjective and objective *relation* of nouns should be indicated in parsing, and in the case of pronouns the names of the cases should be given. Persons of pronouns should be taught by placing before the pupils many sentences in which different forms are used to indicate whether they denote the speaker, the person spoken to, or the person or thing spoken of. The pupils will see that only some pronouns have person, and will call these *personal* pronouns. The cases of pronouns should be taught in a similar manner, and when the various forms indicating the different relations are easily distinguished and named the definition should be given. The inflection will follow, and should be made, as far as possible, by the pupil alone.

The other parts of speech and their properties should be taught in the same way. First present many examples of the fact which it is desired to teach, and when the fact is well understood, lead the pupils to apply the knowledge gained in many different sentences.

Syntax. — The right construction of sentences is the object of the study of grammar, and its rules should be considered as soon as possible after the study of grammar is begun. Greater interest in the study will be awakened when its practical bearing is seen, and a greater variety and amount of practice in correcting false syntax will be had by learning the rules of syntax early in the course. As soon, therefore, as the properties of the parts of speech are known, their rules of construction should be learned. The rules are taught in the same way as are definitions. Put upon the blackboard many sentences like the following : —

> John struck his ball.
> I saw him in the city.
> He taught me to read.
> Etc., etc.

By observing these sentences the pupils will be led to see the changed forms of the nouns and pronouns in different relations, and will also discover that in certain relations the same form is used. From the facts thus learned the rules will be made.

Parsing. — Parsing consists in giving the parts of speech, their kinds, properties, uses, and the rules for their construction. The use of parsing is to apply in a convenient form the facts and principles which have been learned. The form of parsing should be simple, and at first definitions and inflections should be given mainly for the purpose of fixing them in memory. The following form for parsing a pronoun may be used by beginners : —

In the sentence "He came to see me," "me" is a pronoun because it is a word used instead of a noun. (Declined : nom. I, etc.) It is a personal pronoun because it has person ; first person, because it denotes the speaker; singular number, because it stands for one object ; objective case, object of "to see," according to the rule, — A pronoun used as the object of a transitive verb or its participles must be in the objective case.

After some practice of this kind is had, a shorter form may be used, as: "me" is a personal pronoun, first person, singular number, objective case. Rule: A noun or pronoun, etc.

The order for parsing the various parts of speech in the shorter form may be as follows: —

1. Noun: —
   (1) kind,
   (2) number,
   (3) gender,
   (4) case,
   (5) rule of construction.

2. Pronoun: —
   (1) kind,
   (2) person,
   (3) number,
   (4) gender,
   (5) case,
   (6) rule of construction.

3. Adjective: —
   (1) kind,
   (2) (number),
   (3) degree of comparison,
   (4) relation.

4. Verb: —
   (1) kind,
   (2) (voice),
   (3) mode,
   (4) tense,
   (5) agreement,
   (6) rule.

5. Adverb: —
   (1) kind,
   (2) (deg. of comparison),
   (3) relation.

6. Preposition: —
   use.

7. Conjunction: —
   (1) kind,
   (2) use.

Analysis. — While the study of the parts of speech is progressing, there should be taught the various kinds and forms of sentences and analysis as indicated in the outline. The phraseology used in the outline may not be the same as that which is used in the text-book; but

whatever form is used, there should be kept constantly
in mind the purpose of gaining a clear perception of the
thought of the author, and a knowledge of the proper
form and order of elements. Let the progress in analysis be very gradual, allowing each new fact learned to
be reviewed in many sentences. At first the sentences
studied should be of the simplest kind, and when the
elements of such sentences are learned, the same kind
and form of elements may be found in other and more
complex sentences. The following form of analysis will
illustrate the use of terms given in the outline : —

*The tidings of the death of his son filled the old man's heart with
anguish.*

A simple, declarative sentence.

The entire subject is " *The tidings of the death of his son.*"

The simple subject is "*tidings.*"

The entire predicate is "*filled the old man's heart with anguish.*"

The simple predicate is "*filled.*"

" *Of the death of his son* " is an adjective phrase and modifies
"*tidings.*"

" *Of his son* " is an a ljective phrase and modifies " *death.*"

" *The old man's heart* " is an objective phrase, and modifies
"*filled.*"

" *With anguish* " is an adverbial phrase, and modifies "*filled.*"

The form and relation of separate words are given in
the parsing which follows the analysis.

Synthesis. — Composition-writing of all kinds, as
outlined in another place, should be carried on throughout the entire course. In addition to this there may be
practice in combining, contracting and expanding the
elements of a sentence. Such work as the following
will be found profitable : —

Writing sentences having any desired kind and form of element; expanding words into phrases; expanding words and phrases into clauses; contracting clauses into phrases; contracting phrases into words; combining two or more simple sentences into a compound or a complex sentence.

Correction of False Syntax. — Rules of syntax are used not only in forming sentences correctly, but also in testing the construction of sentences already formed. For reasons already given, it is desirable that the practical benefits of the study of grammar should be derived as early as possible. As soon as a rule of syntax is learned, it should be used as a guide in correcting ungrammatical sentences. Many sentences containing violations of a rule just learned, and of rules previously learned, should be placed before the pupils for correction and for the reasons of correction.

To test the knowledge of pupils, and at the same time to make them thoughtful in applying rules, both correct and incorrect sentences may be placed upon the blackboard for them to write out correctly upon paper and to give reasons of correction. This will be found to be much better than to place before the pupils sentences having only incorrect forms which can frequently be corrected "by guess." The following exercise is a good test for pupils who have studied the construction of nouns, pronouns, and verbs.

Write correctly the following sentences, and give reason for every correction made : —

He called to see John and me but neither of us were at home.
Whom do you think I saw in New York?
Who was it that touched the bell? Was it me or James?

Ten men fell into the water and not one of them were drowned.
Every one of the witnesses testifies to the same thing.
Whom do you take me to be?
Do you use Webster or Worcesters dictionary?
Whom did you come with?
He told John and I to come when we was ready.

ARITHMETIC.

ARITHMETIC may be defined as a knowledge of numbers. The objects of its study are, first, to acquire skill in those computations which are of use in the affairs of life; and secondly, to train the faculties of the mind. To gain these ends it is obvious that there should be a careful selection of topics to be taught, and that the topics should be presented in such a way as to secure a proper kind and amount of mental training.

The topics to be presented, and the order in which they should be presented, will be seen in the course of studies. It will be observed that much that is found in many text-books is omitted in the prescribed course. The subjects are limited in order to give needed time to teach and practise upon the more practical parts of arithmetic. Advanced work in mensuration and complicated business problems are also dropped from the course, for the reason that grammar-school pupils are not mature enough to grasp these subjects which would better be taken up in the high school.

Nearly all the faculties of the mind are developed by the study of arithmetic, and we should see that they are developed in an orderly way. While it is doubtless true that the power of reasoning is greatly strengthened by this study, we must be careful not to force it by a too early application to difficult problems. The teacher should keep constantly in mind the necessity of proceeding from the concrete to the abstract, and from the simple to the complex. In computations, first accuracy, and secondly rapidity should be secured. Do nothing for the pupils which they can do for themselves, and always encourage originality, both of thought and of expression.

When the idea is awakened or the course of reasoning made plain, there should be a repetition of the mental act, until the idea or the reason is fixed in the mind. Frequent reviews and drill exercises are therefore necessary, and should be given in such variety of form as will test the pupils' knowledge of the subject and enable them to recognize quickly a difference as well as a resemblance of conditions.

First Steps. — Ideas of number are first gained by means of visible objects. Blocks. splints, shoe-pegs, etc., should be placed in the hands of children as soon as they enter school, and with these objects the various combinations of numbers should be made, beginning with two, and proceeding by slow degrees, until, without the aid of objects, the combinations are known at sight. Addition, subtraction, multiplication, and division should be taught together because it is found that operations by synthesis assist the pupils in analysis, and that the combination and separation by equal parts lead directly to shortened forms of expression. For example, when the pupils see that two put with two makes four, they can learn at the same time that four less two makes two, that two twos are four, and that four divided by two is two.

As soon as possible, the pupils should be led to apply the knowledge of numbers they have acquired. When an operation is performed with the blocks, stories based upon the given combination may be made. In these stories encourage as far as possible originality of expression. Gradually the pupils may be led to make up the stories without the objects, and at last combinations may be expressed without reference to objects. Early in the course, also, practice should be given in solving problems involving the common weights and measures. First with the objects themselves, and afterwards without them, problems of a practical nature may be solved while the pupils are yet learning the simple combinations.

As soon as the pupils acquire a thorough knowledge of the combinations with objects, drill upon abstract numbers may be begun. Generally it is best to keep the practice upon abstract numbers a little behind the practice with objects. For example, while the number eight is being taught with objects, practice in abstract numbers to four may be given. To show how objects may be used in teaching numbers, and how the applications and abstract drill work may be done, the following outline of statements and questions is given. The exercise is intended for a class of first-year pupils who have learned the combinations to seven. They are supposed to be standing around a table, with the blocks before them. The teacher sits at one end of the table, and directs and questions as follows: —

Put one block with the seven blocks. Do you know how many you have now? You have eight blocks. Put one block on the table. Put seven more with it. One block and seven blocks are how many blocks? One boy and seven boys are how many boys? Tell me a story about one and seven. Put six blocks on the table. Put two more with them. How many have you? Put the eight blocks together. Put two of them behind you. How many are left on the table? Eight blocks less two blocks are how many? Tell a story about eight less two. Put eight blocks on the table. Put them into groups of two. How many twos in eight? Put them into groups of four. How many fours in eight? If one apple costs two cents, what will four apples cost? If one orange costs four cents, what will two oranges cost? If you have eight cents, how many oranges can you buy at a cent apiece? How many at two cents apiece? If you have six cents, how many pencils can you buy at two cents apiece? Go to the store with six cents and buy pears at three cents apiece. Tell me a story about two threes. About three twos. About two fours. About four twos. Here are eight mittens; how many pairs? How many horns have three cows? How many ears have four boys? Tell me a story about pairs of shoes. About pairs of bracelets.

How many twos in four? in six? in eight? Look and see how many gills in a quart. How many? How many gills in a pint? How many pints in a quart? in two quarts? If one pint of milk costs two cents, what will one quart cost? What will two quarts cost? If one gill costs one cent, what will one quart cost?

Divide four blocks into groups of two. What is one-half of four blocks? of six blocks? of eight blocks? Divide eight blocks into groups of two. What is one-fourth of eight blocks? One-eighth of eight blocks?

Now without your blocks, quickly: One and one? Two and one? Two less one? Two and what make three? Three less one? Three less two? Two ones and what make three? Three and one? One and three? Four less three? Four twos are how many? How many twos in four? How many ones in four? How many threes in four? One-half of four? One-fourth of four?

It should be understood that it will take several recitations to go over the ground covered by the above exercise, provided that time is given for the stories and for teaching the measures and fractions. It will also be understood that the recitation will not always take this precise form or that the combinations, stories, and illustrations will be limited to what is given above. See that every child is attending to the work in hand, whether it is in teaching, telling stories, or drilling, and when members of the class are inattentive or tired, change the exercise or stop the recitation.

Objects should not be used for teaching numbers beyond 20 in the primary course. Knowing the combinations to 20, all others to 100 are easily learned. In addition and subtraction beyond 20, the pupils are made to see that little work is needed. They have only to apply the knowledge they already have. For example, in the problems $28 + 6$ and $34 - 8$, they instantly recognize the results of $8 + 6$ and $14 - 8$, and have only to think of the tens in getting the answer. At first the teacher leads them to see this; afterwards they do it of their own accord, until adding and subtracting of all numbers less than 10 are done at sight.

In multiplication and division, the pupils should be led to make their own tables from what they know of addition and subtraction. Adding and subtracting by twos, threes, etc., will enable them easily to construct their own tables, and after they have constructed them, they should learn them so well as to be able to multiply and divide numbers at sight.

The plan as laid down for the primary grades includes all combinations to 144, and for the first division of ungraded schools, all combinations to 100. It is not intended in this plan to add or subtract numbers greater than 10 or to use a multiplier or divisor greater than 12. Yet if the pupils become very proficient in this work, it may be well to have them practise in other combinations, such as $28 + 64$; $83 - 25$; 18×4; $64 \div 16$. To add and subtract large numbers, lead the pupils to add or subtract first the tens, and afterwards the units: thus in the problem $28 + 64$, first add 60, then

4. The pupil would say 28, 88, 92. In subtracting 25 from 83, he would say 83, 63, 58. After considerable practice of this kind the computations can be made at sight.

Primary Drill. — To secure accuracy and rapidity of work, it will be found necessary, especially in the third year, to spend much time in drill. It is not enough to recite the tables. Pupils may do this, and still not be able to add, subtract, multiply, and divide *at sight*. Practice upon the combinations may be had in preparing a given lesson, and in the recitation.

In giving work for the pupils " to study " at their seats, the teacher may give a lesson in a book, or put the problems on the blackboard. Time may be saved by putting the problems on pieces of cardboard. These slips may be used by different pupils and classes. The following exercises for study will suggest what may be placed upon the board or cards : —

$$42 + 6 = ? \qquad 38 - 6 = ?$$
$$38 + 9 = ? \qquad 40 - 9 = ?$$
$$41 + ? = 48 \qquad 35 - ? = 29$$
$$? + 26 = 34 \qquad ? - 6 = 32$$
$$8 \times 3 = ? \qquad 42 \div 7 = ?$$
$$9 \times ? = 36 \qquad 36 \div ? = 9$$

Add	6	7			
	4	8	18	6	
	9	5	−9	×8	8)18

The same exercises may be used for drill in recitation. In addition to these the following exercises are suggested.

Add by columns, the teacher or pupil pointing, beginning with very short columns and easy numbers, thus : —

3	5	2	5	7	6	9
2	4	6	4	3	4	8
1	2	3	6	5	8	3
—	—	—	—	—	—	—

The pupil will say one, three, six; two, six, eleven; three, nine, eleven; and so on. Increase the length of columns gradually, until the pupils can add quickly twenty or more numbers expressed by a single figure without mistake.

Another method of drill is to place four columns on the board, thus : —

+ 6	× 4	− 5	÷ 3
7	6	16	26
2	9	19	29
9	3	13	23
3	7	17	27
5	4	14	24
8	5	15	25
6	2	12	22
4	8	18	28

As the teacher points to each number, let the pupil add, subtract, multiply, or divide, as indicated above the columns. By changing the figures above the columns, a great amount of work may be dictated in a little time. The pupils may give the result with or without giving the formula.

Still another method of drill is to place figures near the circumference of a circle, and add until a certain number is reached; or subtract, beginning with a certain number.

Add by 2's, by 3's, etc., beginning with 2, with 3, etc. Subtract by 2's, by 3's, etc., beginning with 40, with 50, etc.

Place in the centre of the circle described above a figure or figures. Point to any figure in the circumference, and require the pupil to multiply or divide. By occasionally changing the figures in the circle, a large number of problems may be given. Keep the attention of every pupil to the recitation of every other pupil, and require answers only as you point.

Practical Problems. — Mention has been made of the advisability of making stories in connection with the learning of combinations. When the combinations are known, they should be applied as soon as possible to practical problems. These problems should contain the common weights and measures, and should be of such a nature as to induce pupils to think. The following problems will suggest what may be given daily during the latter part of the third year in school. Some of the problems will have to be carefully taught with objects before they can be understood by the pupils. Encourage the pupils to give one another original problems of a similar kind.

What will three pints of milk cost at eight cents a quart?

How many cupfuls of milk in a quart, if each cup holds half a gill?

A piece of tape six inches long costs three cents. What will a yard cost at the same rate?

How many apples, at the rate of two for a cent, can I buy for twenty cents?

· What will six apples cost, at the rate of two for three cents? what at the rate of three for two cents?

I buy 12 two-cent stamps at the post-office, and give a half-dollar. What change will be given me?

Eighteen eggs are worth what at twenty cents a dozen?

What will one pound and four ounces of meat cost at twelve cents a pound?

If you should walk six rods north, and then turn and walk eight rods south, how many rods would you be from the place where you first started? how many yards? how many feet?

If a peck of potatoes will last a family one week, how many weeks will two bushels last them?

At one dollar a yard, what will be the cost of a piece of carpeting twenty-four feet long?

Notation and Numeration. — The writing and reading of numbers should be begun in the fourth year, but it is not well to give numbers of more than seven or eight places at this time. Sticks, and bundles of tens and hundreds should be used to teach notation. The sticks may be counted, and the number expressed by figures on the blackboard. Eighteen sticks should be counted as one ten and eight, the ten being bound into a bundle. When two more sticks are placed with them, they will make two bundles of ten sticks each, and should be called two tens, or twenty. When ten bundles of ten sticks each are counted, they should all be bound together into one bundle and called one hundred. As the numbers are thus taught, the expression should be placed upon the board in figures and read. It may not be necessary to teach notation in this way beyond thousands. When this is done, the pupil will see that ten of one denomination will make one of the next higher, and can write and read numbers readily to millions. In the fifth year billions, trillions, and quadrillions should be taught.

Numbers of two places of decimals should be taught and used in the fourth year. Pupils should learn to write decimals at first through a knowledge of writing dollars and cents. When they can write and read numbers in dollars and cents readily, lead them to see that, as there are one hundred cents in a dollar, one cent is one-hundredth part of a dollar, and that one-hundredth is expressed precisely as one cent is when written with a decimal point. Six dollars and one cent is expressed thus, $6.01, and may be read six dollars and one cent, or six and one-hundredth dollars. From this it may be readily seen that any number of cents represents so many hundredths, and may be read as hundredths. The first figure at the right of the decimal point represents the number of dimes, and may be called tenths of a dollar. This may be taught in the same way as hundredths is taught. Numbers of three places of decimals can be taught in the fifth year. As one thousand mills make a dollar, one mill is one-thousandth of a dollar; and therefore one mill, when expressed by figures, may be read one-thousandth.

Fundamental Processes. — At the beginning of the fourth year in graded schools, and of the second period in ungraded schools, the pupils are supposed to have a thorough knowledge of the four fundamental processes to 144 or to 100. They can, without hesitation, add and subtract twelve and all numbers below twelve. They can with equal facility multiply and divide, when the multiplier and divisor do not exceed twelve. They have learned to express in figures the numbers to 144, and can count to one thousand. They have learned to use and to write the fractions $\frac{1}{2}$, $\frac{1}{3}$, $\frac{1}{4}$, $\frac{1}{6}$, $\frac{1}{8}$, in connection with the combinations, and have had much practice in the application of their knowledge of numbers to practical problems.

All of this work should be constantly reviewed in the fourth year, while other things are being taught. As soon as pupils have acquired a knowledge of units and tens in writing numbers, addition of numbers of two figures should be· begun. This should be taught with sticks, beginning with the addition of two numbers that will not require "carrying." We may, for example, wish to add 22 and 21.

22 sticks and 21 sticks are placed in position, properly separated into tens and units. Putting the one unit with two units, we have three units. Putting the two bundles of tens with the other two tens, we have four tens. Answer, four tens and three units, or forty-three. The figures should be written out in proper order, and each result indicated as we go on. Several problems equally easy should be wrought in the same way.

When the pupils have had sufficient practice of this kind, take an easy problem in which the sum of the units is more than nine. Thus, in the problem $24+38$, take the sticks as before, and put the 4 sticks with the 8 sticks, making 12 sticks equal to 1 ten and 2 units. Put together the 10 sticks in one bundle, and add the tens thus, $1+2+3=6$ tens. Answer, 6 tens and 2 units, or 62.

Subtraction can be taught by taking from a given number of sticks a part. Thus, to teach $34-22$, we would take 2 sticks from the 4 sticks and 2 tens from the 3 tens, leaving 1 ten and 2 units, or 12.

To subtract 17 from 35, we should put before the pupils 35 sticks, consisting of 3 bundles of tens and 5 units. Asking them to first take 7 units from the 5 units, they will see at once that they will have to untie

one of the bundles and put the 10 sticks with the 5
sticks, making 15 sticks. Now they take 7 sticks from
15 sticks, and have remaining 8 sticks. 1 ten from 2
tens leaves 1 ten. Answer, 1 ten and 8 units, or 18.

Multiplication and division should also be taught
with objects, each operation being expressed in figures.
It will not be necessary to carry the objective teaching
beyond hundreds, but it will be found useful to have
considerable practice with smaller numbers before numbers of the higher denominations are taken. No number higher than ten thousand should be used during
the fourth year, so as to allow time for a sufficient
amount of drill and for work upon practical problems.

Fractions. — According to the prescribed course,
fractions are taught during the sixth year in the graded
school, or the latter part of the second period in the
ungraded school. Before this, simple fractions have
been taught objectively, and used to some extent in the
various operations. Circles of pasteboard will be found
to be the most convenient means of teaching fractions.
The idea of a fraction should be first taught by presenting the circles cut into halves, fourths, eighths, thirds,
and sixths. The expression may follow, first oral and
then written. Three-fourths will be seen to be three
of the four equal parts into which the circle is divided,
and is expressed by placing one figure above another,
and a line between them. The lower figure will be
seen to express the size of the parts, and the upper figure to express the number of parts taken. Considerable
practice of this kind, with the fractional circles and
expressions, may be followed by giving the terms *denominator* and *numerator*, and having them defined by the

pupils. The same objects may be used in teaching reduction of mixed numbers to improper fractions, of improper fractions to mixed numbers, and of fractions of one denomination to those of another. Care should be taken to occasion the idea before the expression is given. Thus the reduction of $5\frac{1}{4}$ to fourths, $4\frac{3}{8}$ to eighths, $3\frac{1}{6}$ to sixths; of $\frac{7}{2}$, $\frac{8}{6}$, $\frac{9}{8}$, to whole or mixed numbers; of $\frac{2}{4}$, $\frac{4}{6}$, $\frac{4}{8}$, $\frac{8}{12}$, to lower terms, should be known by means of objects before the operation is expressed in writing. When these facts have been presented many times to the pupils, they may be expressed in figures, and the pupils may be led to see the process by which the answers are obtained. For example, in the statement $5\frac{3}{4} = \frac{23}{4}$, the pupils should be led to see, after the fact has been taught by objects, that the answer could be obtained by the following course of reasoning. In 1 there are 4 fourths, in 5 there are 5 times 4 fourths, or 20 fourths; add 3 fourths, and the answer is $\frac{23}{4}$. If it is thought advisable, the rule could be deduced in the same way.

In teaching addition, subtraction, multiplication, and division of fractions, the same method should be pursued. First use the objects, and afterwards express the operations by performing them in figures on the board. Practise much in this way with small numbers before the book is used, and from the problems performed lead the pupils to deduce their own explanation or rule.

To illustrate the method of teaching fractions the following examples are given, one for teaching addition, and one for division. It will be understood that reduction of fractions has been taught before these subjects are reached.

Look at these circles and fractions as I hold them before you. How much is $\frac{1}{2}$ of a circle and $\frac{1}{2}$ of a circle? $\frac{3}{4} + \frac{1}{4}$? $\frac{1}{4} + \frac{1}{4}$? $\frac{1}{4} + \frac{2}{4}$? $\frac{2}{4} + \frac{1}{2}$? $\frac{1}{2} + \frac{1}{4}$? $\frac{3}{4} + \frac{2}{4}$? $\frac{3}{4} + \frac{1}{2}$? $1\frac{1}{4} + \frac{3}{8}$? $1\frac{1}{2} + \frac{3}{4}$? $\frac{1}{2} + \frac{4}{8}$? $\frac{1}{2} + \frac{2}{8}$? $\frac{1}{4} + \frac{2}{8}$? $\frac{1}{4} + \frac{4}{8}$? $\frac{1}{2} + \frac{3}{8}$? Let us now express in figures the answers you give me: $\frac{1}{2} + \frac{1}{2} = 1$; $\frac{3}{4} + \frac{1}{4} = 1$; $\frac{1}{4} + \frac{1}{4} = \frac{2}{4}$; etc.

Do you see how we added the halves and fourths? How did we add the fourths and eighths? Give an example adding halves and fourths, fourths and eighths. Your lesson to-morrow will be these fifty problems on the board (or chart).

The problems given for study are of course similar to those which they have had with the circles in the class.

The first part of the following exercise is designed to show how to teach the division of a fraction by a whole number. The second part illustrates a method of teaching the division of a whole number by a fraction. The directions and questions should be many more than are here given, and each exercise may be enough for two recitations.

Divide this circle into two equal parts; how much in each part? Divide this half-circle into two equal parts; how much in each part? Divide these two circles into four equal parts; how much in each part? Divide these two circles into eight equal parts; how much in each part? Divide this half-circle into four equal parts; how much in each part? Divide one-fourth of a circle into two equal parts; how much in each part? Divide three-fourths into two equal parts; how much in each part? Let us now see what you have done (writing on the board): —

$1 \div 2 = \frac{1}{2}$; $\frac{1}{2} \div 2 = \frac{1}{4}$; $2 \div 4 = \frac{1}{2}$; $2 \div 8 = \frac{1}{4}$; $\frac{1}{2} \div 4 = \frac{1}{8}$; $\frac{1}{4} \div 2 = \frac{1}{8}$; $\frac{3}{4} \div 2 = \frac{3}{8}$.

Who will divide any of these fractions into equal parts and place the result on the board?

Practise in this way with halves, fourths, and eighths, and then with thirds and sixths. When a large number of problems and answers is placed upon the board, lead the pupils to see and express for themselves the fact that we may divide by a whole number by dividing the numerator or multiplying the denominator. When they have done this, give out a large number of simple problems for them to perform before the book is taken.

To divide an integer by a fraction.

Call these circles pies. I have eight pies, and give them to the persons in the room; each person receives four pies; how many persons in the room? Put down on your slate each operation as you find it. I have eight pies, and give to each person in the room two pies; how many persons in the room? I have one pie, and give to each person at the table one-half a pie; how many persons at the table? I have one pie, and give to each person at the table one-fourth of a pie; how many persons at the table? I have two pies, and give to each person at the table one-half a pie; how many persons at the table? etc.

Now let us see what you have on your slate. Yes, —

$8 \div 4 = 2$; $8 \div 2 = 4$; $1 \div \frac{1}{2} = 2$; $1 \div \frac{1}{4} = 4$; $2 \div \frac{1}{2} = 4$; $2 \div \frac{1}{4} = 8$; $2 \div \frac{1}{3} = 6$; $2 \div \frac{1}{6} = 12$.

Keep these upon your slates, and do as many more as you can before to-morrow.

Now call the circles cents. I have four cents (holding up four circles); if apples are one cent apiece, how many apples can I buy? how many at $\frac{1}{2}$ cent apiece? how many at $\frac{1}{4}$ of a cent apiece? If the apples were three times as much apiece, how many could I get; more or less? what part as much? If these apples were $\frac{3}{4}$ of a cent apiece, how many apples could I get? Now let us take eight cents. Who will give us the same kind of a problem? What are the expressions on your slate? Let us put them on the board: —

$4 \div 1 = 4$; $4 \div \frac{1}{2} = 8$; $4 \div \frac{1}{4} = 16$; $4 \div \frac{3}{4} = \frac{16}{3} = 5\frac{1}{3}$; $8 \div \frac{1}{2} = 16$; $8 \div \frac{3}{2} = \frac{16}{3} = 5\frac{1}{3}$; $8 \div \frac{1}{4} = 32$; $8 \div \frac{3}{4} = \frac{32}{3} = 10\frac{2}{3}$.

From this work both the explanation and rule may be deduced by the pupils.

Applications. — From the time the child enters school he is led to apply his knowledge of numbers in making and doing practical problems of various kinds. With a knowledge of common and decimal fractions his work of this kind can only be limited by his immaturity. As the pupil matures, his field of study and practice widens. Some part, at least, of all kinds of business he may know, and the teacher should gather from every source material with which to work; several reference books, both written and mental, should be upon the desk to suggest ways in which the pupils' knowledge of numbers may be applied.

Weights and Measures. — These subjects, according to the prescribed course, are taken in the seventh year. During all the preceding years the pupils have performed problems which involve nearly all of the weights and measures commonly used in every-day life. They will not, therefore, have to spend much time in learning the tables. The metric system, and some parts of the tables of square and cubic measures, and of Avoirdupois and Troy weights, will have to be learned : also miscellaneous facts, such as the weight of different commodities, the number of units in a gross, and score ; number of sheets in a quire and ream, and the value of common foreign coins. All of these tables which will be of use to the pupils should be made and learned by them. When they are learned, they should be reviewed and applied so frequently that the pupils will not have to go to the book for information.

In choosing work for the pupils, give only that which is practical. Omit all parts of compound addition, subtraction, and division, which are rarely or never used.

Do not give impossible areas or volumes to measure or absurd puzzles to solve, but let the work be such as occurs, or may occur, in practical life.

The time may be well spent in the reduction of compound numbers, both ascending and descending, the computation of longitude and time, and the mensuration of surfaces and solids, such as papering and carpeting rooms, measuring boards, wood, bins, etc. Select from two or three books placed upon your table for the purpose such problems as you think most practical and best adapted to your pupils. If the reasoning of any problem is complex, give the same problem first with small numbers, and always encourage the pupil to use blocks and diagrams to illustrate the problems. The practice of illustrating problems by diagrams cannot be too early begun or too constantly insisted upon.

Very much time need not be spent upon the metric system. It is enough to teach by objects the different measures, and to lead the pupils to work enough upon the various applications to see the great saving of time which would follow the introduction of the system. As the denominations are rarely used in practice at the present time, they would be soon forgotten if learned ever so well. Therefore, not so thorough work in the application of metric measures should be attempted as in those measures which are in common use.

Percentage. — The kind of work to be done in percentage is indicated in the best text-books upon the subject. The amount to be done is limited only by the time of the pupil, for very much drill is needed to distinguish readily the various conditions of problems which are classed under the head of percentage. In no part of arithmetic is the necessity greater of passing slowly from the known to the unknown than in percentage. Teach each part of the subject with great care, using familiar illustrations and small numbers. Avoid, so far as possible, all work by rule, but lead the pupil by slow degrees to understand the principle involved in each problem as it is presented. Review frequently, and arrange the problems in such a way as to encourage the pupils to think. Sometimes pupils are directed to look over a "model solution," and to perform all the problems of a given lesson by it — a course which is likely to discourage independent thinking. To indicate how the subjects may be taught, a few illustrative examples are here given. The process of each problem should be indicated upon the blackboard as the answers are found, and when the principle is understood, drill with small numbers upon many similar problems should be given. Present for a lesson problems containing various conditions, so as to induce the pupils to consider carefully each step of the work.

1. *Given the cost and selling price, to find the rate per cent.*
I buy a book for $4, and sell it for $5. What do I gain? What part of the cost is the gain? How many hundredths of the cost is the gain? What per cent?
I buy a book for $5, and sell it for $4. What part of the cost do I lose? What per cent do I lose?

Give other problems of a similar kind containing small numbers.

2. *To find the simple interest of any sum of money.*
I lend you $190. To whom is a favor done? Who should pay whom for the use of it? Money paid for the use of money is

interest. The money loaned is called the principal. Suppose you were to pay me 8 per cent of the principal ($100) for the use of it for one year; what would you pay me? What would you pay me for the use of it for two years? Six months? Suppose you were to pay me 6 per cent a year; how much would you pay me for one year? For six months? For three months? For two months? For one month, or thirty days? For six days? For twelve days? etc.

Suppose I were to lend you $600 at 6 per cent a year; how much would you pay me for six months? For one month? For one day? For four days? For six months and four days?

When this method is well understood, by much practice teach any one of the shorter methods in the same. way, and allow only that method to be used.

3. *Given the sum sent to an agent, and his commission, to find what is expended.*

First teach by familiar examples the terms *commission, consignor, consignee.*

Upon what does a commission merchant always reckon his commission? If he buys goods for $100, and his commission is 2 per cent, what does he get for his trouble? What would be sent him to pay for the cost of the goods and his commission? If I should send my agent $102 with which to purchase goods after deducting his commission of 2 per cent, what would he expend? What would he have for his trouble? The cost of the goods represents how many hundredths, or per cent, of itself? The commission is how many per cent of the cost? What I send him is how many per cent of the cost? How will you get 100 per cent? (If the pupils hesitate here, use the familiar problems like the following : John has one-third more money than James. John has 20 cents; how many cents has James?)

William has 50 per cent more money than Thomas. William has $3; how much has Thomas?

Repeat such problems until the pupils see the principle involved, and can readily perform the problems in which the base is not given.

4. *To assess a tax upon the property of an individual.*

First suppose that $100 is to be raised in a school of fifty pupils, each pupil to pay an equal share without reference to the amount of property he has. What part of the whole amount would each pay? What per cent? How much would each pay? Suppose that the $100 is to be paid by the pupils in proportion to the property they held, and all together had $1,000; how much on one dollar would be raised? If John had $50, what would be his tax? Again, assuming that every one of the pupils should pay one dollar whether he had property or not, how much would be raised in this way? How much left of $100 would have to be raised on the property? How much now would have to be raised on one dollar? What would John's tax be?

Increase the difficulties slowly until large numbers can be easily dealt with.

Notes, bills, receipts, insurance policies, bonds, and other business papers should be brought into the class and used in such a way as to give reality to the work and to fix the principles taught. Parties concerned in business transactions may be personated by members of the class. For example, one pupil may be the maker of a note, another may be the payee, another may be an endorser, another may represent the cashier of a bank. The whole subject of notes, including interest, partial payments, and bank discount, may in this way become real and interesting, and be firmly fixed in the minds of the pupils.

Definitions and Rules. — Definitions and rules should be taught in the higher classes of the grammar grade, not by having the pupils commit them to memory, but by a process of analysis. For example, to teach the definition of subtraction the teacher might take any number, as ten blocks, and take away three blocks to see how many blocks remain. The pupil will observe the process, and define subtraction as "the process of taking part of a number away to find how many are left." Rules are also taught in the same way. Let the pupil observe each step of a given process, and state in general terms the order in which the steps were taken.

The use of formulas should be largely avoided in all grades except the highest. Whenever formulas are used, they should be made by the pupils from principles which are already understood.

Mental Arithmetic. — The use of mental arithmetic is unquestioned. It aids in developing the powers of attention, memory, and reasoning, cultivates the power of language, and greatly assists pupils in their written number work. Oral exercises should be given separately, and also in connection with written arithmetic.

The oral exercises which are given in connection with written arithmetic are mainly for the purpose of illustrating principles, and for drill both in abstract and in concrete work.

Illustrations of the use of small numbers in teaching a new subject or principle have already been given. By concentrating the thought mainly upon the reasoning processes, the pupil is led to see plainly what he could not see if he were dealing with large numbers. Mental exercises should therefore very frequently precede or introduce a regular recitation in written arithmetic, and they may also be given whenever pupils fail to understand a process or the conditions of a problem. For example, there may be some pupils who do not understand the process of finding the present value of a note due at some future time. The principle involved is found to be very simple when such problems as the following are given : —

John has 4 cents, which is $\frac{1}{2}$ as much as James has; how much has James? John has 6 cents, which is $\frac{3}{4}$ as much as James has; how much has James? John has a certain sum of money; after his father gave him $\frac{1}{2}$ as much more, he had 6 cents; how much had he at first?

By giving many problems similar to these, and increasing the size of the numbers gradually, the pupils can readily see that the present value is $\frac{100}{100}$ of itself; and if it gains $\frac{3}{100}$ in six months, it will be worth $\frac{103}{100}$ of its present value in six months. Knowing its value then in money, the present value can be easily ascertained.

When a principle is well understood, it needs to be fixed in the mind by doing mentally many simple problems involving that principle, and others which have been taught previously. For example, when division of fractions is well understood, problems like the following should be given in great number: —

I divide 8 apples equally among some boys, giving each boy $\frac{1}{2}$ of an apple; how many boys received a part?

To how many boys could I give 6 apples, if each boy has $\frac{1}{3}$ of an apple?

How many sticks $1\frac{1}{2}$ feet long can be cut from a stick 6 feet long?

How many bushels of potatoes at $\frac{2}{3}$ of a dollar a bushel can be bought for $6?

Four men earned in one day 8\frac{1}{2}$. If this money were divided equally among them, how much would each man receive?

When coal can be bought for $7 a ton, what part of a ton can be bought for 2\frac{1}{2}$?

Drill follows teaching, and serves to fix in the mind

what is taught. It may consist of practice upon abstract work, in which rapidity is the end sought, or upon concrete work, in which the main object in view is the cultivation of the reasoning powers; or it may combine both of these operations, and aim to promote both thought and rapidity. Besides the means already suggested for drill, the teacher might place upon the blackboard or upon manilla paper drill tables like the following. By extending the tables to 10 or 15, several hundred problems may be given from each table: —

	A	B	C	D	E	F	G	H	I	J	K	L
1	$\frac{1}{2}$	$\frac{1}{2}$	$\frac{1}{4}$	$\frac{1}{3}$	$\frac{1}{6}$	$\frac{1}{9}$	$\frac{2}{4}$	$\frac{18}{4}$	2	$1\frac{1}{2}$	$\frac{2}{3}$	16
2	$\frac{3}{4}$	$\frac{1}{4}$	$\frac{1}{8}$	$\frac{2}{3}$	$\frac{2}{6}$	$\frac{2}{9}$	$\frac{3}{6}$	$\frac{12}{8}$	4	$3\frac{2}{3}$	$1\frac{1}{2}$	13
3	$\frac{4}{8}$	$\frac{2}{8}$	$\frac{1}{4}$	$\frac{3}{6}$	$\frac{1}{3}$	$\frac{3}{9}$	$\frac{2}{8}$	$\frac{16}{6}$	3	$2\frac{1}{6}$	$1\frac{3}{8}$	19
4	$\frac{6}{8}$	$\frac{3}{8}$	$\frac{1}{4}$	$\frac{4}{6}$	$\frac{1}{3}$	$\frac{4}{9}$	$\frac{6}{9}$	$\frac{15}{9}$	8	$5\frac{3}{4}$	$2\frac{2}{3}$	17
5	$\frac{7}{8}$	$\frac{5}{8}$	$\frac{1}{2}$	$\frac{5}{6}$	$\frac{2}{3}$	$\frac{5}{9}$	$\frac{6}{8}$	$\frac{18}{8}$	6	$4\frac{7}{8}$	$3\frac{3}{4}$	14

The table may be used as follows: —

A + B,   B + C,   A + C,   B + E,   B + D,   A + E, etc.
A − B,   A − C,   A − B,   D − E,   D − F,   I − A, etc.
A × B,   B × C,   A × I,   A × J,   A × F,   A × E, etc.
I ÷ A,   I ÷ C,   A ÷ I,   J ÷ I,   A ÷ B,   A ÷ C, etc.

Reduce I pounds to ounces.
Reduce E feet to inches.
What will A pounds of meat cost at L cents a pound? etc.

Besides the oral work which is done in connection with written arithmetic, there should be a few minutes set apart each day for miscellaneous mental practice. The problems given should be of a varied character, sometimes consisting of operations with abstract numbers, in which accuracy and rapidity are mainly sought;

at other times the problems should be of such a nature as will call into active exercise the reflective faculties. As no one book would furnish a sufficient variety of problems, there should be upon the teacher's table several different mental arithmetics, from which to gather and give problems of a proper kind. It will not be found best for the teacher or pupils to read the problems from a book. Let the teacher glance over two or three pages of a book, and select such problems as will induce the pupils to think, giving them in language of his own. Sometimes the problems may be analyzed and explained, and sometimes, especially in examination, answers only may be required. One good method of examining a class in mental arithmetic is to give out the problem slowly and distinctly, ask the pupils to do it mentally and to keep the answer in their minds. After a sufficient time has elapsed for all to do the problem, give the direction, "Write the answer," and after they have had time to write the figures of the answer, ask them to put the pencils down and to take a good position. If the answers are given in large figures, the slates may be examined by having them held up, asking pupils who have the wrong answer not to hold them up.

Explanations. — Great freedom should be allowed in the form of explanations, especially to pupils of the lower grades. The pupils' attention should be directed mainly to the thought, and not to the language, as is frequently the case when complicated and set forms are insisted upon. Sometimes a pupil will understand how to perform a problem, but cannot give the reason. Let similar problems be given with smaller numbers, and the expression of a reason will come in time.

Short Processes. — Always encourage the pupil to perform a problem in the shortest way, provided the problem is equally well understood by the short process. It will be found generally best in the lower grades to have but one method of performing problems of a given kind. In the higher grades, however, the pupils should be encouraged to perform problems with the fewest figures, provided, of course, accuracy is not sacrificed.

GEOGRAPHY.

GEOGRAPHY is a knowledge of the earth on which we live. Physical geography treats of the earth in its natural condition, including land, water, climate, and productions. Political geography treats of the earth as modified by man, its countries, cities, towns, society, religion, government, etc.

Geography may be elementary or scientific. Elementary geography is a knowledge of facts and is pursued in the primary and grammar schools. Scientific geography is a knowledge of causes and relations, and may be begun in the highest class of the grammar or ungraded school and be continued in the high school. It should be said, however, that the facts to be studied in the lower grades may include as much of the relations of cause and effect as are within the comprehension of the pupils of those grades.

Objects. — The knowledge acquired in the study of geography should be a real knowledge of the earth as the home of man, providing for him food, clothing, and shelter, supplying objects for his enjoyment and study, and so being a means of social, intellectual, and spiritual progress. As a means of mental culture, also, the study of geography is of great use. Observation, imagination, memory, judgment, and language are all exercised in the study, and by it the child's interest in the world about him is awakened in such a way as to increase his sympathy and love for his fellow-men.

It is evident that these great objects cannot be attained by learning and reciting facts ordinarily found in a text-book, especially if the facts stand in the pupils'

minds in a disconnected way and unrelated to any experience of theirs or to any direct use.

Preparatory Lessons. — Before geography as a study
is begun, children need to acquire a proper habit of
observation, and to gather facts which will aid them in
their subsequent study. During the first three or four
years, therefore, the plan of study includes lessons in
Form, Place, Plants, Animals, and Minerals, which are
intended to give such knowledge as will make the study
of geography more intelligible and therefore more profitable. The methods to be pursued in these subjects are
to be treated under the head of Observation Lessons.

Local Geography. — Further preparation for the study
of geography is made in the third and fourth years by
lessons to teach geographical ideas and geographical
language. The knowledge thus gained is sometimes
called local geography because much of it is gained by
observation in the locality of the school.

The simpler subjects of the following outline should
be taught during the third year, the more difficult being
delayed until the fourth year, when all preparatory work
should be reviewed.

I. BODIES OF LAND.

1. Hill:
   - base.
   - slopes.
   - summit.
   - hill range.
   - hill system.

3. Plain:
   - field.
   - woods.
   - meadow.
   - swamp.
   - prairie.
   - desert; oasis.

2. Mountain:
   - base.
   - slopes.
   - summit.
   - peaks.
   - mountain range or chain.
   - mountain system.
   - volcano: crater. lava.

4. Table-land.

5. Valley:—   6. Highlands.
   River valley.
   Gorge, or cañon.
   Pass.   7. Lowlands.

8. Coast: {
    beach.
    cliffs.
    bluffs.
    projections: {
        cape.
        promontory.
        peninsula.
        isthmus.
    }
}

9. Islands: {
    continental.
    oceanic.
    volcanic.
    coral.
}

II. BODIES OF WATER.

1. Spring: {
    pure water.
    mineral.
    hot.
    geysers.
}

2. Brook: {
    source.
    branches.
    banks.
    bed.
    current.
    channel.
    mouth.
    water-shed.
}

3. River: {
    source.
    branches.
    banks.
    bed.
    current.
    channel.
    water-falls.
    mouth.
    uses.
    river system.
    river basin.
    water-shed.
}

4. Pond: {
    system.
    basin.
}

5. Lake: {
    system.
    basin.
}

6. Ocean: {
    sea (archipelago).
    gulf.
    bay.
    harbor.
    strait.
    channel.
    sound.
}

III. CLIMATE (weather).

1. Temperature: {
    hot.
    cold.
    temperate.
}

Spring, summer, autumn, winter; day, night.

2. Air and moisture :
{
wind.
vapor.
dew.
frost.
cloud.
fog.
mist.
rain.
hail.
snow.
ice.
}

IV. Soil :
{
loamy.
sandy.
clayey.
fertile.
arable.
barren.
}

V. Productions.

1. Plants :
{
for food.
for clothing.
for building-material : { houses. ships. utensils. }
for fuel.
for medicine.
for oils and dyes.
}

2. Animals :
{
for food.
for clothing : { furs. skins. leather. }
for labor.
for utensils : { ivory. bone. }
}

3. Minerals :
{
for building-material : { houses. ships. utensils. }
for fuel.
for food.
}

VI. People.

1. Races :
- Caucasian.
- Mongolian.
- Malay.
- African.
- American.

2. Occupations:
- agriculture.
- fishing.
- mining.
- manufactures.
- commerce : { exports. imports.

3. Government: { republic. monarchy : { absolute. limited.

4. Religion :
- Pagan.
- Jewish.
- Christian.
- Mohammedan.

5. States of Society :
- savage.
- barbarous.
- half-civilized.
- civilized.

Some of the foregoing subjects will be found difficult to teach satisfactorily. Let it be remembered, however, that no amount of telling or reading can take the place of teaching, and that the teacher may be content to teach very little of a subject, provided the facts are discovered and expressed by the pupils themselves.

Among the most difficult of these subjects to teach is climate, a thorough study of which belongs to a later period. Some ideas of the subject may be gained by calling attention to the temperature and moisture of the atmosphere from time to time, making comparisons of the weather of different seasons and of different places. It may be noted that the temperature is more equable near the sea than at a distance from it, and that it is lower upon a high hill than it is in the valley.

Some general ideas of the formation of dew and rain may be gained by simple experiments. Call attention of children to the fact that some of the water which was left in a dish on the stove the day before has disappeared. Bring out the statement from them that the water has "gone into the air." Call attention to the rising steam, and ask them for familiar instances of the same thing. Give them the name *evaporation*. Hold a cold plate over the steam, and let them observe the drops of water formed on the plate. Call attention to the deposit of moisture on the window-pane in a cold day, and upon the outside of a pitcher of ice-water in a warm room. From these illustrations the children get the idea of *condensation;* and, by a little questioning, they may see that the same conditions exist in the formation of dew and rain as exist when drops of water are seen to form on the plate and pitcher.

Most of the topics in the above outline, under *Bodies of Land* and *Bodies of Water*, may be taught by leading the children to observe the various features of land and water in the vicinity of the schoolhouse. The observation should be made from the schoolhouse at the time of recitation and at recess, or it may be made in little tours of inspection by the school either as a whole or in groups. Frequently it will be found well to direct the attention of children to certain things, and have them bring the results of their observation into the recitation. It will be useful, also, to call attention to their past experiences, and to use the results of their experience in the recitation.

As an assistance both to observation and to memory, it will be found well to draw and to mould representations of the various objects observed, and to have the pupils express correctly, in their own language, all the facts observed.

For the purpose of teaching productions, bring before the class as many specimens of native and foreign products as can be found. From the stores, from the neighboring woods, and from the homes of pupils, there may be obtained a large number of vegetable, animal, and mineral productions, some of which may be kept permanently in the school.

To teach ideas relating to people, first lead the children to think of the condition of the people of their own town and State. Subsequently, by means of stories and pictures, lead them to compare the people of other countries with those of their own country in respect to occupations, religion, government, race, and state.

Plan-Drawing. — Before maps of unknown places are drawn or studied, careful attention should be given to the drawing of plans, first in connection with lessons upon Place.[1] After drawing the outline of various surfaces, and indicating the place of objects upon them, drawing to scale should be begun. One foot to the inch when drawn upon the board, or four feet to the inch when drawn upon the slate, may be a convenient scale for drawing the floor of the schoolroom. Do not assist the pupils much, neither allow them to be discour-

[1] p. 193.

aged for want of assistance. When the floor of the room is carefully drawn, let the different objects — as the teacher's desk, stove, etc. — be indicated upon the plan. As the object is to associate representations with the things represented, the pupils should sometimes be called upon to point out, in the room, certain objects represented upon the plan.

The first plans upon the board should always be made upon the north side of the room; and if made upon the slate, the upper part of the slate should be toward the north. By degrees the pupils may learn that the upper side of the slate or plan represents north, the lower side south, the right-hand side east, the left-hand side west. Objects in the room may now be indicated in the plan by dictation, as follows: Draw the platform on the west end; the stove four feet from the north side; the ventilator near the south-east corner, etc.

Passing from the room, the next step will be to draw the school grounds and neighborhood. Here the progress should be slow, and the steps carefully taken, for there are many important points to be presented, — direction of streets, brooks, and fences, and the location of houses, ponds, hills, etc. A progressive plan may be made, with the schoolhouse as a centre, the pupils drawing, day by day, three or four additional objects, until a complete plan of the neighborhood is made. After this, good maps of the town and country should be studied carefully, and those places which the pupils have seen be particularly noted. There should be a good map of the town and adjoining towns hung up in the schoolroom for occasional reference. If such a

map is not provided, one may be made upon manilla
paper or upon the blackboard.

Much of the plan-drawing should be done in the
third year, in connection with the study of local or
home geography; but it should be reviewed occasionally in the fourth year, that good ideas of maps may be
had before the pupil draws maps of continents and
countries.

As a means of reviewing the subjects which have been
taught in the preparatory lessons, and of introducing
the pupils to the use of topics, topical outlines for the
study of the town should be given. These topics may
include terms which have been taught, and the pupils
should be encouraged to use geographical language in
their recitation, which should be made without questions. The following topics, so far as they belong to
the town studied, may be used: —

1. Outline : boundary (bays, capes).
2. Size : length and breadth.
3. Surface : —
    (1) Mountains, hills, ranges, peaks.
    (2) Valleys, plains.
4. Drainage : —
    (1) Brooks, rivers :
        Source, outlet, branches.
    (2) Ponds, lakes :
        Outlets, inlets.
5. Climate : —
    Moisture, temperature.
6. Soil.
7. Productions : —
    Animal, vegetable, mineral.
8. Industries.

9. Exports and Imports: —
    Railroads.
10. Interesting facts of history.

Study of Maps. — The study of maps of known places may well follow the preparatory observation lessons, and should precede the study or drawing of maps of continents and countries. The maps studied should be of places with which the pupils are familiar, or which they have seen. They should be studied with reference to relative distances (scale) and the location of known objects. They should be compared with maps made by the pupils, and be a means of reviewing lessons upon physical features.

Moulding-Board. — Moulding has the same place in teaching geography as plan and map drawing; *i.e.*, for illustration. It may be used in teaching the natural bodies of land and water, and other parts of local geography *after the real objects have been observed;* also in making relief models and in representing the parts of a continent or section. It will be found especially useful in representing the physical features of a town, adding with bits of cardboard and sticks the principal roads, houses, etc.

GENERAL LESSONS FROM GLOBE AND MAPS.

Earth as a Whole. — In the fourth year, elementary lessons upon the globe should be begun. The subjects to be taught at this time are as follows: —

1. FORM OF THE EARTH.
    Illustrate with clay or croquet ball flattened at two opposite sides.

2. **Motions of the Earth.**

Use knitting-needle or wooden needle for *axis*, and teach the effects of *rotation* and *revolution*. Only the most general and simple facts should be taught at this time. Teach *equator*, *poles*, and *hemisphere*.

3. **Land and Water Hemispheres.**

Draw a line around a globe so as to lead pupils to see that most of the land is in one hemisphere and most of the water in another.

4. **Northern and Southern Hemispheres.**

Show with a globe the relative amount of land and water north and south of the equator.

5. **Eastern and Western Hemispheres.**

Why called old and new worlds?

6. **Bodies of Land.**

The names and relative size and position of the continents should be taught from a mapped globe. Lead the pupils to discover similarity and difference in shape, and character of outline.

7. **Bodies of Water.**

Teach the name and relative size and position of the oceans from the globe. Lead the pupils to see which are in the Eastern, and which in the Western Hemisphere.

8. **Climate,**

Hot, cold, and temperate parts.

9. **Productions and Commerce.**

A few of the principal productions should be named and the climate and localities in which they are produced. Some ideas of commerce, both domestic and foreign, should be given by showing where and how the various productions are carried.

Some of these elementary lessons may best be given by drawing with a crayon upon a plain black globe.

Continents. — When the first lessons upon the earth as a whole are completed, the study of continents should be begun. Books may now be placed in the hands of pupils, but every lesson should first be taught from a mapped globe or a good outline map.

An introduction to the map of the hemispheres and continents is made by opening a globe so that its hemispheres may be placed side by side, and be compared with outline maps of the same.

In these lessons only the most general features should be considered, somewhat as follows : —

(1) Position of continent on globe: show what part is hot, cold, temperate; direction from other continents. (2) Relative size: compare with other continents. (3) Outline: character of coast line compared with other continents; principal indentations; outline drawn by pupils from cardboard models. [See Map-Drawing.] (4) Mountain systems. approximate length and width; comparative height; direction of slopes. (5) Principal rivers and lakes: only a few of the largest; source and outlet; relative length. (6) Most valuable productions : where obtained. (7) Important countries: position in continent; comparative size. (8) Best known cities: position; comparative size. (9) People : races; occupations. [Reading of such books as "Seven Little Sisters" and "Each and All."] (10) Special and peculiar features.

After one continent has been studied, points of resemblance and difference should be constantly referred to, as direction and length of mountain systems, size of rivers, condition of people, etc. In giving the special and peculiar features of a continent, select those which will be of most interest to the pupils, as volcanoes, pyramids, curious animals and plants.

After the outline is traced, it may be kept for the purpose of inserting the various features as they are studied. The order of study is indicated in the following topics, which may need some changes and additions for some of the continents.

I. POSITION.
Surrounding water and land.
Latitude, zones.
II. CONTOUR.
Comparative shape, regularity of coast line.
III. SIZE, compared with other continents.
IV. SURFACE.
1. Highlands : { mountains.
plateaus.
2. Lowlands : { valleys.
plains.
V. INLAND WATERS.
Large lakes and rivers.
VI. CLIMATE.
Comparative temperature and moisture.
VII. PRODUCTIONS.
Vegetable, animal, mineral.
VIII. PEOPLE.
Races, employments, and customs.
IX. POLITICAL DIVISIONS.
Countries, large cities.

Countries and Sections. — After the general features of the continents have been studied, the more important countries and sections should be taken up, beginning with the United States. The sections should be studied and recited by topics as before, the topics being more minute than those of the continents. The study should also be pursued in connection with map-drawing. The pupils' own State and section should be known much more thoroughly than other sections, and should therefore be reviewed more frequently. The industries, states of society, commerce, etc., of other countries should be constantly compared with those of our own country, so as to make the facts learned seem as real as possible.

Interesting facts of history also should be given in connection with places, and, in studying about the cities and productions of a country and the occupations of the people, constant reference should be made to the marine column of the daily or weekly newspaper, where will be found the destination of vessels and the ports from which vessels have sailed, together with what is exported and imported.

Frequent use of pictures should be made in teaching the physical features of a country, its cities, and the manners, customs, and occupations of the people. Scrap-books or alphabetical letter-files may be used for the purpose of preserving pictures cut from illustrated books and papers. With the aid of pupils any teacher can make a large collection of pictures which will be of great value in giving interest and vividness to the subjects taught. Care should be taken to so arrange the pictures that those of a particular section can be easily found at any time.

In teaching and in giving information in any part of geography, let the facts be linked together as much as possible, especially the facts of cause with those of effect. Thus there should be given the names and descriptions of animals together with the climate and physical features of the country in which they live; the position of a country, and its climate; the commercial and manufacturing cities, and their peculiar location with reference to mines, rivers, etc.; the physical conditions of a country, and the character of the people.

On many accounts it will be better to take up large sections for study rather than small sections or single states. Among the advantages of studying large sections are (1) the relative size and position of the states may be better observed; (2) the climate, soil, and productions may be better compared and remembered; (3) trivial and unimportant details are less likely to be dwelt upon. The last point is one of great importance. The really important features of any distant state or country are few, and the time and strength of the pupils should be given to these to the exclusion of such details as the heights of mountains, the length of rivers, absolute areas, capes, small rivers, and insignificant towns. In general it may be said that those features of a country or section should be most emphasized which most affect and represent the life of the country and which most concern ourselves both as a country and as individuals. With this view, topics relating to life should be especially noticed in the study, such as climate and its causes, occupations and habits of the people, land and water communications and what is carried over them, government, and important cities. Certain sections also demand more attention than others, depending upon their importance and their relation and nearness to us. Next to our own State and country, those countries should be most carefully studied which have most to do with us and which are the most highly civilized.

The following topics may be a guide for study and recitation upon countries and sections: —

I. POSITION.
1. Boundaries : $\begin{cases} \text{land.} \\ \text{water.} \end{cases}$
2. Latitude, longitude, zone.

II. SIZE.
1. Length and breadth.
2. Relative size.

III. SURFACE.
1. Highlands : $\begin{cases} \text{mountains:} \begin{cases} \text{systems.} \\ \text{ranges.} \\ \text{peaks} \\ \quad \text{(volcanoes).} \end{cases} \\ \text{plateaus.} \end{cases}$
2. Lowlands.
    Plains : $\begin{cases} \text{interior.} \\ \text{coast.} \end{cases}$

IV. DRAINAGE.
1. Water-partings.
2. Rivers : $\begin{cases} \text{source.} \\ \text{direction.} \\ \text{principal branches.} \\ \text{uses.} \end{cases}$
3. Lakes.
    Location : $\begin{cases} \text{salt.} \\ \text{fresh.} \end{cases}$

V. CLIMATE.
1. Kind : $\begin{cases} \text{temperature.} \\ \text{moisture.} \\ \text{healthfulness.} \end{cases}$
2. Causes : $\begin{cases} \text{latitude.} \\ \text{elevation.} \\ \text{currents :} \begin{cases} \text{air.} \\ \text{water.} \end{cases} \\ \text{nearness to sea.} \end{cases}$

VI. PRODUCTIONS.
1. Fertile and sterile sections.
2. Mineral, vegetable, animal.

VII. PEOPLE.
   1. Races.
   2. Occupations: { agriculture.
                     manufactures.
                     commerce :
             domestic, foreign.
             exports — where sent.
             imports — from what place.
             means :
                 railroads, rivers, etc.
   3. Manners and customs.
   4. Education.
   5. Government.
   6. Religion.
VIII. POLITICAL DIVISIONS.
   States.
   Important cities and towns.
      For what noted?

Mathematical and Physical Features. — In addition to the elementary lessons upon the earth as a whole, given in the fourth year, there should be given in the higher grades more advanced lessons, including motions of the earth, latitude, longitude, and some physical features. As much of the following outline as can be understood should be taught in the sixth and seventh years, the more difficult subjects to be left until the first part of the eighth year, when the whole should be reviewed. The facts learned should be applied to particular sections as they are taken up.

   I. FORM OF THE EARTH.
      Four proofs.
  II. MOTIONS OF THE EARTH.
     1. Rotation (evidences).
        Axis, poles, equator.

Effects of rotation :
   a. with axis horizontal.
   b. with axis upright.
   c. with axis oblique.
2. Revolution (evidences).
Effects of revolution :
   a. with axis upright.
   b. with axis oblique.
Tropics and polar circles : cause of location.
Zones, parallels, meridians.
Variation in the length of day and night in different
   parts of the earth.

III. LATITUDE AND LONGITUDE.
   1. Length of degree on large circles; on small circles.
   2. Latitude; measured where and from what?
   3. Longitude; measured where and from what?
   4. Difference in longitude and time.

IV. LAND SURFACE.
   1. Formation of continents.
   2. Coral formations.
   3. Volcanic effects.
   4. Causes of depression and elevation of surface.

V. WINDS.
   1. General cause.
   2. Kinds and causes of each :
      (1) Trade winds.
      (2) Monsoons.
      (3) Cyclones.
      (4) Local winds.
   3. Uses of winds.

VI. WATER MOVEMENTS.
   1. Springs: kinds and causes.
   2. Waves, what and how caused.
   3. Tides :
      Kinds, causes of each.
   4. Ocean currents :
      (1) Kinds and causes.
      (2) Polar and equatorial.

(3) Principal currents.
(4) Influence in navigation.
(5) Influence upon climate.
(6) Take imaginary voyages to show effects of ocean currents.

VII. CLIMATE.

Formation of dew, mist, fog, clouds, rain, snow, frost, hail.
Amount of rain, how affected in various parts of the earth.
Temperature depends upon what.

VIII. SOIL (sub-soil).

1. Thickness.
2. Composition.
   (1) Loam.
   (2) Sand.
   (3) Gravel. } Character of each.
   (4) Clay.
   (5) Organic matter.
3. How made.
   (1) Water freezing in crevices of rocks.
   (2) Effects of atmosphere.
   (3) Effects of running water.
   (4) Effects of roots and rain.
   (5) Effects of insects.
4. Kinds.
   (1) Calcareous.
   (2) Sandy. } Character, and how made.
   (3) Clayey.
5. Fertility.
   (1) Depends upon what.
   (2) Degree of fertility.
6. Adaptation of soil to different plants.

These subjects should be carefully taught each day *before* they are "studied" in a book. For means of illustrating and teaching some of the topics the teacher should consult good reference books and use simple apparatus.

To teach the motions of the earth and their effects in producing a variation in the length of day and night and change of seasons, use a ball with a cardboard disk to separate the light and dark hemispheres. The ball should have a knitting-needle for an axis, and be placed in various positions before a lighted lamp to represent the sun. By rotating the ball with the axis in an upright and in a horizontal position, and placing the disk between the light and dark hemispheres, there may be shown the lighted hemispheres and the relative length of day and night, if the axis of the earth were in those positions. Incline the axis $23\frac{1}{2}$ degrees towards the north, making both motions of the ball (rotation and revolution), and there are represented many useful facts, such as the relative length of day and night in different parts of the earth, three causes of change of seasons, cause of position of tropics and polar circles, difference of longitude and time, and the position of the sun in various parts of the earth at different times of the year. To teach some of these and other points, it would be well to have a blacked ball upon which chalk-marks may be made.

To teach the causes of winds, place a bit of lighted candle on a piece of glass. Over it place a lamp-chimney so that the chimney will project over the edge of the glass. By holding a thread at the bottom and at the top of the chimney, the facts may be observed that cold air moves toward the flame below, and that warm air ascends. From this illustration, and from others showing the unequal heating of the earth's surface by the sun, the pupils may learn the causes of some local winds, and of the surface and upper currents, north and south, changed by the rotation of the earth into constant northeast and southeast winds, or trade winds.

Map-Drawing. — After careful practice in plan-drawing, and observation of good maps of the town and county, the pupils are prepared to begin the drawing of maps. In giving the first lessons upon continents the globe should be used, and it would be well for the teacher to prepare pasteboard outlines of the continents. These outlines will give a good idea of the relative shape and size of the continents, and afford at the same time models for tracing. When the outline of a continent is traced, the different parts may be represented as they are studied, as mountain systems, rivers, and productions.

In the sixth year, when the study of the United States is taken, the pupils should draw the outline, first by copying, and afterwards from memory. Fine and artistic efforts should not be attempted in any part of the course, — the object being merely to fix in the mind facts that are learned. Direction, distance, and location are in this way impressed upon the mind as they can be in no other way. The first efforts in imitation may be by tracing upon thin paper. Afterwards the pupils may attempt to copy with the map before them, and then see what they can do from memory. The first attempts at memory drawing will be very crude, but the pupils should be encouraged to try, and generally it will be found to be agreeable employment. The first topic in the study of the United States will be "outline." At the time of recitation each pupil may draw the outline upon the slate or board from memory, and indicate the boundaries — natural and artificial — by initial letters. For example, Gulf of Mexico, Chesapeake Bay, and New Brunswick may be indicated by G. M., C. B., N. B. Day by day the map should grow as new topics are taken up. A progressive map may be kept by the pupils on paper or placed upon the board; but they should be ready to draw each day all that has been previously studied; so that at the close of the lessons a completed map may be made by every pupil, embracing the principal mountains, rivers, cities, and production areas.

In the seventh year, when latitude and longitude have been studied, the preparatory study may include parallels and meridians. With the book open, the teacher by skilful questioning may draw out from the pupils many facts in regard to distances and latitude; afterwards by a little direction the pupils may draw, free-hand, the parallels and meridians, which will be sufficiently accurate for all practical purposes. They will then be prepared to draw the outline, imitating the map in the book. When this has been done two or three times, the map may be drawn from memory, *without the parallels and meridians.* In recitation, also, the drawing of parallels and meridians from memory should not be attempted, the outline only being drawn, with no construction lines. In the pupils' study, in which the map is drawn by parallels and meridians, the shape and relative dimensions of the country are impressed upon the mind, and when they draw the outline from memory, the shape and dimensions are found to be sufficiently accurate.

It may be well sometimes to indicate the high and low land by different colored crayons, as for instance, shades of brown and green. When the topic "productions" is reached, areas of the principal products may be indicated by enclosed lines. The climate and animals of a given section may be indicated by small printed or ·written words.

Memory maps of any given subject, such as surface, drainage, productions, or cities, may be called for at any time, and the pupils by constant practice should be ready to answer the demand. For example, a river map of Europe may be drawn from memory, as a review lesson, the names or their initials being written or printed. In the same way examinations may be made. More can be indicated upon a map in a single hour than could be written out in three hours.

It will be seen that the drawing of maps, both in study and recitation, constitutes an important part of the work in geography as here laid down. The reasons for emphasizing map-drawing will become apparent as a saving of time, an increased interest in the study, and superior results are seen.

The Recitation. — What has been said of the advantages of topical study and recitation applies with peculiar force to geography. Outlines, more or less minute, should be given to the class as a guide to study. The same outlines should also be a guide to each pupil's recitation, the teacher giving as little assistance as possible. A review of the previous lesson or lessons may be given during the first few minutes of the recitation, so as to connect together related subjects.

When a pupil has told all that he can of a given topic, encourage the rest of the pupils to ask questions of the one who has recited. It will, of course, be understood that the answers to such questions, as well as the facts given in recitation, need not necessarily be found in the text-book, but may be gathered from all reference books to which the pupils have access. Very often a part of the class may be sent to the board, and the rest take slates, for the purpose of drawing the outline of the country studied, and indicating, or representing, such facts as have been learned, as mountains, rivers, cities, etc., each pupil reciting as all draw. In drawing the outline of a country, for example, one pupil may mention the body of adjacent water or land and the direction of the boundary line as the class draw; then another pupil may continue the description. They may proceed in like manner with the other topics, following the order in which they were learned. In this form of recitation it will be seen that the teacher says very little, most of the talking being done by the pupils.

The question and answer method, by which the teacher uses many more words than the pupils, should very rarely be used. After a country has been studied, a page of map-questions may be given out for a lesson. In the recitation of such a lesson one pupil may read the questions for the pupils whom the teacher designates to answer. Or each pupil may be asked to write five questions, and after he has answered one he may give another to another pupil, naming the pupil who is to answer after the question is given.

In the map-questions and in other lessons the outline wall-maps may sometimes be used, one pupil pointing out the places named. Generally, however, the answers should be given without the map being in sight. An occasional exercise with the outline map will be found profitable, in which the teacher points upon the map to certain places, which the pupils name or about which they tell what they know.

Geographical Reading. — After a subject or country has been studied by topics, there should be class reading of journeys and other descriptions for the purpose of gaining interesting and useful information. At least one-third of the time given to geography, and some of the time set apart for supplementary reading, should be given to such reading. It is not necessary for every pupil in the class to have a book. Three books, or even one book, passed from one pupil to another, will suffice. Half a dozen good books of travel upon the countries studied should be accessible to every teacher of the grammar grade. They will do much to give interest to the study and direct the future reading of the pupils.

HISTORY.

THE chief objects to be kept in mind in teaching history are : (1) to create an interest in history and a taste for reading it; (2) to teach important facts of history so that they will be remembered ; (3) to show the relation of past events to the present in such a way as to prepare pupils for the varied duties of life ; (4) to cultivate the powers of memory, imagination, and reflection ; (5) to cultivate language.

Preparatory Work. — Story-telling and story-reading should precede the formal study of history, and may be begun very early in the course. True stories of celebrated persons, especially of their child life, will be interesting and instructive to children of the primary school. During the fourth and fifth years in school the stories should continue to be largely about persons, and may be somewhat disconnected ; that is, no special effort need be made to follow in chronological order the history of our country, the main purpose being to make enduring impressions upon the pupils, of the principal characters in history, and to create an interest in them. The story may be sometimes told by the teacher, and sometimes read after a few of the principal facts have been told. Sometimes one pupil may read the story to the rest, and sometimes — perhaps oftener than in any other way — the pupils may read in turn at sight. All of these exercises should be followed by talking and writing upon the subjects given, in order to encourage attention, to fix the points in the minds of pupils, and to cultivate the power of expression.

During the sixth and seventh years in school, story telling and reading should be continued, but in a more systematic manner and with a wider purpose in view than during the preceding years. To teach what history is, and to lead the pupils into the possession of historical ideas as a basis for subsequent study, will now be the purpose of the teacher. Ideas of peaceful life, of war, and of government, are best gained by observation of present affairs, by reading and hearing what has transpired in the past, and by comparing what is heard with what is known from observation.

Begin, then, by calling the attention of pupils to the necessary accompaniments of peaceful life, — useful employments, schools, government, religion, etc. Lead them to state in detail what they see in every-day life about them, and what is transpiring at the present time in places remote from them. Several talks of this kind will bring out all the essential ideas of peaceful life, and make the pupils realize that history is a real thing of the present as well as of the remote past. When this has been done, lead them to compare the present condition of their neighborhood and country with what it was in early colonial times. Have them read stories of the early settlements, dwelling especially upon the privations that were endured, the absence of schools, railroads, and telegraph, the primitive home life, and the means of travel.

The local history of the town or neighborhood should be first considered. There are few places which have not most interesting stories connected with them. The more personal and real these stories are, the better. After the pupils have read and talked about the early history of their own neighborhood and State, let them do the same with the history of other places, it being kept constantly in mind that the story should convey a vivid impression of real life. Pictures will aid the pupil to get a clear idea of some things which cannot be well described by words. Photographs of places, and pictures cut from illustrated papers and pasted upon cardboard, coins, and relics of every description, — all will be found to be a valuable aid to the teacher of history.

The same method of teaching ideas of war should be used as is used in teaching ideas of peace. In the stories read and talked about, the causes of wars, their necessity, and the methods of warfare should be considered. It would not be well at this stage to dwell much in detail upon campaigns and battles.

Ideas of government, the objects of government, the different kinds of government, and the duties of citizens, should be taught in connection with stories illustrating both peace and war, and with what exists in their own town, State, and country.

During the latter part of the seventh year, one elementary book of United States history may be read through in regular order, for the purpose of getting a connected account. As before, the reading should be followed by talking and writing, in which the principal events are brought out clearly in the pupils' own language. All the while, the geography of the section talked about should be carefully studied from outline maps. Progressive maps, with changes in the boundary, may be drawn by the pupils. Chronological tables may also be made, consisting of the dates of the most important events. If the dates of five or six events of a century are kept in mind, all other events may be distinguished as occurring before or after one of these dates. For example, if the time of the landing of the Pilgrims is known, some other events could be remembered as occurring either before or after that event.

Topical Study.—At the beginning of the eighth year in school, history should be taken up as a distinct study. Instead of one book being used for study, it is better to have several, each pupil deriving the benefit of the study of others from different books. Topics should be arranged carefully by the teacher, and placed upon the blackboard. These topics can be copied by the pupils into topic-books provided for the purpose. Some time will be needed and not a little direct assistance before the pupils can use the topics as they should be used in study, and before they can give long and connected statements in their own words.

The following general outline may be a guide of work to be attempted during the eighth and ninth years : —

I. AMERICA BEFORE COLUMBUS.
    Traces of inhabitants : Northmen.
II. DISCOVERERS AND EXPLORERS.
    1. Spanish.
    2. English.   } Important discoveries and explorations.
    3. French.
    4. Dutch.
III. ENGLISH SETTLERS.
    1. In New England.
    2. In Middle States.
    3. In Southern States.
        (1) Permanent settlements.
        (2) Cause of settlers coming.
        (3) Life of people.
            Manners, customs, laws, religion.

       (4) Government.
       (5) Growth and change during colonial period.
       (6) Wars.

IV. THE FRENCH IN NORTH AMERICA.
V. THE REVOLUTION.
VI. THE CONFEDERATION.
    1. Reasons for.
    2. Principal events.
    3. Defects.
VII. THE UNITED STATES.
    1. The Constitution.
       (1) Formation and adoption.
       (2) Features.
       (3) Amendments.
    2. Presidential administrations.
       (1) When begun, length.
       (2) Principal events.
    3. Internal progress.
       (1) Population.
       (2) Industries.
       (3) Productions.
       (4) Exports.
       (5) Education.
       (6) Inventions.
    4. Wars.
       (1) England(1812).   ⎰ Cause.
       (2) Mexico.   Duration.
       (3) Civil.   Principal events.
                                 Result.

The topics of the general outline will have to be elaborated somewhat as the various subjects are reached. The following topics, for example, may be given upon "The French in North America."

    1. The territory acquired.
       (1) What region.
       (2) By whom discovered and settled.

(3) First settlements.
(4) Time (relative).
2. Government.
    (1) Kind.
    (2) Results.
3. Loss of territory.
    (1) Claims.
    (2) Allies.
    (3) Opponents.
    (4) Parts abandoned, and when.

The following topics for the study of wars may be used : —

1. Parties.
2. Cause.
3. Occasion.
4. Elements of strength and weakness.
5. The campaigns.
    (1) Plan.
        a. Objective points. Where? Why?
        b. Routes.
        c. Forces and commanders.
        d. Advantages and difficulties.
    (2) Movements.
    (3) Decisive battles.
    (4) Results.
    (5) Consequences.
6. Results of the war.
7. Consequences of the war.

The Recitation- — A short time should be taken at the beginning of each recitation for reviewing such topics of past lessons as have any connection with the lessons of the day. Such reviews will also fix in mind the important facts which have been studied.

To bring out the points clearly, and to make the study interesting, maps and diagrams should be in con-

stant use in the recitation. Engraved maps may be
consulted, but special attention should be given to the
drawing of maps by the pupils. Progressive maps, or
maps which grow with the study of a section, may be
made from day to day, and the pupils should be ready
to draw at any time rapid sketches, which will illustrate the relative position of places, the movements of
armies, or the growth of territory.

In recitation, the pupil should be expected to take a
topic and tell, *in his own language*, what he has ascertained in regard to it, with as little interruption as possible. After he has finished his statement, the other
pupils may add anything which has been omitted, correct any misstatement which has been made, or ask
questions to bring out the points more clearly. If
there are several different books in the hands of the
class, the statements made by the various members will
vary considerably. One will give a story not told by
the pupil who first recited. Another will show the relation which the event described bears to others. Still
another will derive from the event a practical lesson for
our own people and time. All will help to make the
story more complete and more likely to be remembered.
Emphasize especially those features which are directly
related to present affairs, or which may lead the
pupils into a higher appreciation of their duties as
citizens, and give them a better understanding of those
duties.

A recitation in history properly conducted will encourage the pupils to gather information from all available sources. The gazetteer, cyclopædia, biographies,
and histories of various kinds will be sought and read

for the purpose of gaining and giving all possible information upon the topics to be recited. Such study and recitation will encourage a spirit of investigation and tend to the formation of a habit of using reference books, which will be of incalculable service to pupils after they leave school.

Selections of poetry and prose bearing upon the subjects studied may be memorized and recited with great profit to the pupil. Patrick Henry's "Appeal" and Mrs. Hemans's "Pilgrim Fathers" have done more for some pupils than all else they have studied. Feelings of patriotism may be excited and the imagination may be stirred in this as in no other way.

Topical Reviews. — In the latter part of the ninth year, and occasionally at other times, topical reviews should be given consisting of the details of a single subject. The following outlines may be suggestive of the manner of taking up reviews in which the history of a single subject is traced with comparatively few details : —

INDIANS.

1. What territory occupied, past and present.
2. Mode of living.
3. Claims to the soil.
4. Government support.
5. Present condition and prospects.

SLAVERY.

1. Origin.
2. Slave trade.
3. Early opposition.
4. Recognition in Constitution.
5. Louisiana purchase.
6. Missouri Compromise.

7. Abolitionism.
   Garrison, Phillips.
   John Brown, Lovejoy.
   Emancipation.
   By individuals.
   By state.
   By country.

EXTENSION OF TERRITORY AND SETTLEMENT.

1. Settlement of Kentucky and Tennessee.
2. Settlement of the Northwest.
3. Louisiana purchase.
4. Florida purchase.
5. Settlements west of the Mississippi.
6. Annexation of Texas.
7. Mexican War.
8. Settlement of the Pacific coast.
9. Purchase of Alaska.
10. Settlement of the Southwest.

Biographical reviews, especially of the lives of those persons who have had a prominent part in the affairs of the country, will also be found interesting and useful. Many of the leading features of history will in this way be brought out clearly and be connected in such a way as to make them remembered. The following names are suggested for review: —

John Smith, Columbus, Cabot, Cortez, La Salle, Wolfe, Washington, Braddock, Lafayette, Franklin, Adams, Putnam, Jefferson, Madison, Clay, Webster, Scott, Lincoln, Grant, Garfield.

In these later lessons upon a country, it will be well to encourage the pupils to ask questions in recitation, the answers to which they have previously looked up. Much interest will in this way be developed and the pupils will be encouraged to consult reference books at home, in the public library, and in the schoolroom.

Historical Reading. — One of the chief objects of the study of history in school is to awaken an interest in the subject to such an extent as to induce persons to read good books of history and biography after they have left school. Doubtless this object is gained, to a great extent, by following good methods of study and by frequently reading good books in school. Yet more than this may be done, first by directing the outside reading of pupils, and secondly by encouraging such reading by means of special exercises. There should be given to the pupils a list of books, both of biography and history, suitable for them to read. If any of the books named are not in the public or school library, the teacher should use his influence to have them put there. Generally trustees of libraries are very glad of such suggestions, and are willing to co-operate with teachers in leading the young to read good books.

A course of reading by subjects may be laid out for a term, and once a week, perhaps on Friday afternoon, thirty or forty minutes may be well spent in questioning pupils upon what they have read. For example, the subject for one week might be *The Mound-Builders*. The pupils would be asked what they have read upon the subject during the past week or at any previous time. From one and another of the pupils information of where the Mound-Builders lived, what they built, use of mounds, what is found in them, and where they are now seen, together with such a description of the utensils discovered as will lead the pupils to infer the condition and occupations of this curious people. Such exercises help the pupils to gain valuable information, and will also stimulate them to read upon the subject to be discussed.

Another means of stimulating pupils to read is to give out historical or biographical subjects for composition. Knowing that they are to write upon a given subject, they will read with the view of gaining all the information they can. For some reasons it may be well to have such compositions written during a specified time in school.

Historical Recreations. — It will be useful to take half an hour occasionally for a game or for miscellaneous questioning. One way of spending the time would be to have each pupil bring in five questions somewhat out of the usual course; such as, "Whose dying words were, ' Don't give up the ship'?" "Was Washington ever wounded in battle?" "Who was ' Rough and Ready'?"

A useful game is to have each pupil assume some character of history, and by a story or a little account of himself lead others to guess who he is. Another game consists in having one of the pupils leave the room, while the others select for him some historical character. On his return he is to guess from the remarks of his mates what character he represents. By careful management these games will prove profitable and interesting to all.

PHYSIOLOGY AND HYGIENE.

HYGIENE, or a knowledge of the means of preserving health, should be especially emphasized in the primary and grammar grades, and only such parts of anatomy and physiology should be taught as will help· pupils to a good understanding of the laws of health. In the primary school, observation of external parts alone should be made; and only as pupils are prepared to observe should the structure and function of the various internal organs be taught.

Means. — By means of parts of animals, procured at the butcher's, the structure of nearly all parts of the body can be taught. If a manikin is not provided, good anatomical charts should be near at hand for constant reference. As the various parts of the body are studied, their location should be pointed out by pupils, either upon their own bodies or upon the bodies of others.

While books may be in the hands of pupils of the higher grades, the teacher should under no circumstances allow the pupils to memorize and repeat what is not clearly understood.

Outline and Methods. — Instead of laying down a definite amount for each term and year, the following general outline is given for the teachers of all grades above the primary.[1] Only the most general features of the subjects should be taken up in the lower grades, the study and observation being more minute as the pupils grow in maturity and in ability to comprehend

[1] The course for primary grades is given upon page 195.

the functions of the various parts. For the daily study it will be necessary to subdivide the topics.

A few suggestions in regard to methods of teaching are added to each subject. Other suggestions will be found in good text-books, several of which should be upon the teacher's table for reference.

I. *Waste Matters of the Body.*

Show by observation that water and carbon constantly escape from the body through the breath, and that salt escapes by means of perspiration. To show the existence of carbonic acid in the breath, breathe into lime-water, and observe the same effect as when lime-water is mixed with carbonic acid. This is shown by thrusting red-hot coal into a dry test-tube and adding lime-water to the gas generated.

II. *Food and Drink.*

Show by observation and experiment the principal kinds of food, as the albuminous foods, sugars and starches, fats, and mineral foods. Hints of methods will be found in any good text-book of physiology. In directing the observation of pupils, keep constantly in mind the purpose of showing what kind of food is best to build up the body, to repair waste, and to supply heat.

III. *Digestion and Assimilation.*

1. Organs and parts : —
    (1) Name; (2) location; (3) construction.
2. Process of digestion.
3. Hygiene.
    Conditions of health in respect to eating, drinking, and exercising. Effects of use of tobacco.

Examine structure of teeth procured from a dentist; also teeth of lower animals. For location and external shape, let the pupils look into one another's mouths, and, with the aid of a mirror, in their own mouths. Dissect a cat, rabbit, or frog, to see the location and structure of organs. Make drawings, and compare with chart. Get specimens from the butcher's, and examine structure. Examine bits of pig's stomach to see coats and openings of gastric tubes.

Consult text-books for experiments to show the action of saliva, gastric juice, bile, and pancreatic juice upon various kinds of food. Lead pupils to know what food is most nutritious, and length of time taken for digestion. Let the pupils infer *reasons* for laws of health in relation to care of the teeth, manner of chewing the food, times of eating and exercising, kind of food to be eaten, times of drinking, etc.

IV. *Circulation.*

1. Organs and parts : —
   (1) Name; (2) location; (3) construction; (4) function.
2. Composition and uses of blood.
3. Hygiene : —
   (1) Nature and causes of diseases of organs.
   (2) Health of organs in relation to food, exercise, clothing, and air.
   (3) The use of tobacco and alcohol.

Dissect a sheep's heart to show its structure and the position of parts. Refer to text-book and chart for guide in dissecting and in finding the parts. Make drawings of parts discovered, and compare with chart. Observe with microscope the blood circulating in frog's foot. Listen with the stethoscope to the heart-beats. Notice pulse in the wrist and in other parts of the body. For experiments to show the composition of the blood, consult good text-books.

V. *Respiration.*

1. Organs and parts : —
   (1) Name; (2) location; (3) construction; (4) function.
2. Breathing : —
   Action of inspiration — expiration.
3. Voice : —
   (1) Organs; (2) sound and speech.

4. Hygiene : —

   (1) Action of air in lungs.

   (2) Cause and prevention of disease; ventilation; disinfectants; loose clothing; exercise.

Listen to respiration with stethoscope in inspiration and expiration. Note the difference. Examine carefully a sheep's lungs and windpipe attached. Distend lungs with air, and examine. Examine sheep's windpipe; cut lengthwise in front and behind to show vocal cords; notice the cartilages that form the larynx.

VI. *Muscles and Tendons.*

1. Structure and arrangement.
2. Kinds.
3. Action and use.
4. Hygiene.

   Health and strength of muscles in relation to exercise, rest, food, pure air.

Examine boiled lean beef to observe fibres, bundles, and connective tissue. Get sheep's leg with hoof on to show the structure and action of tendons; also, to show the contraction and relaxation of muscles. Examine the tendons of a fowl's leg and foot. Let the pupils locate muscles, and observe the action of tendons and muscles upon their own bodies. Let the pupils infer from the construction and use of muscles the need of exercise; also, the proper amount and kind of exercise.

VII. *Bones.*

1. The skeleton.
2. Composition and structure.
3. Periosteum.
4. Cartilage.
5. Joints and ligaments.
6. General uses.
7. Hygiene.

   Food; exercise.

Dissolve mineral matter of bones by soaking them in weak muriatic acid. Destroy animal matter by burning. Examine bone with microscope. Examine partially decayed bone. Cite instances to illustrate circulation of blood in bones and the growth of them. Have pupils infer the general uses. Examine with knife and forceps joints, coverings, and cartilage procured at the butcher's.

In examining the skeleton, the number, form, and position of the bones should be noted, and so far as it seems best the name of each bone may be given. The common name should be given in preference to the scientific name. Encourage pupils to feel of bones to ascertain their shape in every part, and have them infer the motions and other uses of parts from a knowledge of their shape and structure.

If the school does not own a skeleton, it may be borrowed from a physician. If none can be procured, examine bones of lower animals. Use charts constantly.

VIII. *Nervous System.*

1. Organs and parts : —
    (1) Name; (2) location; (3) construction; (4) function.
2. Hygiene: —
    (1) Name and cause of disease.
    (2) Health of organs, how preserved. Occupation, recreation, sleep.

Dissect a calf's brain, and compare parts observed with diagram. Let pupils infer from the structure and function of the brain and nerves the need of rest and sleep, the time in which rest should be taken, the duration of mental exercise, and the kind of food and clothing needed. The effect of the use of tobacco and alcohol upon the nerves should be inferred from observation of its use, from what is known of the nervous system, and from familiar experiments.

IX. *Senses.*

1. Touch	Organs and parts : —
2. Sight	Structure.
3. Hearing	Function.
4. Taste	Hygiene.
5. Smell	

By experiment show what parts of the body are most sensitive.
Let pupils infer the cause and reason.

Show by experiments the assistance which the senses give one
another in giving impressions.

Dissect the eye of an ox or a codfish to observe the structure.
Let the pupils infer from the structure causes of disease and the
kind of care which should be taken of the eyes.

X. *Skin.*

1. Structure and use of parts : —
   (1) Cuticle, hair, and nails ; (2) true skin ; (3) perspiration-
       tubes ; (4) oil-tubes.
2. Complexion.
3. Hygiene : —
   (1) Diseases and their causes.
   (2) Healthy condition of skin in relation to general health.
   (3) Cleanliness ; clothing.

Examine skin with microscope. Scrape off cuticle with a sharp
knife. Observe blisters and callous places. Examine perspiration-
tubes on palm of hand with microscope ; also, hair and finger-
nails. Let pupils infer from the use of parts the kind of care
needed.   •

Dissection. — Reference has been made in the above
outline to the dissection of a cat or rabbit. To do this
well it will be necessary for the novice to get some
assistance either from books or from some one who has
had practice in dissecting. The following suggestions
copied from *The American Teacher* may be of assistance
to some teachers.

[A blow on the temple will kill a rabbit; for a cat, with its
proverbial "nine lives," chloroform may be used. This can be
given on a sponge, placing the animal in a close box, or by putting
it down the throat by means of a pipette. Experience proves that
the village doctor is often glad to encourage the study of physiology by thus preparing the animal for dissection. If the subse-

quent work is tenderly and reverently done,—as it should *always* be,—the pupils will have a fuller appreciation of the " fearful and wonderful" way in which the Creator has fashioned the human body than is possible from the mere study of the book. No teacher should undertake this work who cannot thereby increase the reverence of his pupils for the "temple of the soul," and thus disarm all criticism upon dissection as "developing cruelty."

Materials. — A rabbit or cat; a board large enough to hold the animal when stretched out; hammer and tacks; a sharp knife and scissors; a needle, strong thread, and a pair of light forceps.]

1. Place the animal upon its back, on a board, holding it in position by driving a tack through each paw.

2. Parting the fur, carefully slit the skin with the scissors from the neck to the posterior part of the chest; make short cross-cuts at the end of this slit, and draw back the skin with the fingers, being very careful not to disturb any of the tissues or organs beneath.

3. See and feel the trachea and larynx under a thin layer of tissue; note, on each side and "just behind the angle of the lower jaw," the external jugular veins.

4. Between the trachea and each of these veins, just under the tissue layer, lies a muscle (sterno-mastoid). Study its position, and the meeting of the two; the subject of muscles is often a puzzle to the pupil, his ideas thereon being very misty.

5. Clear away on the left the thin layer of tissue, being very careful *not to prick a vein*, so as to get blood upon the specimen. If any small branch must be cut, tie it in two places first, and cut between. Another muscle (the sterno-hyoid) will now be seen, between the sterno-mastoid and the trachea. Pull the latter muscle outward, trace slowly and carefully with the fingers through the connective tissue between the two muscles, and the carotid artery and some large nerves will be found. Be sure that the pupils see the latter, and understand clearly that nerves are tangible cords, not mere "impressions."

6. Cut the sterno-mastoid muscle where it joins the breast-bone, turn it one side, gently lift the carotid artery in your forceps and trace it forward, separating it with care from adjoining parts, till you reach its division at the angle of the lower jaw. Following

up the external carotid artery, find the submaxillary gland, "a soft, roundish mass about the size of a hazel-nut." Note its slender duct passing into the mouth. A little farther along, the artery is crossed by a tendon and nerve.

7. The large pneumogastric nerve is nearly parallel to the carotid artery; upon it, near the skull, is a ganglion.

8. Repeat this dissection on the right side, then cut across the inner ends of the muscles from the chest to the shoulders, and, turning them outward, note the arteries, veins, and nerves passing to the trunk and fore limbs.

9. Raise the front end of the sternum in your forceps, cut through the muscles and rib cartilages on each side, turn back the sternum, cut it across near the lower line of the chest cavity, and remove it. Notice the diaphragm (size and shape), the pericardium inclosing the heart, and the collapsed lungs. Carefully dissect away adjoining parts, turning heart and lungs as needed, so as to trace the main blood-vessels.

10. Continue the cut of the skin into the wall of the abdomen, make cross-cuts, and reflect the skin and muscles.

Note shape and position of the œsophagus, stomach, intestines, and liver.

In many respects, the frog is the best animal from which to learn the structure and arrangements of the internal organs of the human body. To kill the frog, put it into a little alcohol, or into a mixture of ether and water, in a closed bottle or fruit-jar. Lay aside the skin with a sharp knife, and lead the pupils to see and describe the arrangement of organs; also, so far as they are able, to examine the structure of each part.

This work will be found very profitable, and is within the power of every teacher to do.

Emergencies. — Special lessons should be given in the higher grades to show what may be done in times of emergency before the physician arrives. A knowledge of what to do when the body is cut or injured in any part, when poison is taken, and when a partially drowned person is taken from the water, might be the means of preserving a valuable life, and at no time can such knowledge be more advantageously given than while the structure and functions of the organs are being taught. Detailed directions, found in any good text-book upon physiology, should be frequently reviewed.

Use of Tobacco. — In connection with the lessons in Physiology and Hygiene, the effects of the use of tobacco upon the system should be clearly and forcibly explained. The character of the constituents of tobacco — carbonic acid, ammonia, and nicotine — should be taught, and their effects upon the stomach, lungs, blood, brain, and nerves, be made known. The teacher should dwell especially upon the harm which smoking and chewing tobacco have upon young people, not only in its physical effects on account of the delicacy of tissues, but also in its mental and moral effects.

Use of Alcohol. — The effects of alcohol as a poison may sometimes be forcibly shown objectively, even to little children. In primary grades, however, most of the instruction in the effects of the use of alcohol must consist of citing examples of the direct injury which has been done, and of telling and reading proper stories.

In the higher grades, in addition to the means employed in the lower grades, more direct teaching of the subject may and should be done. The following outline of lessons prepared by Mr. Arthur C. Boyden, of the Bridgewater (Mass.) State Normal School, shows what may be done in the grammar school: —

These lessons are intended to suggest a method of teaching the effects of alcohol on the human body. Each part of the subject is introduced by simple experiments from which the teacher may derive the points to be impressed. For the grammar grade selection of the more important parts may have to be made, but for the higher grade all the points can be taught, understood, and explained. In the primary grade preparation for this work should be made by simple lessons on the parts and systems of the human body, and by stating in simple terms the more apparent facts in regard to the effects of alcohol.

I. ORIGIN OF ALCOHOL.

1. In Fermented Liquors.

Experiments. — Exp. 1. Add molasses to water in a bottle till it is of a deep brown color, then add a teaspoonful of yeast, allow it to stand in a warm place for a day or two. Obs. The mixture has the odor of alcohol, later a sour, acid odor; the mixture has a sharp taste. Inf. The little yeast plant has changed the sugar of the molasses to alcohol; this will change to an acid if left alone. Call the yeast plant a "ferment," and the process of changing "fermentation."

Exp. 2. Allow apple juice to stand exposed to the air for a few days. Obs. The liquid has the odor of alcohol, also the biting taste. Later it has a sour, acid taste like vinegar. Inf. Very small ferments from the air have changed the sugar of the apple juice to alcohol. Call the liquid "cider." The alcohol will change to vinegar if left exposed to the air.

Cider is formed by the fermentation of apple juice in the air.

Wines are formed by the fermentation of grape juice, etc., in the air.

Ales and *Beers* are formed by the fermentation of the sugar of grains. (Malt liquors.)

Alcohol is an essential constituent of all these fermented liquors. Nature will change it to an acid if left to itself.

2. In Distilled Liquors.

Exp. 3. Heat cider or wine in a test-tube over an alcohol lamp, pass the steam through a glass tube into a bottle which is wrapped in a wet cloth to condense this steam. Obs. The odor and taste are more marked than in the fermented liquors; often there is a bitter taste. Inf. The condensed liquor is stronger than the fermented liquor, and is changed into new substances oftentimes. Call this process of evaporating and condensing "distillation," and the resulting liquid a "distilled liquor."

Brandy is distilled from wines.

Gin is distilled from beer, and flavored with juniper berries.

Whiskey is distilled from the wort of fermented grain.

Rum is distilled from fermented molasses.

II. PROPERTIES AND USES OF ALCOHOL.

Exp. 4. Examine alcohol for its color, odor, and taste. Place a little on the hand. Obs. Alcohol is a transparent liquid, has a strong odor and a biting taste. Inf. The rapid evaporation of the alcohol makes the hand feel cool; it is a volatile liquid.

Exp. 5. Place a little in a spoon, apply a lighted match. Obs. It burns with a blue, hot flame. Inf. Alcohol is inflammable because it unites easily with the oxygen of the air.

Exp. 6. Shake a little powdered resin in alcohol. Obs. The alcohol changes to the color of the resin; finally the resin disappears. Inf. Some resinous substances are soluble in alcohol.

Exp. 7. Mix a little oil of turpentine with alcohol; shake. Obs. The turpentine mixes with the alcohol. Inf. Alcohol will mix with some oils.

Exp. 8. Add alcohol to the white of an egg (albumen). Obs. The alcohol changes the moist mucilaginous albumen to a white, stringy solid. Call this "coagulation." Inf. Alcohol coagulates albuminous substances by extracting the water from them.

Properties. — Alcohol is a transparent liquid, — odorous, — has biting taste, — is volatile. It dissolves many resinous substances — and mixes with most oils. It is inflammable — great affinity for oxygen. It coagulates albumen — attraction for water.

Uses (resulting from these properties). — External application to allay inflammation. Alcohol lamps for heating purposes. A solvent for gums in preparing varnishes. In preparation of perfumery, medicine, etc. Preservation of museum specimens.

III. Effects of Alcohol on the Human Body.

1. Alcohol impairs Digestion.

Exp. 9. Place with the finger a little alcohol on the inside membrane of the mouth (a mucous membrane); repeat this several times. Obs. The membrane stings, the saliva flows freely, finally there is a dry, puckery feeling. Inf. Alcohol inflames the membrane, excites the flow of the liquid which it secretes, and absorbs the moisture in it.

Application. — The lining membrane of the mouth also lines the stomach and the other organs of the digestive system. A small amount of alcohol will cause a profuse flow of the gastric juice and passes very rapidly into the blood. A larger amount inflames and irritates the lining membrane of the stomach. A continued use weakens the quality of the gastric juice by the unusual and irregular flow, also impoverishes the blood from which it comes. It irritates the constantly inflamed membrane of the stomach, leading to an ulcerous condition and chronic inflammation. (See Dr. Sewall's diagrams, p. 44 of the Standard League Documents, No. 3, 36 Bromfield Street, Boston.)

Exp. 10. Add alcohol to raw meat; also rub some meat in water till it is well colored with blood. Add alcohol to this blood. Obs. The liquid is full of white particles, and the meat seems hard. Inf. The alcohol has coagulated the albumen of the meat and blood.

Exp. 11. Add alcohol to some of the pepsin of the gastric juice. Obs. The pepsin contains white, stringy particles. Inf. Alcohol coagulates pepsin.

Note. — To prepare the pepsin, get from the butcher the inside membrane of a pig's stomach ; cut into fine pieces, and soak it in glycerine for a few hours. The glycerine dissolves the pepsin; strain through a fine cloth. Prepared pepsin can be bought of the druggist.

Application. — Pepsin is the active solvent of the gastric juice. Alcohol tends to harden the food and coagulate the pepsin, thus retarding digestion. Continued use tends to chronic indigestion and to the intensifying of any diseases of the digestive system.

2. Alcohol absorbs the Water of the Body.

Exps. Refer to Exps. 8 and 9.

Alcohol not only absorbs water from the albumen which it coagulates, but the whole system floods it with water to dilute it and render it less harmful. Hence alcohol absorbs the water of the saliva, of the gastric juice, of the blood, of the tissues, and of all the secretions. This soon results in a craving for fluid to supply the body, really a "thirst" for water requiring time for its absorption throughout the system, but temporarily satisfied by more exciting.

3. Alcohol destroys the Blood-Corpuscles.

Exp. 12. Prick with a pin under the finger-nail and draw a drop of blood. Place this on a bit of glass, and examine with a magnifying glass. Observe the way in which the little blood-corpuscles are arranged. Touch them with the smallest amount of alcohol. Obs. The corpuscles are of an irregular shape, and have lost part of their color. Add more alcohol. Obs. The corpuscles are in an irregular mass of a whitish color. Inf. Alcohol coagulates the albumen of the corpuscles, and dissolves the coloring matter. Refer also to Exp. 5.

Application. — Alcohol at once enters the blood, seizes the oxygen that the red corpuscles are carrying to the various parts of the body, dissolves the coloring matter, and coagulates the albumen of these corpuscles. Hence the blood partially fails in its work of carrying new matter to the tissues and in eliminating the waste matter. The result is a clogging of the system with effete matter, poisoning of the blood, diseases of the skin, liver, and kidneys. The retarding of the combustion within the body lowers its temperature in direct proportion to the amount of alcohol taken.

4. Alcohol ruins the Blood-Vessels.

Observe the crust of earthy matter on the inside of bottles of grape wine. Inf. The earthy matter which was soluble in the grape juice is thrown down by the alcohol in the wine.

Application. — The mineral matter which is being carried by the blood to the bones is precipitated by the alcohol and forms a crust in the blood-vessels and in all the tissues, making them weak and brittle. As a result blood-vessels burst under any unusual strain, and apoplexy results.

5. Alcohol paralyzes Nerve Matter. (A narcotic.)

Exp. 13. Etherize or chloroform a frog by soaking a wad of cotton and putting it in his mouth, or place a spoonful of ether in a jar of water and immerse the frog. When insensible, carefully cut open the skin and flesh of the leg till the nerve is exposed. Touch a drop of alcohol to the exposed nerve. *Obs.* The nerve becomes stiff and white, the trembling of the limb ceases. *Inf.* Alcohol has paralyzed the live nerve matter.

Application. — A small dose of alcohol causes incipient paralysis of the nerves of the tissues and brain ; this causes an extra activity for the purpose of diluting and expelling the poison from the system, manifested by the "animated appearance, the throbbing of the arteries, the flush of the face, and the sparkle of the eye." This paralysis also numbs any feelings of pain, apparent benefits arising from previous paralysis. The paralysis of the nerves controlling the muscular walls of the capillaries weakens their elasticity; at the same time the heart increases its action : hence the blood tends to remain near the surface, and an extra radiation of heat takes place — a second reason for the lower temperature of the body.

Increase the dose, and the paralysis of the brain increases in this order : 1. Of the delicate nerve matter of the superior brain (cerebellum), blunting the highest functions, reverence, modesty, love, etc.; its reflex action is the loss of control of the connecting nerves; thus moral power fails, and the lower nature is supreme. 2. The part of the brain controlling voluntary motion is paralyzed ; at the same time the nerves of sensation are paralyzed, resulting in an insensibility to pain and injury; this goes on till a person is "dead drunk." 3. The last part of the nervous system affected is that which controls the involuntary actions, breathing, etc.; this paralysis causes death.

Continued use leads to a degeneracy of nerve matter and tissue by the constant paralysis and repair, because the structure of the nerve matter is changed; hence "disorders occasioned by the strain imposed on the system, diseases traceable to the general degeneration of the system, and diseases which might otherwise be averted or resisted"; finally the insatiable demand for alcohol, diseases of the nerves, delirium and death.

OBSERVATION LESSONS.

BESIDES the objective work required to be done in connection with the teaching of all the common branches, there should be given regularly in all primary and grammar grades and in the ungraded school, observation lessons upon minerals, plants, and animals. It should be understood that the aim of these lessons is not so much to teach many facts as it is to cultivate the pupils' powers of observation, and to awaken an interest in, and a love for, the things of nature that lie directly about them. Let this part of the work therefore be slowly and carefully done. Use no book in the recitation, give out no lessons to be learned, and tell nothing to the pupils which they can ascertain for themselves by their own observation. Learning one fact by their own unaided powers is better than memorizing a hundred facts which have been given them.

Do not let the fact that you have not much knowledge of science discourage you from making the effort to teach the subjects required to be taught in these elementary lessons. With three or four elementary books of science from which to learn some facts and methods of illustration, any teacher can after a little time conduct the exercises so as to secure good results. Again, let it be urged upon you not to use books in teaching these lessons, but have the pupils study objects only. Make a careful preparation of every lesson, even though the subject be familiar, and so far as possible provide each pupil with something to do or to see. Have a definite object in your mind in presenting a lesson, avoiding the aimless and irrelevant conversation which is frequently carried on in a lesson of this kind. Avoid a uniform question and answer method, and do not encourage or allow the use of set and formal expressions. The "Model Lessons" found in books and periodicals should serve as a hint only of what may be done. No two lessons should be conducted precisely in the same way. The best object lessons are those in which there is the freest expression of what the pupils actually see.

Do not extend the lessons beyond the point at which the pupils' interest flags, nor rob the lessons of their proper time. It will be well to have a definite time allotted to them. Two ten-minute lessons every day in the primary grades, or during the first three years, and two lessons a week, of thirty or forty minutes each, or one lesson a week, an hour in length in the higher grades will give time to do much valuable work. In order to give each subject a proper share of time, and give the teacher something definite to work by, the following arrangement of subjects and times is suggested:—

First Year. — First Half.

Plants, 8 weeks.	⎫	*Form,* 4 weeks.	⎫	
Place, 8 weeks.	⎬ A.M.	*Color,* 4 weeks.	⎬ P.M.	
Human Body, 4 weeks.	⎭	*Qualities,* 8 weeks.		
		Size and Weight, 4 weeks.		

First Year. — Second Half.

Plants, 8 weeks.	⎫	*Form,* 4 weeks.	⎫	
Animals, 4 weeks.	⎬ A.M.	*Color,* 4 weeks.	⎬ P.M.	
Place, 8 weeks.	⎭	*Human Body,* 8 weeks.		
		Size and Weight, 4 weeks.		

Plants, 8 weeks.		*Form*, 8 weeks.	
Human Body, 4 weeks. } A.M.		*Color*, 4 weeks. } P.M.	
Place, 8 weeks.		*Qualities*, 8 weeks.	

Plants, 8 weeks. ⎫
Human Body, 4 weeks. ⎬ A.M.
Place, 8 weeks. ⎭

Form, 8 weeks. ⎫
Color, 4 weeks. ⎬ P.M.
Qualities, 8 weeks. ⎭

SECOND YEAR. — SECOND HALF.

Plants, 8 weeks. ⎫
Animals, 4 weeks. ⎬ A.M.
Place, 8 weeks. ⎭

Form, 4 weeks. ⎫
Color, 8 weeks. ⎪
Wt. and Meas., 4 weeks. ⎬ P.M.
Human Body, 4 weeks. ⎭

THIRD YEAR. — FIRST HALF.

Plants, 8 weeks. ⎫
Place, 4 weeks. ⎬ A.M.
Home Geog., 8 weeks. ⎭

Form and Color, 8 weeks. ⎫
Human Body, 4 weeks. ⎬ P.M.
Animals, 8 weeks. ⎭

THIRD YEAR. — SECOND HALF.

Place and Home Geog., ⎫
20 weeks. ⎬ A.M.

Form and Color, 8 weeks. ⎫
Human Body, 8 weeks. ⎬ P.M.
Animals, 4 weeks. ⎭

GRAMMAR GRADES.

Plants. — From April to November.
Animals. — From November to April.
Minerals. — From November to April.
Astronomy. — From April to November.
Physics. — From November to April.

For the Observation Lessons, ungraded schools should be divided into two sections, each section being taught separately, and upon subjects required for graded schools. The following arrangement of topics and times is suggested for

UNGRADED SCHOOLS.

To the younger pupils give two short lessons daily.
Plants or Animals. — Once a week.

Size and Weight, or Qualities. — Once a week.
Color or Form. — Once a week.
Place or Home Geography. — Once a week.
Human Body. — Once a week.

To the older pupils give one long lesson a week upon plants from April to November, and upon animals or minerals from November to April.

COLOR.

The apparatus for teaching color should consist of different-colored worsteds, papers, cards, pigments, etc. A color-chart will also be a valuable aid.

Differences and resemblances of colors should be taught by having the children select colors differing from and resembling a given color. The name of the color should then be given, and the pupil be asked to select that color from among others, and to point to it in any part of the room. At the end of the first year the pupils should be able to distinguish and name all of the common colors, as indicated in the Course of Studies. Color and form may be taught together by using different-colored cards of various shapes.

In the second year shades, tints, and hues of common colors should be taught as before, with their names: scarlet, pink, crimson, straw, indigo, purple, lavender, salmon, buff, etc. Matching colors, shades, and tints will be found to be a useful exercise. Envelopes containing various colored bits of paper may be given out, from which the pupils may select a color to match a given color held up before them. At the end of the second year pupils should be able to distinguish and name all of the common colors, and their tints and shades.

Color and form should be taught together in the second year, considerable time being given to the making of designs in which forms and colors are combined.

In the third year there should be some practice in mixing pigments of different colors. Orange from red and yellow, green from yellow and blue, and purple from red and blue, should be produced before the pupils, either by mixing the pigments or by passing the sunlight through pieces of colored glass. Hues should also be produced by mixing pigments of unequal proportions, as, for example, a reddish hue of yellow from the mixture of a very little red with yellow.

Prismatic colors in proper relations should be shown from a glass prism in a sunny window, or from a soap bubble. An imitation of the solar spectrum should be made by the children by arranging threads of worsted upon any surface, or by drawing them through perforated cardboard. In the same way, scales of colors from the lightest tint to the darkest shade should be made.

Colored designs in connection with the study of form should be made, special care being taken to have the lessons properly graded. These lessons should be preceded and accompanied by lessons to teach harmony of colors. If the teacher does not know the harmonic or complementary colors, he should consult good books upon the subject, and show the children what colors are harmonious and how the complementary colors may be found.

Much information may be given in connection with the color lessons as to the different plants and metals used for dyes, emblematic colors, colors of horses, etc.

Further and more explicit suggestions to teachers will be found in Miss Crocker's " Lessons on Color in Primary Schools."

FORM.

See Drawing, page 252.

PLACE.

The subject " Place," in the Course of Studies, is intended to include position, distance, and direction, all the lessons to be constantly illustrated by plan-drawing.

Teach use of the terms of relative position by having the children place an object, as a small pasteboard square, in different relations to a book or upon the desk. This should first be done in imitation of the teacher, and afterwards from dictation. Statements expressing the relative position of two objects may sometimes be made by the children.

The following will indicate some of the work which children should do during the first year: —

The (square) is

on, under, over, below, above, behind, before, at the right of, at the left of, in front of, in the centre of, at the right side of, at the left side of, at the right-hand corner of, at the left-hand corner of, at the upper right-hand corner of, at the middle of the right side of, at the middle of the front edge of, etc.,   the desk.

Little drawings of the top of the desk, with an object upon it in different positions, should be made by the children, the teacher first showing how upon the blackboard.

The relative position of different objects in the school-room should be described; as, "The teacher's desk is in the front part of the room," "The clock is above the blackboard," "John sits behind me," etc. As soon as the points of compass are learned, the statements in regard to position may be extended; as, "There are two windows on the north side of the room," "The stove is near the northwest corner of the room," etc.

Relative distances should be taught at first, such as the relative length and width of two books, of two tables, of the length and width of the room, etc. The inch, foot, yard, and rod should be shown by actual measurement, and much practice should be had upon estimating lengths by these standards. Lines upon the slate and board, of an inch, a foot, and a yard in length, should be made many times by the children, the work being tested and corrected by the aid of a measure. Various distances within sight of the children should be first estimated, and afterwards ascertained by measurement. This work may well be continued throughout the course.

The points of compass (cardinal and semi-cardinal) should be taught early in the course, and applied in all the Place lessons of the primary grade. It is well to place upon the floor of the room lines indicating North, South, East, and West. Teach, and have your pupils tell, the direction in which the rows of seats extend, the road, the fences, etc. ; also, the direction which an object is from any other object, using the terms North, Northeast, etc.

Other suggestions of methods to teach Place are given under the head of Plan-Drawing.[1]

[1] p. 143.

HUMAN BODY.

It is not natural or well for young children to examine very minutely the structure and functions of the various parts of the body; nor can they learn with profit many of the reasons of the laws of health. It is important, however, that they know by observation the external parts of the body, well enough at least to lead them to compare the parts with corresponding parts of the lower animals, and to know the proper use and care of the various parts.

Considerable information will have to be given in these lessons, although the pupils should be led to ascertain and infer as many facts as possible from observation. They should locate the parts as they are named by pointing at or touching their own bodies and the bodies of others. Sometimes parts of lower animals should be brought before the class for observation, as for example when the structure of muscles or the shape of bones are taught. Charts and pictures should also be near at hand for constant reference.

Much use of simple illustrations and stories should be made in giving lessons upon hygiene to young children, especially upon the effects of the use of tobacco and alcohol. The various primary physiologies now published, will be found very suggestive to teachers in respect to both matter and method. As a rule, these lessons should be taught orally, no use being made of books by the pupils.

The following topics, prepared by Dr. Larkin Dunton, of the Boston Normal School, will be found useful as showing what subjects should be taught in the primary grades and the order in which they should be taught.

First Year.

I. *Parts of the Body.* 1. Head, neck, and body or trunk. — 2. Arms, right and left. — 3. Legs, right and left. — 4. Limbs. — 5. Position of body compared with that of common animals. — 6. Arms, wings, and forelegs compared.

II. *Parts of the Head.* 1. Crown, back and sides. — 2. Hair, combing and brushing. — 3. Face, complexion, and washing the face. — 4. Ears, right and left.

III. *Parts of the Face.* 1. Forehead, temples, cheeks, chin, and lips. — 2. Eyes, eyebrows, eyelashes, and eyelids. — 3. Nose, nostrils, and bridge of the nose. — 4. Mouth, teeth, and tongue; cleansing the teeth.

IV. *Neck.* 1. Throat and back of the neck. — 2. Protection and cleanliness.

V. *Parts of the Body.* 1. Back, chest, and stomach. — 2. Shoulders, sides, and hips.

VI. *Arms.* 1. Movements. — 2. Joints; shoulders, elbows, and wrist. — 3. Upper arm, forearm, and wrist.

VII. *Hand.* 1. Back, palm, thumb, and fingers. — 2. Joints, fists, and knuckles. — 3. Forefinger, middle, ring, and little fingers, and thumb. — 4. Motions, strength, and use. — 5. Nails and their uses. — 6. Cleanliness; paring and biting.

VIII. *Legs.* 1. Motions, proper walking, and hip, knee, and ankle joints. — 2. Thigh, shin, calf, and foot.

IX. *Feet.* 1. Sole, instep, heel, ball, and arch. — 2. Tight and short shoes, and cold and damp feet. — 3. Cleanliness of feet, and neat shoes and stockings.

Second Year.

X. *Eye and Sight.* 1. Color of the eyes. — 2. White of the eyes, iris, and pupil. — 3. Change in the pupil for light. — 4. Bony socket and eyeball. — 5. Eyelids, eyelashes, eyebrows, winking, and tears. — 6. Too little and too much light, and reading at twilight. — 7. Holding work too near, looking cross-eyed, and cleanliness.

XI. *Ear and Hearing.* 1. Sounds known by the ear; transmitted by the air and by solids. — 2. Direction, pitch, and quality of sounds. — 3. Shape of the ear, internal ear, and cleanliness of ear. — 4. Care of the ear: cold draughts, pulling, and shouting into. — 5. Listening attentively, and eavesdropping.

XII. *Nose and Smell.* 1. Odors: pungent, aromatic, spicy, etc. — 2. Use of smell: determining good food, pure air, etc. — 3. Scent in animals compared with smell in man. — 4. Colds, draughts, ventilation, cleanliness, etc.

XIII. *Tongue and Taste.* 1. Tongue and saliva. — 2. Kinds of flavors: bitter, sweet, astringent, etc. — 3. Chewing gum, tobacco, etc. — 4. Hot drinks and strong drinks. — 5. Thirst, and proper time to drink.

XIV. *Touch.* 1. Use of fingers, and delicacy of touch. — 2. Rough, smooth, etc.; cold, hot, etc.; shape, size, etc. — 3. Cleanliness, blisters, callouses, etc.

THIRD YEAR.

XV. *Teeth.* 1. Enamel, crown, and root. — 2. Cutting teeth, eye-teeth, and double teeth. — 3. Two sets, shedding, and number. — 4. Cleansing: how and how often. — 5. Effects of hot drinks, candy, pickles, biting hard substances, etc.

XVI. *Skeleton.* 1. Skull, spine, ribs, etc. — 2. Structure of bones, hollow and light. — 3. Kinds of joints, why joints move easily, and danger from pulling.

XVII. *Muscles.* 1. Appearance; lean meat. — 2. Attachment to bones. — 3. Action of muscles. — 4. Exercise, proper kinds of play and work, and rest.

XVIII. *Skin.* 1. Elasticity, pores, and perspiration. — 2. Cold draughts and proper clothing. — 3. Cleanliness: bathing, dandruff, etc.

XIX. *Circulation.* 1. Where the blood is, uses of the blood and heart, and the pulse. — 2. Arteries and veins. — 3. Tight bands, tight clothes, warmth and exercise, wounds.

XX. *Respiration.* 1. Pure and impure blood, windpipe and lungs, how to breathe. — 2. Pure air, and how to get it. — 3. Odors and dust, clean bodies and clothes, and out-of-door exercise.

XXI. *Digestion.* 1. Use of teeth and saliva, eating slowly, drinking when eating. — 2. Proper kinds of food and drink; tea, candy, pickles, etc. — 3. Regular and late meals, chewing gum, etc.

PLANTS.

It will be seen in the Course of Studies that some of the topics of Plant Lessons which are prescribed for grammar grades, are also prescribed for primary grades. The reason of this arrangement will be seen when it is understood that in the primary grades only the most general and obvious features of a plant are to be observed, and that while a simple classification is made by pupils of the lower grades, the attention there is mainly given to developing the observing powers.

In the first year, little more than what some of the children already know should be taught, the chief objects being to awaken an interest in the plants themselves, and to encourage a spirit of investigation. Lead the children to recognize some simple differences and resemblances in common plants in respect to size, length of stalk or trunk, and size, color, and shape of the flower and leaf. For example, statements like the following might be drawn from the children, while a buttercup and an anemone are being examined : —

> They grow at different heights from the ground.
>
> The flower-leaves of the butter-cup are yellow, and those of the anemone are white.
>
> The flower-leaves of the buttercup are wider than those of the anemone.
>
> They are not fragrant.

When any plant is examined and talked about, encourage the children to bring other plants similar in respect to shape of leaves, color of flower, etc. The teacher should sometimes assist the children in their observation, by drawing shapes and parts of the leaf and flower; and the children should be encouraged to draw the various shapes as they are observed.

Many of the most common trees, shrubs, and wild flowers should be examined in the way described during the first year.

In the second year, the principal parts of the plant and of the root, stem, bud, leaf, and flower should be observed, the pupils noting resemblances and differences as before. When the different parts are recognized, the names of the parts should be given by the teacher and written upon the blackboard; and as the facts are learned, they should be put into sentences by the pupils. For example, the children may observe the facts (the teacher giving the names) and afterwards put them into sentences as follows: —

> The parts of a flower are the calyx, corolla, stamens, and pistils.
> The parts of the calyx are called sepals.
> The parts of the corolla are called petals.

The following facts may be learned in the same way during the second year: —

I. *Stems, Stalks, or Trunks.*

1. Shapes:
   - round.
   - three-sided.
   - four-sided.

2. Parts:
   - bark.
   - wood.
   - pith.
   - threads.
   - fibres.

3. Colors: { green.
              { red.
              { brown etc.

4. Uses.

II. *Leaves.*

1. Shapes: { oval.
             | oblong.
             { egg-shaped.
             | heart-shaped.
             { needle-shaped, etc.

2. Color: { green.
             { red.

3. Parts: { stem.
             { blade: { apex.
             {   { margin.
                        { surface.

4. Veins: { net-veined.
             { parallel-veined.
             { forked-veined.

5. Shapes of margin: { plain or even.
                       { wavy.
                       { toothed.

6. Kinds of surfaces: { smooth.
                       | rough.
                       { woolly.
                       | hairy.
                       { silky.

III. *Buds.*

1. Kinds: { leaf-bud.
             { flower-bud.

2. Shape: { round.
             { cone-like.

3. Color.

4. Parts: { germ.
             { (scales).

IV. *Flowers.*

1. Shapes: —

Rose-shaped, bell-shaped, trumpet-shaped, cross-shaped, wheel-shaped, funnel-shaped, etc.

2. Parts :
$\begin{cases} \text{calyx, sepals.} \\ \text{corolla: petals.} \\ \text{stamens.} \\ \text{pistils.} \end{cases}$

3. Colors :
$\begin{cases} \text{red.} \\ \text{blue.} \\ \text{white.} \\ \text{pink.} \\ \text{scarlet, etc.} \end{cases}$

4. Shapes of petals and sepals. 5. Number of petals and sepals.

From the common trees, shrubs, and wild flowers, the children should observe the most obvious peculiarities of each, and try to find others having similar peculiarities.

As the parts are observed, the children should put the facts they have learned into a simple description, like the following: —

This flower has a light-colored stem and heart-shaped leaves.
It has five green sepals and five light blue petals.
The petals are all of the same shape.
It is called a violet.

Similar descriptions should be made of many of the common plants of the neighborhood. Do not insist upon or encourage a set form of description, but let the pupils exercise freedom and originality in giving the statement of facts which they have observed.

In the third year some of the interesting facts connected with the history of plant life should be observed. Put various kinds of seeds in water and in the earth, and watch their development from day to day. Let the children notice that the seed contains the germ of the plant, and that the root grows downward, while the stalk grows upward. Let them see also that the leaf-buds have a hard covering like varnish, and that some of them have scales on the outside and a woolly lining on the inside. The development of the flower-buds, flowers, and fruits should also be observed. Most of these lessons would best be given in the spring of the year.

During September and October of the third year the uses of each part of the plant may be observed, especially of the common plants used for food. In this way the classification of fruits, vegetables, and grains may be made and their various differences and resemblances noted. The growing and ripening grains will afford excellent means of observation.

The study of plants in the Grammar grades should be more minute than in the Primary grades. Parts of the plant which were not before observed are now noticed and additional names are given. The following hints for elementary plant lessons, suggested by Mr. George H. Martin, will assist teachers in the selection of topics and in methods of teaching.

The Roman numerals indicate the grade in which the lessons should be given — although teachers of Primary grades will find the simpler parts of the outline none too difficult for their pupils.

OUTLINE OF STUDY.

IV. *Lessons to teach the Parts of a Plant.*

1. To teach to *name* the parts.
    Root, Stem, Leaves, Hairs, Buds, Flowers, Fruit, Seed.

2. Teach to *describe* the parts.
    ROOT.   The root lives in the ground.
    STEM.   The stem bears leaves.
    LEAVES.   The leaves grow on the stem.
               The leaves are thin.
               The leaves are flat.
               The leaves are green.
    HAIRS.   The hairs grow on the leaves and on the stem.
    BUDS.   The buds grow on the stem.
               The buds are full of little leaves.
               Leaves grow from buds.
    FLOWERS.   The flowers grow on the stem.
               The flowers are bright colored.
               The flowers smell sweet.
    FRUIT.   The fruit grows on the stem.
               The fruit has seeds in it.
    SEEDS.   The seeds grow in the fruit.

3. Teach to *name* and *describe* the parts of a leaf.
    Petiole, Blade, Stipules, Veins.
    PETIOLE.   The petiole is narrow.
    BLADE.   The blade is broad.
    STIPULES. The stipules are like little blades.
               The stipules are at lower end of the petiole.
    VEINS.   The veins are in the blade.
               The veins are hard.

4. Teach to *name* and *describe* the parts of a flower.
    Sepals, Petals, Stamens, Pistils.
    SEPALS.   The sepals are on the outside of the flower.
               The sepals are green.
               (All the sepals form the *Calyx*.)

PETALS.   The petals are next inside the calyx.
            The petals are bright colored.
            (All the petals form the *Corolla*.)
STAMENS.   The stamens are next inside the corolla.
            The stamens have two parts.
                One part is like a thread. (Call this the *Fila-*
                ment.)
                The other part is on the top of the filament.
                (Call this the *Anther*.)
                In the anther is a yellow powder. (Call this
                Pollen.)
PISTILS.   The pistils are in the middle of the flower.
            The pistils are larger at the bottom and the top.
                (Call the large part at the bottom the *Ovary*.
                Call the large part at the top the *Stigma*. Call
                the part between the *Style*.)
                There are some little bodies in the ovary. (Call
                them *Ovules*.)

V. *Lessons to teach History of Plant Life.*

1. EMBRYO.
     Illust. A bean soaked a few hours in water.
     There is a little stem in the seed.
     There are two little leaves in the seed.
     There are two thick parts to the seed.

2. GROWTH.
     Illust. Bean-plants in different stages.
     A root grows down from the seed into the ground.
     A stem grows up from the seed.
     The two thick parts come above the ground.
     The two little leaves unfold and make larger leaves.

3. BUDS.
     Illust. Same as above.
     There is a bud between the two leaves.
     This bud opens, and a stem, and more leaves grow from it.
     The plant keeps growing from buds.

4. FLOWERS.

Illust. Pear, apple, or cherry flower-buds.

The flowers come from flower-buds.

5. FRUIT.

Illust. Apple, pear, or cherry flowers as the petals are falling away.

The ovary grows.

The other parts of the flower fall away.

The ovary makes the fruit.

6. SEEDS.

The ovules in the ovary make the seed in the fruit.

Home Study. — Cover the surface of water in a tumbler with cotton. On this place seeds of different plants, — bean, corn, flax, and others, — and put in the sunlight. Observe carefully daily, and report germination of each kind, and subsequent changes.

VI. *Lessons to teach Differences in Parts of Plants.*

Note. — The order of the study of the parts is unimportant, and may be determined by the season. Stems may be studied earlier than leaves or flowers.

1. DIFFERENCE IN STEM.

Illust. A section of stem of elder one inch long.

(*a*) In structure. The elder stem is soft inside.

The elder stem is soft outside.

The elder stem has a hard ring between.

Call the soft part inside *Pith*.

Call the hard ring *Wood*.

Call the outside part *Bark*.

Illust. A section of banana stem one-half inch long.

The banana stem has hard threads scattered through a soft part.

The thread looks like the wood in the elder.

(*b*) In shape.

(*c*) In color. } Teach these topics as above.

(*d*) In surface.

2. DIFFERENCES IN ROOTS.

Illust. Beet, Grass, Dahlia.

(*a*) In constitution.　The beet root is fleshy.

　　　　　　　　　　The grass root is fibrous.

(*b*) In shape.　The dahlia root has several parts.

　　　　　　　The beet root has only one part.

3. DIFFERENCES IN LEAVES.

Illust. A variety of leaves.

(*a*) In shape.　The geranium leaf is round.

　　　　　　　The grass leaf is long and narrow.

　　　　　　　The white birch leaf is pointed at the top.

　　　　　　　The plum leaf is round at the top.

　　　　　　　The horse-chestnut leaflet is broad at the top.

　　　　　　　The horse-chestnut leaflet is narrow at the base.

　　　　　　　The maple leaf is broad at the base.

　　　　　　　The madeira-vine leaf has an even edge.

　　　　　　　The chestnut leaf has an uneven edge.

(*b*) In shape.

(*c*) In surface.

(*d*) In color.

(*e*) In size.

(*f*) In venation.

(*g*) In composition.　⎬ Teach these topics as above.

(*h*) In phyllotaxy.

(*i*) In vernation.

(*j*) In completeness.

(*k*) In form, size, etc.,

　　　of petiole.

Note.—Have shape, venation, composition, phyllotaxy, and vernation of leaves shown by drawing on slate or board.

4. DIFFERENCES IN FLOWERS.

Illust. Such flowers as can be obtained for the purpose.

(*a*) In arrangement of parts:

　　　The lilac flower has the sepals united.

　　　The lilac flower has the petals united.

　　　The lupine flower has the stamens united.

The apple flower has the pistils united.
The violet flower has the stamens on the end of the stem.
The apple flower has the stamens on the calyx.
The lilac flower has the stamens on the corolla.
The apple flower has the calyx attached to the ovary.

(*b*) In color.
(*c*) In odor.
(*d*) In size.
(*e*) In number.
(*f*) In arrangement on stem.
(*g*) In order of opening.
(*h*) In completeness.   } Teach these topics as above.
(*i*) In symmetry.
(*j*) In regularity.
(*k*) In number of parts.
(*l*) In shape of parts.
(*m*) In arrangement of parts in
         bud.

Note. — Have size of flowers measured. Have symmetry, regularity, and shape of parts shown by drawings.

5. DIFFERENCES IN FRUITS.
    Illust. Such fruits as can be obtained.
    (*a*) In condition when ripe : Oranges are juicy.
                                     Apples are fleshy.
                                     Grapes are pulpy.
                                     Corn is dry.
    (*b*) In size.
    (*c*) In surface.
    (*d*) In color.
    (*e*) In flavor.   } Teach these topics as above.
    (*f*) In shape.
    (*g*) In openings.
    (*h*) In constitution.

6. DIFFERENCES IN SEEDS.
    Teach differences in number, size, shape, color, surface,
    arrangement, germination, number of cotyledons.
    Have shapes shown by drawings.

VII. *Lessons to teach Differences in Habits of Plants.*

(a) In position : The elm grows erect.

The squash lies on the ground.

The grape climbs by stem tendrils.

The ivy climbs by rootlets.

The pea climbs by leaf tendrils.

The bean twines. In what direction ?

The hop twines. In what direction ?

(b) In growing : The elm grows tall with one woody stem.

The currant grows low with several woody stems.

The peony grows low with soft stem.

(c) In fruiting.

(d) In locality.

(e) In storing food.

(f) In branching.   } Teach as above.

(g) In blooming.

(h) In multiplying.

VII. *Lessons on the Uses of Plants.*

1. What part of plant is useful? For what?

Illust. — The potato plant.

The underground stem of potato is used for food. Starch is obtained from it.

2. In what ways useful?

(a) For food : It is nutritious.

It has not a strong flavor.

It is easily cultivated.

It yields abundantly.

(b) For starch : It contains much starch.

Note. — Care is needed in these lessons to adapt the subject and the method to the capacity of pupils. The lesson outlined above is not suited to youngest pupils.

VIII. *Lessons on Special Subjects.*

FOREST TREES.

Illust. — The chestnut-tree.

(*a*) SIZE. The chestnut is a tall tree with long, spreading branches.

(*b*) STEM. It has one straight stem.

(*c*) BARK. The bark is gray, hard, and close; has long parallel cracks.

(*d*) LEAVES. The leaves are very long.
The length is   times the breadth.
They are long and pointed at the top.
The edge has hollows separated by sharp points.
The leaves are paler on the under side.
They have a short leaf stem.

(*e*) FRUIT. The fruit is covered with a bristly burr and contains from one to three nuts.

(*f*) WOOD. The wood is coarse-grained and has large pores.

ANIMALS.

Some of the lessons on animals may have to be given by means of pictures, although, so far as it is possible to do so, the animals themselves, either alive, stuffed, dried, preserved in alcohol, or mounted, should be brought before the pupils for observation. Generally, the preserved specimens will be found better for class use than the living animals. A collection of specimens should be in a cabinet close at hand, the pupils being encouraged to add to it a few specimens each year.

The work involved in collecting and preparing specimens for observation may deter some teachers from carrying on these lessons; but if a beginning is made, and the co-operation of pupils is secured, there will be little danger of failure on this account. Some of the specimens may be found all ready for observation, as the crab, starfish, coral, sponge, and a few of the insects. Stuffed birds may be bought for a small sum of a taxidermist, and a few of the animals needed may be procured at the provision store. A large number of the animals, however, will have to be caught, killed, and prepared for class use by the teachers and older pupils.

Insects may be caught with a net made of a stick, hoop, and mosquito netting. For killing the insects, have a bottle of chloroform, ether, or benzine, with a camel's-hair brush attached inside to the cork; or they may be killed by throwing them into a bottle containing cotton saturated with ether. When they are dead, they may be dried and mounted upon cards or slices of cork, with pins thrust through the thorax. For some purposes, it will be found best to preserve the insects in alcohol. When this is done, let the insects be soaked in water for a time before using, to take out the alcoholic odor. Further suggestions for mounting and preserving specimens will be found in any good text-book of zoölogy.

If one specimen for each pupil cannot be provided, allow three or four pupils to look at one specimen; or if there is only a single specimen for the entire class or school, have the specimen examined by the pupils in groups.

In all grades, both teacher and pupil should use the pencil and chalk freely in drawing the shapes of the several parts, and in locating the parts, *after they have been observed.*

The use of animals, and the importance of kindness toward them, should be impressed upon children of all ages in connection with these lessons.

Primary Grades. — The first lessons should be upon those animals which are most familiar, as the cat, dog, horse, cow, rabbit, hen, duck, pigeon, frog. These and a few others of which these are types, will be all that it will be well to observe during the first year. In these early lessons only the most obvious features of each animal should be considered, as, for example: the number and shape of ears; number and shape of legs; number and shape of toes or claws; kind of covering; uses of parts; etc. It will be remembered that parts of the human body are studied in the primary school.[1] This work will greatly assist in the observation of parts of the lower animals, and should go on at the same time.

In the second and third years, observation and comparison of common animals, including domestic animals and the common fowls, birds, and insects, should be continued. The observation and naming of parts should occur throughout the course, care being taken not to tell what the children can see for themselves, and not to proceed too rapidly. Such animals and specimens as can be most easily procured should be observed. *What* the children observe is of far less consequence than the fact that they *do* observe some animal every day in a proper way. It may be necessary to direct the attention of children to certain animals which cannot conveniently be brought into the schoolroom. Their observation of such animals will have to be made out of school hours, the facts observed to be subsequently stated in recitation.

Only the most prominent parts of insects should be

[1] p. 195.

observed at this time, such as the head, thorax, and abdomen; feelers, eyes, wings, and legs. Interesting facts and stories may be told or read to children in connection with the lessons upon insects.

Resemblances and differences in the parts and habits of animals should also be taught during the second and third years. These lessons may be pursued in the following order : (1) resemblances and differences in many parts of two animals; (2) resemblances and differences in a few parts of three animals ; (3) resemblances and differences in single parts of several animals. The resemblances and differences in the habits of animals may have respect to manner of locomotion, of getting food, and of eating and drinking.

In comparing animals, resemblances are given first; afterward, differences. Let the children draw their own inferences.

As an illustration of what points are to be developed in these early lessons, the following examples are given. The questions and statements merely indicate the kind of observation which may be made.

·1. *To teach resemblances and differences in parts and habits of two animals.* — Compare hen and duck, as to size, shape of head, length and shape of bill, comb, shape of body, shape of legs, size and shape of wings, thickness of feathers, tail feathers, condition of feet, habits in getting food, habits in walking, habits in eating and drinking.

2. *To teach resemblances and differences in several parts of animals.* — Compare horse, cow, and sheep as to (*a*) size; (*b*) covering; (*c*) teeth ; (*d*) tail; (*e*) horns, etc.

Write complete sentences.

3. *To teach resemblances and differences in animals in respect to one part.* — What animals have hair ? What have wool? What

have feathers? What birds have long bills? What birds have short bills? What have straight bills? What wide? What narrow?

In the same way teach differences of animals as to (*a*) mouth; (*b*) feet; (*c*) ears; (*d*) wings.

Grammar Grades. — The aim of the work during the fourth and fifth years is mainly to lead pupils to observe for themselves the parts of several animals. It will be well at this stage to have some system or order in the observation. The animal should first be examined as a whole, and afterwards in parts, in regular order. Some facts respecting the size, form, surface color, position, and uses, should be observed and stated by the pupils, the teacher merely directing the observations and correcting errors.

The names of animals to be observed are given in the course for graded schools. The observation of each of these animals — or others of which these are types — should be as minute as time and the ability of pupils will permit. Only a few points should be observed at each lesson, care being taken to allow time for every pupil to observe each point. Complete statements of facts observed should be made by the pupils, but they should be given freely and naturally.

To show what it is possible for pupils of the lower grammar grades to see, and also to show a good method [1] of directing their observation, the following lessons are given. They are by Miss J. M. Arms, of Boston.

THE LOCUST, OR "GRASSHOPPER."

The children may begin the study of insects with the locust, or "grasshopper," as it is commonly called, because it is a good type

[1] For method, see the forthcoming *Guide for Science Teaching*, No. VIII., by Alpheus Hyatt.

of the whole class of insects, and is familiar to them. To insure the best success, each child should be provided with an alcoholic specimen, which may be pinned to a small strip of cork to aid in handling. The children observe the body first, afterwards the parts fastened to the body. By questions the teacher leads the children to tell her that the body is long, and that a part of it is round. She asks, " Is it round like a ball, or round like a tube ? " [showing ball and tube], and they answer, " Round, like a tube."

They tell her that the body is yellow, brown, and red. She asks, " Are the two sides alike or unlike ? " They think the sides are alike, so that the locust has a right and left side, like their own bodies.

They say that the body is divided into three parts, — a head, a "tail," which the teacher calls the abdomen, and between these two parts, a middle and larger part, which (having taken the lesson on the lobster) they think is the thorax.

Having observed and described the body, as a whole, they next observe the three parts more closely. The head, they say, is long in an "up and down" direction, and the teacher gives the word vertical, and writes it on the board. They say that it is narrow, that it has two " horns " which the teacher calls " feelers," and that it has two "things" which they think are eyes, one on each side.

Before this they have noticed that the head moves quite freely up and down, or in a vertical direction, and sideways; also, that when the head moves, the forward part of the thorax moves.

Observing now the thorax, they often describe the forward part as a cape. [We have noticed that little girls are very apt to call it " a cape," and little boys " a saddle."] · They think that the thorax looks somewhat "like a box," flat on the lower side, with "queer marks" on it, and with lines on the sides. The teacher gives the word "seams" for these lines, so that the thorax is seamed. The children find that the legs and wings are fastened to this part of the body.

The "tail" is longer than the head and thorax. The children see lines running round it.

The teacher asks, " What have I in my hand ? " The children answer at once, " A ring."

" Is it a gold ring?" " No, it is a paper ring."

" What is this?" asks the teacher. " Three or four paper rings fastened together with tissue-paper."

" Do the rings move upon each other, or are they fastened so tightly together that they cannot move?" " They move upon each other."

" Now look at the locust's 'tail,' and tell me something more about it." Most of the children are pretty sure to say that the " tail " is ringed, and that the rings move upon each other. Some count six rings, others seven, and two or three are sure there are eight. The number of rings is a matter of little importance, as it is difficult to make out, and is, therefore, work for older pupils.

The children next see the line or crease running from the thorax to the end of the " tail." Above the crease on each side they see, if their eyes are very keen, a row of tiny slits. These, they are interested to know, are the breathing-holes of the locust. This offers an opportunity to the teacher to speak of the wonderful little tubes and sacs which the locust possesses, and which, when filled with air, lighten the weight of the body, and help the insect to fly. At the end of the " tail " they see the organ which is used for boring holes in the earth in which the eggs are deposited. For this reason the organ may be called an egg-depositor.

Having carefully observed the body, they are ready to examine the parts fastened to it. They say the feelers are long, like " big threads," and " made of little pieces." Below the feelers they find the upper lip, with the two hard, dark-brown " teeth " beneath, and back of these, four little organs they often call " whiskers," but which the teacher tells them are organs used, possibly, in obtaining food.

The children are too young to make out the three pair of mouth-parts satisfactorily. A blackboard drawing will show these parts, if the teacher wishes to resort to such a drawing, but I prefer to pass over the subject till the children are old enough to find the mouth-parts and make their own drawings. It often happens that some member of the class has seen a locust eat, and can tell the others how it bites and chews grass, and how the " teeth " move sideways instead of vertically, like their teeth.

Looking at the parts fastened to the thorax, every child can describe the three pair of legs. Every child sees that each leg is made of pieces which move upon each other, so that the leg is jointed. Every one finds that each leg has two little hooks at its end, the use of which each must try to find out when the summer comes again. Every one sees that the last pair of legs is longer and larger than the other two pair, and are prettily marked. Many are eager to tell their teacher that the locust jumps with these legs, and all agree that the insect is a good leaper.

In the lesson on the lobster, the children have seen the feelers, mouth-parts, and walking-legs on a large scale, and can better understand the structure of these parts in insects.

The children spread out the wings on one side. The first or upper pair they say are long, narrow, brown, with stiff "things" in them, which the teacher calls "veins." They cannot see objects distinctly through them. These the teacher calls "wing-covers." The second or lower pair they say are broad, white, with stiff veins in the longest part, and "little veins" in the shortest part. They can see objects distinctly through them. They say these wings are folded like a fan, and lie straight with the body. The teacher calls them true wings. The children compare the true wings with the wing-covers.

Observing the egg-depositor, they say there are four distinct parts that are hard and strong; two of these parts curve upward, and two downward.

After the observations are finished, simple drawings and written descriptions are required.

OUTLINE OF THE LESSON ON THE LOCUST.

1. *Body.* General description : long; tube-like; yellow, brown, red; two sides alike. Divided into three parts: head, thorax, tail.

Parts described: (1) *Head:* long vertically; narrow; bears two feelers; has two eyes; set upon a neck; moves vertically and sideways. (2) *Thorax:* box-shaped; forward part like a cape; flat on lower side; seamed; bears legs and wings. (3) "*Tail*": long; ringed; has two rows of breathing-holes; bears organ for depositing eggs.

2. *Parts fastened to the Body.* One pair feelers : long, thread-like. One pair "teeth" : brown, stout, notched, move sideways.

Two pair thread-like organs. Three pair legs : jointed, hooked, of unequal length and size ; last pair (leaping-legs), long, large, strong. Two pair wings (wing-covers and true wings). Wing-covers brown, stiff, not transparent, veins large. True wings white, transparent, folded like a fan, lie straight with body. Egg-depositor, — four distinct parts, — stout, curved, horny.

THE DRAGON-FLY.

When the locust is familiar, the dragon-fly is observed in the same order, and afterward compared with the locust.

We will omit the observations on the dragon-fly, and pass to the comparative work.

The children tell their teacher that the dragon-fly is like the locust because it has a long, tube-like body ; because the two sides of the body are alike ; because the body is divided into three parts, which they are now ready to call the head, thorax, and "tail." They say that the head has two eyes, like that of the locust ; that the thorax, or middle part, bears the legs and wings ; that the "tail" is long and ringed.

They also see that the dragon-fly resembles the locust in having one pair of feelers, an upper lip, and one pair of dark "teeth." They are not sure of the little organs back of the "teeth," but they are sure that the dragon-fly has three pair of legs and two pair of wings, like the locust. They also see an egg-depositor at the end of the tail.

When the children look for differences, they are quick to say that the body of the dragon-fly is longer than that of the locust, and that the three parts look, as a little child once told me, "as if they were not put together very tight," which is another way of saying that the parts of the dragon-fly are not as closely consolidated as those of the locust. They say that the head is shorter vertically, and broader ; the eyes a great deal larger ; the head "ever so much looser," or, as the teacher says, much more loosely attached ; the thorax more hunch-backed ; the "tail" more slender.

They also say that the feelers are shorter ; the legs smaller, and more nearly equal in size ; the wings longer, more finely veined, and more useful as flying-organs. They have come to this last conclusion by their own efforts, unaided by the teacher.

After these comparisons have been made, the children draw the inferences that the dragon-fly bites its food, and that it is a good flyer, and not a leaper.

In this way the interesting habits of insects, and their wonderful powers of adaptation, are brought out clearly.

The following statements of facts, prepared from observation of specimens by pupils of a normal school, will be helpful to some teachers. Pupils of grammar-school age may not be able to observe all the points that are indicated in the notes; but with a good magnifying-glass most of the facts may be ascertained and expressed by the pupils.

With a good elementary text-book as a guide, similar notes upon other animals may be made. It is advisable for teachers to examine a specimen, and to note the various points to be observed, before the lesson begins.

THE COMMON ANT.

Color. — Brownish red.

Size. — About one-fourth of an inch long.

Parts. — Three divisions: head, thorax, and abdomen.

The head is about one-fourth the size of the whole animal, and is slightly triangular in shape, looking at it in front. There are two eyes, one on each side of the head. Projecting from the front of the head, near the eyes, are two antennæ, which are twice jointed, the second joint being notched. The mouth is provided with strong jaws, called mandibles, for tearing the food, and underneath are the inner jaws.

The thorax connects the head and abdomen, and is smaller in diameter than either of the other parts. It is covered on the top by a shield-shaped portion. The juncture of the thorax and abdomen is very slender, and consists of one knob, or ring.

The ant has three pairs of legs, all placed upon the thorax. The legs are five-jointed, the first joint being the smallest; and from the third is a projection called the spur. The spur on the two front legs is larger than on the others. The last joint is notched, or toothed, a great many times.

The abdomen is marked by rings, which separate it into six segments. These segments differ in size, the last one being the smallest; and the effect is to make the abdomen taper to a point. These segments allow of the abdomen's being bent very easily. The sides of the abdomen are covered with little hairs.

THE DOR-BUG.

Size. — About seven-eighths of an inch long and one-half of an inch wide.

Form. — Oblong in shape, slightly rounded at both ends.

Color. — Dark brown on the upper side; yellowish brown on the under side.

Parts. — Three parts: head, thorax, and abdomen.

The head is the smallest of the three parts. All the divisions of the body are jointed. It has two compound eyes, one on each side of the front part of the head. Between the eyes are the *antennæ*, which are about one-fourth of an inch long, and have little oblong knots at the end. They are used as feelers. On the forward portion of the head are the mouth-parts. These are so small that only the jaws can be seen, and those with the greatest difficulty. The jaws come from the sides of the mouth.

To the under side of the thorax are attached three pairs of legs. The legs of the first pair have three parts. The division nearest the body is smooth, and larger than the other two. The middle division is shorter, and notched. The last division is jointed, notched, and at the end has two little claws. The notches and claws enable it to fasten itself to objects. The second and third pairs of legs have the same structure as the first pair. On the upper side of the thorax are two pairs of wings. The outer pair are brown, oblong, pointed at the back, glossy, and firm of texture. This pair is attached to the second segment of thorax. Under this is a pair of gauzy wings. The second pair are larger, are shaped like half a lilac leaf, and have several strong veins running through the thin tissue. One strong vein extends along the straight edge, and enables the wing to cut more easily through the air. This pair is attached to the third segment of thorax. When at rest, they are folded under the thicker wings, which protect them. The back of each wing folds under the front part, and both cross under the shield-wings.

The abdomen is oval in shape. It has divisions, or segments. The largest segment is near the thorax. From this they diminish in size to the end of the body.

BLACK SPIDER.

Black, with some brown markings upon it. Width, not including legs, about one-fourth of length. —— of an inch long.

Body consists of two principal parts of about the same size, connected by a small, narrow part. On the forward part of one of the large divisions is the head, which is simply a continuation of the division. On the top of the head are a pair of eyes about one-eighth of an inch apart: below these, on the front part of head, are another larger pair of eyes nearer together; and below these, on the lower part, are four more eyes, arranged in a horizontal line. From the lower part of the head projects downward a pair of jaws which are long and strong. On the end of each jaw is a little hook pointing inwards. In the end of each hook is a tiny hole. Passing a pin between the jaws, teeth are discovered on the sides of the jaw nearest together. These teeth extend about half-way up the sides of the jaws. Under the jaws is the mouth, which has a lower lip, but no upper lip. Attached to the back of the upper end of each jaw is a jointed part, or feeler, consisting of four joints. On the under side of the forward division (*cephalo thorax*) are four pair of legs. They are seven-jointed. The first pair are larger than any of the others, the second pair next in size, the third pair are the smallest. The legs are covered with little black hairs, especially numerous on the lower joints.

The second large division (*abdomen*) is almost spheroidal in form, and on the upper side is covered with hairs. On the under side of the abdomen, on the end nearest the thorax, is an opening on each side of which is a semicircular slit. Below these parts on or near the end are projections arranged in the form of a circle.

CLAM.

1. *Shell.*

(1) Three to five inches long, two inches wide. Ovate and convex in shape. Edge entire. Thinnest part near the edge. Broader end called anterior end; narrower end called posterior end. If posterior end is nearest you and hinge is up, the part of shell to the right will be the right valve; the part of shell to the left will be the left valve. (2) On the inside of shell there is a narrow band of dull white near edge; broader band of glossy white inside of this, from which a portion projects toward centre at posterior end. In centre a dull white portion, at anterior end, is a glossy white elliptical spot. At posterior end is a glossy white circular spot. (3) The outside of shell is dull white in color. There are concentric rings which grow farther apart as they near the edge. Rather rough surface. (4) In the hinge there is a projection from left valve; depression on right valve.

2. *Live animal.*

(1) Mantle. Covers the outside of valves except where worn in exposed parts. Internal parts covered by mantle, which serves also as lining for valves. The part of mantle exposed when valves are opened is thickened and of a darker color. (2) Muscles. Lying near inner end of shell is a thick muscle which protects the interior from injury. A dark brown elastic substance placed where the two valves fit into each other serves to keep the valves apart. The anterior adductor is attached to the glossy spot in the anterior portion of the valves; composed of many thread-like bands of muscle which serve to close the valves. The posterior adductor is attached to a circular portion in posterior end. (3) Siphon. Projection from posterior end; tubular in shape; can be extended during life eight or ten inches; dark colored, covered by mantle; tough texture; two openings leading into tubes; little fringe around openings. (4) Gills. Extending from between two anterior openings of siphon to beyond hinge of valves; fan-like in shape; marked with parallel ridges extending from base to

edge; both gills same form and size; edge entire. Two similar gills below the body. (5) Body. Same size as gills; light color with dark streaks; thickened and rounded in form; projection at anterior end (foot); attached to line of division. (6) Ribbons. Anterior end of body; length the width of gills; thin and narrow; all alike; two above and two below the body. (7) Mouth. Dark colored spot situated where four ribbons unite; entrance into body. (8) Foot. At lower anterior end of body; thickened tough projection; expands on absorbing water; protrudes from slit in muscle. (9) Slit. Situated in lower anterior portion of muscle which lies around edge of shell.

CORAL.

Materials. — Pieces of the skeleton of one kind of coral, enough for each pupil to have one piece. A whole mass of the same kind of coral, if it can be obtained. The Galaxea coral is a particularly good one for study because the parts are large.

Observation of Skeleton of Galaxea. — It is white, composed of little cylindrical tubes imbedded in a white porous substance. When scratched with a knife-blade, the tubes and porous substance are equally marked. When a bit of each is placed in a separate glass with a little muriatic acid, the acid froths, and the bit of coral is dissolved. [We infer from the equal hardness and the like behavior with muriatic acid that both parts of the skeleton of coral are of the same material. Both are carbonate of lime, the same substance as marble.]

The tubes rise from above the coral about one-fourth or one-third of an inch. At the top the tubes are about one-eighth of an inch in diameter, the edge is uneven, and the sides of tubes are marked with longitudinal lines. Inside the tubes are six large partitions, extending longitudinally from the circumference to the centre. Six shorter and thinner ones, alternating with these and extending not quite to the centre, and in some of the tubes twelve very short partitions alternating with the twelve longer ones.

The tubes show the same partitions where broken off at the bottom of piece of coral as at the top of tubes. At the bottom the tubes are smaller than at the top, and they tend toward each other. Occasionally in the bottom of piece the tubes are united.

From the rough and broken appearance of pieces we judge that they are parts broken from a large mass.

ANGLE-WORM.

Materials. — A live angle-worm for each pupil placed in a white plate which has been rinsed in cold water and left wet. One live angle-worm placed on a dish of moist earth. For more minute examination, worms killed and hardened by lying in alcohol, one for each pupil. A pot of moist earth with a small plant of grass or clover growing in it, and several live angle-worms for children to observe habits.

OBSERVATION OF LIVE ANGLE-WORM ON PLATE. — *The angle-worm has no distinct head or limbs*, is cylindrical in shape, —— inches long, —— inch through, light reddish brown on the upper side, paler on the lower side, often iridescent, and marked by lines encircling it, which divide it into *many rings or segments.*

Toward one end of the body is a thicker portion in which the rings are less distinctly marked. [This thicker part is called the *saddle.*] The end of angle-worm which is nearer the saddle is forward as the worm moves, and on the under side of the first segment is a hole. [The mouth. This forward end of angle-worm is called the *anterior* end, and the part of worm back of saddle the *posterior* end.]

On the upper side a dark line extends through the middle, and when the worm shortens itself, this line is crinkled. [This dark line is the *food-tube,* or intestine, seen through the skin of worm, and made dark by the earth which the worm swallows. The mouth opens into the food-tube, and there is a small opening from the food-tube in the last segment of the body.]

Lying above the food-tube is a slender red *line,* which also is crinkled when the worm shortens itself. [*This tube holds* red *blood,* and is called the *heart.*]

The worm stretches out both ends of the body, and, on the plate, does not succeed in moving onward much in either direction.

OBSERVATION OF ANGLE-WORM ON MOIST EARTH. — The worm makes anterior part of body more pointed, stretches it out, fastens it in earth, and draws posterior part of body up to position of anterior part. Then repeats the movements in the same order, and so moves along.

EXAMINATION OF WORM HARDENED IN ALCOHOL. — The worm is a light slate color, is shorter and more stiff and tough than the live worms, with the segments much nearer together. The three parts of worm, anterior part, saddle, and posterior part, can be seen more plainly.

On each side of worm are two parallel lines of little dots. When the angle-worm is held between the thumb and finger of one hand, and drawn through the fingers of the other hand, these little dots are felt as points projecting from the sides of angle-worm. These points are the ends of tiny bristles which the angle-worm uses as hooks to fasten the forward part of his body until he has brought the back part of body up to the position of the forward part.

OBSERVATION OF ANGLE-WORMS LIVING IN POT OF EARTH. — As angle-worms work only in the dark, all that can be seen of their habits is the castings left on the surface of the earth, and possibly some change which the worms have made in the position of pebbles and sticks on the surface. If children can be induced to keep angle-worms at home, and to watch them just at dusk, they may succeed in seeing them come from their burrows, and, when disturbed, return to them, closing the burrow with a pebble or chip. They can also prove that angle-worms perceive light, by suddenly bringing a light near when they are out of burrows.

In the latter part of the fourth year, something of the growth and change of insects should be taught. The best illustration of this change is perhaps the butterfly. To secure the best results, several lessons should be given at different times upon the various changes which are observed. Show a leaf or twig containing the eggs of the insect, and encourage pupils to bring other specimens of the same kind. The same may be done with the young, just after they have emerged from the egg. The full-grown caterpillar and the cocoon can be easily found, and will be interesting objects of study. By putting the cocoon into a box with holes in it, the growth of the butterfly may be seen; or, better still, by putting the caterpillar into a glass box, with some of the leaves of the tree upon which it was found. The various stages of development may be observed until the butterfly is formed. The same may be done with other insects, as the frog, fly, mosquito, June-bug, potato-bug. Some practical lessons may be taught in connection with the food of the maggot, grub, and caterpillar, and the time and place in which injurious insects deposit their eggs.

During the seventh year, the pupils learn by observation to group animals according to resemblances of parts and habits. The animals which have been previously examined, and others, both familiar and unfamiliar, are to be classified first by pointing out the *essential*, characteristics of fishes, frogs and toads, reptiles, birds, and mammals. So far as possible this classification should be made by the pupils' own observation.

The varieties of birds and mammals may then be distinguished, the class giving as much time to the examination of specimens as time will permit. The most valuable part of this year's work, as indeed of the work of all grades, is the observation of adaptation of structure to use. Lead the pupils constantly to infer the special use of each part as it is observed, and knowing the habits of certain animals, to infer and prove the necessary structure of the various organs and parts.

The prescribed course provides for minerals to be taught only during a part of two years, — the sixth and eighth years of the course. Not much can be done in this time, but enough, it is hoped, to enable the pupils to know some common minerals by name and to know how to distinguish them.

It is thought best in these elementary lessons to confine the study to the solids or rock forms and to direct attention especially to those rocks which are most common. The first two or three lessons may be given to teaching what a mineral is. By comparing the mineral form with the vegetable and animal forms, it will be seen that one is organized and that the other is unorganized, and that a fragment of the mineral, unlike that of the animal or vegetable, has the same properties and composition as the whole.

The next step is to teach the difference in minerals in respect to, —

1. *Natural form.*	4. *Lustre.*
2. *Structure.*	5. *Transparency.*
3. *Hardness.*	6. *Color.*

Other distinctions, as streak, refraction, polarization, phosphorescence, and those qualities which are tested by heat and chemicals are important, but may be deferred to the high-school course.

To teach difference in natural form, compare, with reference to form of crystals. Rock salt, quartz, sulphur, alum, ice (snow) may be good specimens in which the form of crystals may be easily observed. If it can be done, the formation of crystals in the fusing and cooling of sulphur would be interesting and instructive. A few simple technical names of crystal forms may be learned; as, *cubic, hexagonal, pyramidal*, etc.

To teach structure, puncture the mineral with a knife or some pointed instrument to see if it has cleavage or can be readily split up into thin layers like mica, talc, gypsum, and slate, or into fibres like asbestos, or into little cubes like galenite.

No definite degree of hardness can be taught in these elementary lessons. Test with the point of a knife or of any hard metallic substance, the hardness of the mineral and give the names *hard, medium hard, soft*. Talc, gypsum, and zinc would be called soft; quartz, feldspar, and topaz would be called hard. Other minerals could be compared with these.

To teach lustre, take three minerals, as galenite, feldspar, and jasper, and show, or rather have the pupils see and say for themselves, that galenite is bright, or has lustre; that feldspar is less bright, or has less lustre; and that jasper is not bright, or has no lustre. To give technical names to the different kinds of lustre, compare the lustre of various minerals with lead, glass, and pearl. If the mineral is like lead in lustre, it has a metallic lustre; if like glass, it has a vitreous lustre; and if like pearl, it has a pearly lustre.

To teach difference in minerals in respect to transparency, the mineral may be placed before the eye, and if objects can be seen through it, it is said to be transparent. If only light can be seen through the mineral, or objects very dimly, it is said to be translucent. If neither objects nor light can be seen through the mineral, it is said to be opaque.

While these differences are being observed, the pupils
are learning incidentally the names of the common minerals. But it is not enough for them to know the
names of a few minerals. If it can be done in these
early lessons, it is desirable that they should learn to
distinguish minerals when they see them, or at least to
be able to distinguish a few.

For example, to teach to distinguish quartz, we should
if possible place before each pupil a specimen of quartz,
with such other appliances as will lead him to examine
it with reference to the qualities already spoken of.
He will see, and by being given the terms can say, that
the quartz has crystals in the form of a hexagonal
prism or shaft, terminated by a hexagonal pyramid;
that it has no cleavage; that it cannot be scratched with
a knife, and that it scratches glass easily; that it has a
vitreous lustre; that it is transparent, translucent, and
opaque; that it is commonly colorless and white.

Although the chief object is to lead the pupils to
observe, it would be well to give with the teaching
such information as will be of interest or value. For
example, when the color of the quartz is observed, it
would be well to tell the pupils that when quartz crystals are purple, they are called *amethyst*, and that
quartz occurs also in uncrystallized or massive forms,
in which case, when colored and translucent, it is called
carnelian and *agate;* and when opaque, *jasper, opal*,
and *flint*. An inspection of specimens of these minerals
will greatly add to the interest of the pupils.

Knowing so much of quartz, it will not be a difficult
matter for the pupils to distinguish that mineral from
others, and it would be well to have some time given

to the work of examining various minerals for this purpose.

Of course such work is necessarily slow. Two or three lessons may be profitably given to *quartz.* An equal number of lessons may be given to each mineral named in the following outline of lessons prepared by Mr. Chas. P. Worcester.

1. GALENA (Lead Ore). — (1) Form : cubic.   (2) Cleavage : good, cubical; *i.e.,* it divides and subdivides readily into cubes.   (3) Hardness : can be scratched readily with a knife.   (4) Lustre : metallic.   (5) Opaque.   (6) Color : blue gray.

2. PYRITE (Iron Pyrites). — (1) Form : usually cubic.   (2) No cleavage.   (3) Cannot be scratched with knife.   (4) Metallic lustre.   (5) Opaque.   (6) Color : brassy yellow, or yellowish white.

3. HALITE (Rock Salt). — (1) The crystalline form of salt that is mined is cubic.   The coarse crystals sold as rock salt are from salt water by evaporation, and are of the square hopper-shape.   (2) No cleavage.   (3) Can be scratched with the nail.   (4) Vitreous lustre.   (5) Transparent or translucent.   (6) Colorless : white or stained brown or red.   (7) Taste : salt.

4. FLUORITE (Fluor Spar). — (1) Form : cubic, or modified cubic; *i.e.,* cubic with the edges bevelled or the corners cut off.   (2) Some cleavage, clipping the corners of the crystal.   (3) Can be scratched with the knife.   (4) Vitreous lustre.   (5) Transparent or translucent.   (6) Color : white, bluish, or of various colors.

5. CORUNDUM (commonest form is emery.   Sapphire and ruby are rarer forms of this mineral). — (1) Form : sometimes rhombic; *i.e.,* as if originally a cube which had been flattened out by a diagonal pressure exerted on one edge, but more often massive; *i.e.,* without crystalline form.   (2) No cleavage.   (3) Very hard; quartz can be readily scratched by it.   (4) Vitreous lustre.   (5) Opaque.   (6) Usually black.

6. MAGNETITE (Magnetic Iron Ore). — (1) Form: octohedron usually; i.e., the crystal formed as if by the union of two four-sided pyramids, base to base. (2) No cleavage. (3) Can with difficulty be scratched with knife. (4) Metallic lustre. (5) Opaque. (6) Color: black. (7) In a powder it is strongly attracted by a magnet.

7. ASBESTOS. — (1) Form: silky, flexible threads. (2) Cleavage: fibrous. (3) Lustre: silky. (4) Opaque. (5) Grayish white.

8. HORNBLENDE. — (1) Form: usually rhombic or six-sided prisms. (2) No cleavage. (3) Slightly softer than quartz. (4) Vitreous lustre. (5) Opaque. (6) Color: black or greenish black. (7) Often a constituent of granite, syenite, and gneiss rocks.

9. GARNET. — (1) Form: usually well-defined dodecahedrons; i.e., twelve-sided crystals. (2) Cleavage: not good. (3) Hardness: about like quartz. (4) Lustre: vitreous or dull vitreous. (5) Transparent, translucent, or opaque. (6) Color: red or brown.

10. MICA (commonest variety, Muscovite). — (1) Form: not readily made out. (2) Cleavage: perfect, into flexible leaves of indefinite thinness. (3) Can be scratched with the nail. (4) Transparent. (5) Vitreous lustre. (6) Color: gray and yellow.

11. FELDSPAR (commonest variety, Orthoclase). — (1) Form like that of a book that is flattened out by a diagonal pressure applied on one edge. (2) Cleavage good; usually in two directions parallel with the crystal faces. (3) Usually somewhat softer than quartz, but with difficulty to be scratched with a knife. (4) Lustre: vitreous or pearly. (5) Opaque, or rarely translucent. (6) Color: usually white, may be stained brown or red.

The main constituent of granite, syenite, gneiss, and the most important of the common rocks.

12. TOURMALINE. — (1) Form: hexagonal prisms, usually of a roughly triangular cross-section. (2) No cleavage. (3) Hard as quartz. (4) Vitreous lustre. (5) Opaque. (6) Color: brown black.

13. TALC. — (1) Form: not easily made out; often massive. (2) Cleavage: when crystalline, good in one direction. (3) Very soft; feeling very characteristic, soft and soapy. (4) Pearly lustre. (5) Opaque. (6) Color: gray.

14. SERPENTINE. — (1) Form: massive. (2) No cleavage. (3) Can be scratched with the knife, but not with the nail. (4) Lustre: dull, waxy. (5) Opaque or translucent. (6) Color: dark green.

15. GYPSUM. Varieties: fibrous (satin spar); massive (alabaster); burned (plaster of Paris). — (1) Form: sometimes in single rhombic crystals, but more often in flat crystals, in general shape like an arrow-head. Such are called twinned crystals, and are really modified single crystals of the regular form. Imagine a regular rhombic crystal to be cut in two by a diagonal plane, and then one-half the crystal rotated on the other, half-way round, and you have the twinned crystal. (2) Cleavage: perfect. (3) Can be scratched with the nail. (4) Lustre: vitreous, pearly, or dull. (5) Transparent, translucent, or opaque. (6) Color: white or brown.

16. CALCITE. Varieties: transparent crystals (Iceland spar); massive (marble, limestone); burned (lime). — (1) Form: usually hexagonal pyramids or rhombohedrons, with only half as many faces as hexagonal pyramids. (2) Cleavage: perfect, parallel to the faces of the rhombohedral crystal. (3) Can be readily scratched with the knife, but not with the nail. (4) Lustre: vitreous. (5) Transparent, translucent, or opaque. (6) Color: white, or variously stained.

ASTRONOMY.

In the twenty lessons assigned for this subject comparatively little can be done. Not all of the work, either, can be purely observational, some of the facts being known only by inference, or upon the authority of others. The first few lessons may include subjects which have already been partially taught in connection with geography. These facts should be reviewed, and other facts learned with as much minuteness as the ability of the pupils and time will permit. The following outline of topics and questions will indicate in a general way the subjects of study, and the order and methods of presenting them. The Roman numerals indicate the order of lessons. Some of the observations will have to be made in the evening, and results be brought into the class.

I.–V.

1. FORM OF EARTH.
   Proofs. — (*a*) Vessel coming in sight. (*b*) Shadow of earth in eclipse. (*c*) Horizon, a circle. (*d*) Voyage around the world.
2. SIZE OF EARTH.
   Diameter. Circumference. (Illustrate by time of railroad train.)
3. MOTIONS OF EARTH.
   (*a*) *Rotation.* — Evidences. Effects. (Illustrate by ball in sunlight. Lighted hemisphere changing — why? Observe effects with axis of ball in various positions: 1st, horizontal, and toward the sun; 2d, upright; 3d, oblique. Illustrate sunrise, noon, sunset, midnight, in the same way. Practise with globe, and find relative times for different places.)
   (*b*) *Revolution.* — Illustrate with ball and lamp and paper disc. Axis inclined 23½° toward the north. Why does the sun rise and set at different times? Why is the sun higher at noon in the summer? Which pole is in sunshine in June? In December? When is sun directly over equator? Effect in length of day in different parts of the earth. Length of day at the equator. At the north pole. Change of seasons caused by what? Show by illustration that three conditions must exist. Place tropics — why 23½° north and south of equator? Polar circles — why 23½° from poles? Orbit of earth. Plane of orbit. Why does sun seem to move? Lead pupils to observe difference in path of sun.

VI., VII.
THE SUN.

Comparative size. Distance from earth. (Illustrate by railroad train.)

Spots. — What supposed to be? Change of form indicates what?

Eclipses of Sun. — How caused? Kinds. Illustrate, and draw conclusions from pupils.

VIII., IX.
THE MOON.

Light, caused how? Cause of phases? Illustrate. Distance from the earth? Position and names of spots? Spots indicate what? Probable appearance from the moon of our earth? Eclipse explained.

X.-XII.
PLANETS.

Appearance and movements of planets that are in sight? Names? Planets in sight at different seasons? Relative size of each? Comparative length of year? Comparative length of day? Moons and rings? Which planets have phases? Conjunction of planets? Probability of habitation?

XIII.-XX.
FIXED STARS.

Appearance, how different from planets when seen through telescope? Why? Give idea of distance by railway train. Do they change their relative position as do the planets? Cause of difference. Position and names of stars of first magnitude. Constellations observed and named; position of stars noted. Results of observation brought into the class.

PHYSICS.

In conducting lessons in Physics the teacher should be careful to lead the pupils to correct conclusions through their own observation. The observation is what is actually seen, and should not be confounded with the experiment which precedes it nor with the inference which follows. The experiments should be made by, or in presence of, the pupils, with simple apparatus. To show the order and character of the work which may be done, and the kind of apparatus used, the following outline of topics for twenty lessons is presented. It is taken largely from the elementary course pursued in the Bridgewater (Mass.) State Normal School.

The Roman numerals indicate the lessons, but sometimes not so much can be done.

I. MATTER, BODY, SUBSTANCE.

Exp. 1. Place a pencil upon the table. Put another in the same place without moving the first. Obs. Cannot do it. Inf. Pencil takes up room [occupies space].

Exp. 2. Fill a bottle with water. Put more in. Obs. Cannot do it. Inf. Water occupies space.

Exp. 3. Close one end of a glass tube. Press other end into the water. Obs. Water does not *fill*. Inf. Air occupies space.

Call anything that occupies space "matter." Call a limited portion of matter a "body."

Exp. 4. Taste salt and sugar. Obs. The taste is different. Inf. They are different kinds of matter.

Exp. 5. Feel of soap and stone. Obs. They feel different. Inf. They are different kinds of matter.

[In the same way smell of coffee and of tea; examine color of leaf and bark; strike on wood and glass, etc. Bring out the inference that they are different kinds of matter.]

Call a kind of matter a "substance."

[Much of the time of the first lesson may have to be given to leading the pupils to distinguish the difference between an experiment and an observation, and to lead them to make correct inferences. If care is not taken, they will be inclined to infer too much.]

II. Changes in Matter.

Exp. 1. Examine a match. Obs. A red end with peculiar smell, a yellow tip, white wood. Inf. Made of different substances.

Exp. 2. Burn and then examine. Obs. Smell goes off with the smoke, red and yellow disappear, also the white wood; a soft, black substance is left. Inf. Change of substance. Call such a change in matter a "chemical change."

Exp. 3. Drop a match. Obs. Change of place.

Exp. 4. Examine the dropped match. Obs. Looks the same as at first. Inf. No change of substance. Call such a change a "physical change."

Exp. 5. Leave a match on table. Obs. No change. Inf. Change must have a cause.

Call a cause of change in matter "force."

Call a cause of chemical change in matter "chemical force."

Call a cause of physical change in matter "physical force."

Call the knowledge of physical force and its effects "physics."

Call the knowledge of chemical force and its effects "chemistry."

Exp. 6. Tear paper with fingers. Obs. A change in paper. Inf. Force exerted by fingers caused the change. Call this "muscular force."

Exp. 7. Take plaster of Paris, wet and pour out on glass plate. Obs. From powder it soon becomes solid. Inf. Force holds the parts together. Call this force "cohesion."

Call any force that draws or holds bodies together an' "attractive force."

Exp. 8. Mark with lead-pencil on paper. Obs. Particles of lead stick to the paper. Lead and paper are unlike. Inf. Force holds the unlike parts together. It is an attractive force. Call this force "adhesion."

Exp. 9. Drop a pencil. Obs. The pencil moves downward to the floor. Inf. Force causes it to fall. It is an attractive force. Call this force "gravity."

III. Changes in Matter.

Exp. 1. Hold a piece of sealing-wax near the flame of a match. Obs. Wax softens and melts. Inf. Force caused this change. Call this force "heat."

Exp. 2. Prepare two pieces of paper with nitrate of silver. Keep one in the dark. Obs. No change of paper in the dark.

Exp. 3. Cover part of other with card, and expose to light. Obs. The part exposed to the light turns dark. Inf. Force caused this change. Call this force "light."

Exp. 4. Burn a match. Obs. Wood changed to different substance. Inf. Force caused this change. Call this force "chemical affinity."

Exp. 5. Put a knife-blade on magnet. Touch it to some iron tacks. Obs. Tacks are drawn to knife. Inf. Force caused this motion. It is an attractive force. Call this force "magnetism."

Exp. 6. Rub a stick of sealing-wax with a piece of dry flannel, and bring wax near bits of paper. Obs. The bits of paper are drawn to the wax. Inf. Force caused this motion. It is an attractive force. Call this force "electricity."

Exp. 7. Touch a metal button to cheek. Obs. Button feels cold.

Exp. 8. Rub button briskly on sleeve, and then touch to cheek. Obs. Button feels warm after rubbing. Inf. By using muscular force "heat" is produced.

Exp. 9. Rub sealing-wax with dry flannel, and bring near bits of paper. Obs. Paper is drawn to wax. Inf. By using muscular force "electricity" is produced.

Exp. 10. Burn match, and while burning look at it; hold a hand near it. Obs. Flame is bright; hand is warmed. Inf. By using chemical affinity "heat" and "light" are produced.

Exp. 11. Bring a match near the flame of a burning match. Obs. Match kindles and burns. Inf. By using heat "chemical affinity" is formed.

These forces are so related to each other, that by using one we may get some of the others.

IV. STATES OF MATTER AND QUALITIES OF BODIES.

Exp. 1. Place a pebble on the table. Press it with the finger. Obs. No change. Inf. Body tends to keep its form; parts held together firmly. Call such a body a "solid."

Exp. 2. Place drop of water on the table, and press it with the finger. Obs. Water spreads out, and the parts move away from one another. Inf. The parts are held together loosely and move freely among themselves. Can change its form easily. Call such a body a "liquid."

Exp. 3. Boil a little water in a test-tube over a candle-flame. Obs. Steam rises and disappears in the air. Inf. Parts are not held together, and tend to separate without pressure. Call such a body a "gas."

Call liquids and gases "fluids."

Exp. 4. Pass the finger along edges of a book. Obs. The finger can move up or down, right or left, forward or backward. Inf. Body extends in three directions. Say that the book has "extension."

Exp. 5. Repeat Exp. 4. Obs. The finger can move only a certain distance in each direction. Inf. The extension is limited. This gives the book "form" or "shape."

Exp. 6. Close the fingers of one hand around one finger of the other hand. Take out finger, leaving an opening. Put other hand in. Obs. Cannot do it. Inf. Hand occupies more space than the finger. Call the amount of space occupied by a body its "size" or "volume."

Exp. 7. Put book on table; put another in same place without moving the first. Obs. Cannot do it. Inf. The two books cannot occupy the same space at the same time. Say that the book has "impenetrability."

Exp. 8. Put book on table; push it. Obs. The body moves. Inf. A body can be moved. Say that the book has "mobility."

V. Qualities of Bodies.

Exp. 1. Put book on table; do not touch it. Obs. The book does not move. Inf. The book cannot move itself. Say that the book has "inertia."

Exp. 2. Hold book in the hand. Obs. Hand is pressed downward. Inf. Book presses hand downward. Call this pressure "weight."

Exp. 3. Tear a piece of paper; tear each piece. Obs. The piece is divided into parts; each piece is divided into parts. Inf. The body can be divided indefinitely. Say that the body has "divisibility."

Exp. 4. Look at a bit of sponge. Obs. There are open spaces in sponge. Call these "pores."

Exp. 5. Put a drop of water on table; dip into it a bit of blotting-paper. Obs. The water disappears in the paper. Inf. There are open spaces or pores in the paper. Say that these bodies are "porous," and have "porosity."

Exp. 6. Fit a cork into a test-tube or a bottle; through this cork pass tightly a glass tube; fill bottle and part of tube with water; tie string around tube at surface of water; set bottle in dish of hot water, or wrap around it a cloth wet in hot water. Obs. The water rises in the tube. Inf. The parts have separated from each other. Say that the body has "expansibility." [By experiments with a soft cork infer that the body regains its form by its own effort. Say that the body is "elastic," and has "elasticity."]

VI. Effects of Force.

Exp. 1. Place a marble on table; strike it with finger. Obs. Force exerted; marble moves. Inf. The force caused the motion.

Exp. 2. Rest the book on the hand, just above the table; take away the hand. Obs. Downward pressure on the hand; the book falls. Inf. The force which caused the book to fall caused the pressure.

Exp. 3. Place book on floor; lift it to the table. Obs. Force exerted; work done. Inf. The force does work; force causes "motion" and "pressure," and "does work."

Exp. 4. Put marble on table; strike it with finger just hard enough to move. Obs. Marble moves.

Exp. 5. Put book on table and strike it with same force. Obs. Book does not move. Inf. Something prevents motion.

Exp. 6. Place smooth paper on sleeve; move finger along paper and then along sleeve. Obs. Motion is lessened when sleeve is reached. Inf. Something lessens motion. Call anything that prevents or lessens motion a "resistance."

Exp. 7. Hold a marble in one hand and a bullet in the other. Obs. Bullet is heavier than the marble.

Exp. 8. Place each on the table. Obs. Neither moves. Inf. Both have inertia.

Exp. 9. Strike marble with little force; strike bullet with more force. Obs. Marble does not move; bullet does not move. Inf. Inertia is a "resistance."

Exp. 10. Strike marble with just force enough to move it; strike bullet with same force. Obs. Marble moves; bullet does not move. Inf. Heavier body offers more resistance — has more inertia.

Exp. 11. Place book on table and apply force enough to move it. Obs. Book moves. Inf. Book has inertia; inertia overcome.

Exp. 12. Put another similar book on first, and apply the same force. Obs. No motion. Inf. Two books have more inertia than one. The more matter, the more inertia. [In the same manner, by experiments with paper, rough and smooth, a stick and a marble, lead the pupils to infer that, (1) air offers resistance; (2) surface of paper offers resistance (friction); (3) pressure increases the friction; (4) cohesion offers resistance; (5) body tends to keep moving (inertia); (6) force has "direction" and "intensity."]

VII. Properties of Motion.

[Apparatus needed : *marble, pencil, shingle, bullet, filbert, brick.*]

Teach following properties of Motion : *Direction, Velocity, Momentum, Energy.*

The various inferences from experiments observed will be, (1) The motion has direction. The motion is the same as the direction of the force which produced the motion. (2) The greater distance was passed in the same time because more force was applied. (Call the distance passed in a given time "speed" or "velocity.") (3) The marble in motion exerted force. It got this force from the hand. (Call the force of a body in motion "momentum.") (4) Inertia of shingle greater than momentum of marble. (5) Momentum of bullet more than momentum of marble. The heavy body has more momentum than a light one moving at the same rate. (6) Inertia of book greater than momentum of marble. (7) The body has more momentum because its velocity is greater. The momentum depends upon the force used. (8) The motion of the brick enabled it *to do work.* (Call the power to do work "energy.")

VIII. Effect of Several Forces acting together.

(1) In same direction. (2) In opposite direction. (3) At an angle. (4) Parallel. (5) Unlike. (6) Equilibrium.

Exp. 1. Suspend a pulley, and over it pass a cord; to one end attach a two-ounce weight; attach a two-ounce weight to other end. Obs. The first weight is held up.

Exp. 2. Take off second weight. Obs. The first weight falls.

Exp. 3. Raise second weight a little with the hand. Obs. The first weight moves downward. Inf. The second weight holds up the first weight.

Exp. 4. In place of second weight attach two one-ounce weights. Obs. The first weight is held up.

Exp. 5. Raise small weights with hand. Obs. The first weight moves downward. Inf. Two one-ounce weights do same work as two-ounce weight *in same direction.* Each force does same work as when acting alone.

[In the same way show that a three-ounce weight in one direction, and a one-ounce weight in an opposite direction, do the same work as a two-ounce weight in the direction of the three-ounce weight. Each force (in opposite direction) does same work as when acting alone.]

Exp. 6. Place a marble on the table; snap it directly to the right, then directly forward, and observe the motion in each case.

Exp. 7. Snap it in both directions at same time. Obs. The marble moves in a direction between two former motions; it moves in a straight line. Inf. Each force does the same work as when acting alone.

Exp. 8. Take a piece of lath one foot long, make a hole in the middle, and suspend by a string; make similar holes one inch apart on each side, first hole one inch from the middle; make hooks by bending pins, and suspend from each of the holes. Mark off with a ruler a piece of sheet-lead one inch square, and cut several of them; make a hole in one corner of each, and put in a thread to suspend it by. With this piece of apparatus show, (1) Equal weights at equal distance from middle do same work. (2) By doubling the distance of the weight from middle, we make it do double the work. (3) By doubling the weight at the same distance, the work done is doubled. (4) By doubling both weight and distance, four times the work is done.

IX. Cohesion and Adhesion.

Exp. 1. Press two bullets together. Obs. They come apart easily. Inf. Cohesion does not act.

Exp. 2. Scrape one side of each bullet; press together, and pull apart. Obs. They do not come apart easily. Inf. Cohesion holds them together.

Exp. 3. In a tumbler of hot water slowly put powdered alum; continue till alum begins to fall to bottom of tumbler. Obs. Alum disappears in the water.

Exp. 4. Take a twig from some plant, clean, and hang in the water; let the water cool quietly. Obs. The particles of alum have been brought together again; the body has a definite form. Inf. Cohesion has acted; cohesion has arranged the particles in a definite way.

[In the same way teach the following effects of Cohesion: *Hardness, Tenacity, Elasticity, Flexibility, Ductility, Malleability, Brittleness.* Also lessons on Adhesion, showing that solids adhere to solids, that solids and liquids adhere, and that solids and gases adhere.

X., XI. Gravity.

Direction, Supporting Forces, Centre of Gravity, Stability.

To teach *Direction*, give the following experiments, having pupils observe and infer as before. — Exp. 1. Take one end of a string in each hand; hold left hand still, moving right hand toward the right; stretch the string; do the same upward; do the same downward.

Exp. 2. Tie a stone to one end of a string, and hold other end in hand.

Exp. 3. Draw circle upon paper, and from two points outside draw lines straight toward the circumference; extend these lines into the circle.

To teach *Supporting Forces.* — Exp. 1. Place on table a soft lump of salt; on this place a heavy book.

Exp. 2. Place the same book on a small stone. (Cohesion overcomes gravity.)

Exp. 3. Moisten finger, touch to bit of paper, and raise finger. (Adhesion overcomes gravity.)

Exp. 4. Bring steel pen near a knife-blade, and remove the hand.

Exp. 5. Rub knife-blade on magnet, and repeat No. 4.

Exp. 6. Bring bits of paper near a stick of sealing-wax, and remove the hand.

Exp. 7. Rub wax on sleeve, and then repeat No. 6.

To teach Centre of Gravity. — Exp. 1. Place book on table.

Exp. 2. Balance a pencil horizontally on finger.

Exp. 3. Cut pasteboard in form of a triangle; make a hole near each end; tie in a string to hold it by; make a plumb-line, and suspend string and plumb-line from the same finger; mark on the pasteboard the direction of the plumb-line.

Exp. 4. Suspend from each corner, and repeat No. 3.

Exp. 5. Rest the pasteboard on the point of a pin at the point of intersection of the lines.

Exp. 6. Make a pin-hole at this point, put pin through, and turn body into different positions.

Exp. 7. Suspending pasteboard by a string, draw body to one side.

To teach Stability. — Exp. 1. Rest a small piece of board on end; overturn it by turning it on one corner; observe force used, and motion of centre of gravity.

Exp. 2. Overturn by turning on edge; observe as before.

Exp. 3. Balance pencil on point of finger.

Exp. 4. Move it in either direction.

Exp. 5. Suspend a plumb-line from hand.

Exp. 6. Move body either way, then free.

Exp. 7. Roll a marble on table.

XII., XIII. WEIGHT.

In this lesson explain principle of *Balance* and *Steelyard* by simple experiments.

Take same stick as in study of parallel forces; cut two pieces

of sheet-lead exactly two inches square; hollow in middle to make
little pans; make a hole in each corner of each, and by threads
from corners suspend from hooks on each end of stick. Call this a
Balance. Suspend by middle string; in one pan put one lead
weight, in other pan put some sand.

Take a piece of lath and make a balance with unequal arms,
like a steelyard; from longer arm hang a stone, and call it P.
Hang one weight on hook on short arm; move stone till they balance. Mark place 1; put 2, 3, 4, 5 weights, and mark place where
P balances. Hang piece of wood from hook, and move P till they
balance. (Each pupil should construct his own balance.)

XIV. PENDULUM.

Suspend a bullet by a fine thread from a fixed support.

Exp. 1. Draw it to one side; free it.

Exp. 2. Draw it a little to one side, and free. Count oscilla-
tions for fifteen seconds.

Exp. 3. Repeat, only drawing farther.

Exp. 4. Make string six inches long. Oscillate, and count as
before.

Exp. 5. Make string twelve inches long. Repeat.

XV. EFFECT OF GRAVITY ON LIQUIDS.

By experiments show that, (1) Gravity causes water to fall. (2)
Falling water has momentum. (3) Gravity causes water to run
down hill. (4) Running water has momentum.

To teach the effect of gravity on liquids supported, give the following experiments: —

Exp. 1. Tie a piece of thin rubber on one end of an Argand
lamp-chimney; fill chimney with water.

Exp. 2. Fit a cork tightly into other end of chimney; through
a hole in cork pass a glass tube with a bend near one end; hold
chimney horizontally, and partially fill tube with water.

Exp. 3. Fill tube wholly.

Exp. 4. Cut a piece of lead a little larger than lamp-chimney;
suspend by a string through a hole in the middle; insert chimney

in a jar of water, and hold lead close to the bottom by the string through the chimney; release the lead.

Exp. 5. Release the lead near the surface.

Exp. 6. Close one end of a tube with finger, and press open end into a jar of water.

Exp. 7. Remove the finger.

[The facts to be shown by these experiments are, that water presses downward and laterally; that pressure depends upon depth of water; that within the water there is upward pressure; and that upward pressure at the bottom of tube is due to the downward pressure of the water around it. Prove also that water tends to have the same level, and that pressure is transmitted through the water downward, laterally, and upward.]

XVI. Loss of Weight. Floating Bodies.

By familiar experiments show that a body immersed in water weighs less than out of it; that upward pressure of water supports a part of the weight; that the body displaces its own volume of water; that loss of weight equals weight of water displaced. Also show that lead is heavier than equal volume of water; that a body sinks because it is heavier than an equal volume of water; that a body floats because it is lighter than an equal volume of water; and that heavier liquids hold up the lighter.

XVII. Pressure and Elasticity of Atmosphere. Barometer.

With an Argand chimney, covered at one end with rubber, show that atmosphere presses the rubber downward, upward, and laterally. Also, by pressing open end of chimney into water, show that air in the tube is compressed; that the compressed air is elastic.

To illustrate principle of barometer : —

Exp. 1. Take an empty horse-radish bottle, having a tight-fitting cork, and partly fill with water. In the cork make two holes for two glass tubes. Through one put a bent glass tube. Close one end of a long straight tube with a cork, fill with water, insert, and pass through other hole so that the open end shall be below the level of the water. Obs. The water stays in the tube above the level of the water in the bottle. Inf. The pressure of the atmosphere on surface of the water in bottle holds up the water in the tube.

Exp. 2. Through tube draw air from bottle. Obs. Water falls in the tube.

Exp. 3. Admit air again. Obs. Water rises in the tube. Inf. The height of water in the tube varies with the pressure of the atmosphere.

XVIII.-XX.

The time of these three lessons may be well spent in making siphon, common lifting-pump, and forcing-pump. With lamp-chimney, corks, leather, and small pieces of wood, the pupils can by degrees construct the pump, and explain all the principles involved.

INFORMATION LESSONS.

IN addition to the information given in connection with the regular lessons, there should be taken ten or fifteen minutes daily for what may be called an information lesson, in which facts of a general character are given.

PRIMARY GRADES.

In the primary grades the information should be of a very simple character, the aim being to lead the children to think and inquire about common things around them. Frequently the subjects talked about may be suggested by the observation lessons. Interesting facts which cannot be gathered by the child's observation may be told; as for example, the description of wild animals or the kind of life half-civilized and savage people lead, or the kind of plants which grow in tropical regions. Sometimes the information may be given in answer to questions. Two or three questions may be written on the blackboard, to be answered the following day. What the children cannot answer should be supplied by the teacher.

The following questions may be of some assistance to teachers of primary and ungraded schools: —

What is flour made of ?
Why do we plant trees?
Where does the rain come from, and where does it go to?
Of what are baskets made? Boxes? Bags?
When the tin wears off, what is left?
What is a grocery? A dry-goods store?
What would you probably see in a farm-yard?
Name some articles made of iron. Of wood. Of tin.
Why do people gather hay in summer? Why do they dry it?
Why should we be kind to animals?
Tell me all you know about hay. Corn. Flour.
Of what use is a thermometer? A weather-vane?
Tell me something the horse can do. The dog. The cat.
What animal does mutton come from? Veal? Beef? Pork?
What becomes of snow when it melts?
Should we stare at strangers? Why not?
Tell me the names of the different kinds of birds you have seen.
Why do we not see the stars in the daytime?
Where and how is coal obtained? Wood? Oil? Cheese? Paper?
Where does tea come from? Sugar? Rice? Raisins?
What do people use for fuel? For light?
Name the different modes of travelling.
Where do the different kinds of fruit we eat grow?
What would you find at the seashore?
How are ships useful to us? How large are they? Of what are they made?
Of what is each article of our dress made?
Name the country, State, county, and town in which you live?
Who is President of the United States? Governor of this State?
What is it to be useful? Selfish? Benevolent?

What is meant by a flock? A drove? A swarm?

Mention a polite act. Some rude acts. Some kind acts.

What plays do you like best? What books?

Of the objects you have seen to-day, which are natural and which are artificial?

Tell the seasons of the year, and some pleasant things of each.

Name the days of the week. The months of the year.

If everything you can see were taken out of the schoolroom, of what would it still be full?

If the sun does not shine in the room till afternoon, which way does the room face?

Why are the 22d of February, the 17th of June, and the 4th of July, holidays?

What do we call the young of the goat? Of the horse? Of the cow? Of the cat?

From what are bricks made? How?

Of what is bread made?

Where do potatoes grow? Apples? Strawberries? Blueberries?

Where does the moon get its light?

Why do we not see the moon in the daytime?

Who is meant by grandfather? Grand-daughter? Uncle? Aunt? Cousin? Nephew? Niece?

How long does it take the minute-hand of a clock to go round once?

How many things does it take to make a dozen? A score?

Of what are buttons made? Glass? Cotton cloth? Woollen cloth? Linen cloth? Leather?

GRAMMAR GRADES.

General information for older pupils should take a wide range, including subjects which may be classed under the following heads: —

1. News of the day or week. 2. Civil government. 3. Animals, Plants, Minerals. 4. Morals and Manners.

The amount of time to be given to each of these subjects cannot be definitely prescribed, it being well in such a matter to be guided by circumstances.

At the time of the town, city, or State election, considerable attention to civil government should be given; and when interesting or important events are transpiring, it would be advisable to spend more time upon the newspaper exercise. Sometimes the observation lessons may excite such an interest in natural history as to make it desirable to give two or three general exercises a week upon information connected with animals, plants, and minerals. Generally, however, it will be well to be guided by the rule of having two lessons a week in News, one in Civil Government, one in Natural History, and one in Morals and Manners.

Newspaper. — An excellent opportunity is afforded to study geography, history, and all the political and social questions of the day, by means of the daily or weekly newspaper. There is a variety of ways in which this exercise may be conducted. Three or four pupils may be appointed to give at each lesson an abstract of the news, with such explanations and comments as they can give. Or volunteers may be called for from the entire school to give some item of news. Care should be taken that the news selected or related be of an important or useful character. Merely exciting and unimportant events should be passed by, one object of the exercise being to interest the pupils in that part of the newspaper which is of most importance to them, and to lead them into good habits of reading the newspaper.

Sometimes it may be well for the teacher to give the items of news, asking one and another of the pupils to locate certain places spoken of, and to tell what they can in explanation of the events related. For example, certain acts of Parliament or of Congress may be spoken of, such as home-rule or the tariff. The pupils could be asked what legislation had been attempted before, and what would be the possible effect of the present law. Events in Russia or Greece might suggest questions of boundary, government, religion, and labor or other social questions. Atlases and maps should be consulted by the pupils to ascertain the location of places unknown to them.

The following topics may be suggestive : —

Acts of Congress, Parliament, and other legislative bodies. Existing wars : progress and cause. Expeditions and their purpose. Market reports. Shipping news : arrivals and departures ; exports and imports. Important court decisions. Results of elections.

Civil Government. — For the purpose of giving pupils a better idea of government, and of instilling into their minds high ideas of the duties of citizenship, regular instruction should be given in the grammar . grades upon the following topics : —

Duties, manner of election, and time of service, of Selectmen, Assessors, School Committee, Town or City Treasurer, Collector, Aldermen, Mayor, County Commissioner, Sheriff, Register of Deeds, Judges, Members of State Legislature, Governor, Secretary of State, Attorney-General, State Treasurer, Members of Congress, President, Members of Cabinet.

Names of officers elected at the last National, State, and town elections.

Necessity and use of government and law.

Duties of citizens in respect to the laws.

Advantages of co-operation and arbitration.

Laws in relation to schools, to property, highways, etc.

The civil service. Foreign service.

Existing political parties. Principles of each. History.

Animals, Plants, Minerals. — The time of the observation lessons is given mainly to observing things

in nature. Such lessons will constantly suggest other
interesting matter, which may be told the pupils, or
which the pupils may learn from books. Such subjects
as the following will profitably occupy the attention of
the pupils at least once a week : —

Habits of animals, both wild and domestic.
Uses of animals, alive and dead.
Manner of growth and culture of all articles of food, including
tropical fruits, spices, grains.
Description, value, and use of precious stones and other
minerals.

Sometimes questions like the following may be given
out, to be answered by the pupils or teacher on the
following day : —

How is salt got from sea-water?
What is saltpetre, and what is its use?
How is gunpowder made?
What is phosphorus, and what is its use?
What is soda, and what is its use?
What is potash, and what is its use?
How is lime obtained?
What is marble? What kinds are there, and where found?
What is chalk? Plaster of Paris?
How are lead-pencils made?
What is peat, and how is it prepared for fuel?
What is coal made from?
What is petroleum or kerosene oil, and how is it prepared for use?
How are bricks made? Earthenware?
Of what and how is porcelain made?
How is glass made? How is it made into bottles, goblets, etc.?
How are school-slates and slate-pencils made?
How is iron got from the ore?
What is wrought iron?
What is steel? Uses?
What is bronze? Kinds and uses?

How are pins made?
How are looking-glasses made?
Where do we get lead from? How obtained?
What are stereotype plates, and how are they made?
What is tin? How used?
Of what and how are coins made?
How is gold obtained from rocks? From sand?
Uses of nickel?
What is dynamite, and how made?
How are macaroni and vermicelli made?
How is starch made, and what is its use?
What is malt? Its use?
What is the difference between fermented and distilled liquors?
What is sago? How made?
What is tapioca? How made?
Place and manner of growth of the gourd? the leek? garlic? cauliflower? peanuts? pineapples? dates? figs? raisins? banana? pomegranate? tea? coffee? cloves? etc.
What is candy made of? What ingredients are unhealthful?
How is camphor made? Uses?
From what is gum arabic made? India rubber?
How does flax grow, and what is made from it? Hemp? Cotton?
What is tow? Jute?
Describe cambric; lawn; muslin; canvas; nankeen.
How and from what is lace made? Calico?
From what and how is paper made? Different kinds of paper?
Uses of oak? Maple? Willow? etc.
How is resin made, and what are its uses? Tar? Lampblack?
Place, manner of growth, and uses of mahogany? Ebony? Bamboo? Logwood? Palm?
Manner of making cheese?
What are Durham cattle? Ayshire? Alderney? Jersey?
How are candles made? Soap?
Difference between woollen goods and worsted goods?
What kinds of woollen goods?
What is felting?
How are carpets made? Different kinds of carpets?
How is leather made? Uses?

Kinds of fur, and where obtained?
Uses of ivory? How obtained?
How is wax made, and what are its uses?
How and where is silk made?
What is velvet? Satin? Brocade? Gauze? Crape?
What is obtained from the whale?
What is mother-of-pearl, and what are its uses?
What are shell cameos?

DRAWING.

Form. — The study of Form is a necessary accompaniment of drawing, and is begun in the first year of school. The apparatus needed for the Form lessons given in the primary grades are sphere, cube, cylinder, pyramid (rectangular and triangular), prism (triangular and square), cone, spheroid. Forms similar to those already named should be provided as they are needed, as rubber ball, orange, boxes, dice, lead-pencil, top, etc. Clay and proper conveniences for moulding should also be provided. It would be well for the pupils to have small forms for close observation, and the teacher to have a large form by which to direct the attention of pupils. The first few lessons will consist of simple comparison of familiar objects with respect to form. An object (as a ball) may be presented, and the pupils be asked to find another object like it in form. In this way resemblances and differences of form may be observed before the forms are named or before the parts are examined.

The first object for particular study is the sphere. It is first presented as a whole, and the following facts are observed and expressed by the pupils : —

It is round.
It will roll in all directions.
It has an evenly-curved surface.

The teacher then gives the name of the object, and the pupils say, "It is called a sphere."

The cube and cylinder are next presented, and facts observed as follows: —

1. General shape.
2. Number of surfaces (faces).
3. Form of surfaces.
4. Equality of surfaces.
5. Edges:
   (*a*) number; (*b*) kind; (*c*) equality.
6. Corners:
   (*a*) number; (*b*) kind.
7. Things which its form enables it to do.
8. Similar forms:
   (*a*) to the entire object; (*b*) to each part.

The object is then moulded in clay, and the surfaces drawn upon the slate or paper. It will be seen that the study of surfaces, lines, and angles will be carried on in connection with the study of solids. The simple names, plane and curved, straight and curved, square, blunt, and sharp, may first be used in describing the surfaces, edges, and corners.

After the sphere, cube, and cylinder have been studied, they may be divided into two or more sections, and the parts may be studied in the same general way as the original wholes. The triangular and square prism, pyramid, the cone, and spheroid are next taken in order, and studied as were the cube and cylinder. The introduction of more technical names may be begun at this point, as the names of the angles and triangles:

also diameter, diagonal, circumference. Invention may also be begun here, color being combined with form. The sticks or colored paper of different shapes may be placed in order, beginning with the most simple designs, and proceeding slowly in complexity. At first the pupils will require considerable aid from the teacher. By degrees the pupils will be led to depend more upon themselves, until the designs are entirely original.

The following plan of Form lessons pursued in the Practice Department of the Framingham (Mass.) Normal School will be found helpful to teachers who can give more attention to the study of Form than is indicated in the Course of Studies. The outline is prepared by Miss Ellen A. Williams, critic teacher of the school.

FORM.

PRIMARY SCHOOL. — FIRST YEAR.

It is best not to take up this subject during the first three months of the child's attendance at school, as he has so many other new things to learn. Some lessons in Color should also precede those in Form.

After the child has learned the *name* of the form, and has become familiar with its use in little oral sentences, — "The sphere is on the table," "Mary gave the sphere to the teacher," etc., — he should learn *by his own observation* the following points about each form, and should also be led to tell truthfully, in his own words, the result of each observation.

Note.— At first too much stress should not be laid upon the child's ' form of expression ; but as the work progresses through the different grades, great care should be taken to draw from him *exact* and *concise* statements.

Subjects of First Year's Study. — The sphere, cube, and cylinder. The first course of lessons should deal with these forms as wholes ; that is, without dividing any of them.

Name: Spelling learned from written word. Perfect familiarity with the spelling should be secured by having the child write a sufficient number of short sentences containing the name.

Form: Sides — number of, shape, relative size, and relative position. Edges — number of, kind, relative length, relative position, and formation. Corners — number of, kind, and formation.

Appearance of form from different points of view when at rest.

Appearance of form from different points of view when twirled.

Things which its form enables it to do.

Naming of objects of approximate form which they have seen, bringing as many to class as possible.

Drawing of free-hand pictures of plane surfaces bounding the solid.

Drawing of free-hand outlines of objects of approximate form.

Moulding in clay the perfect form.

Moulding in clay simple objects of approximate form.

Copying in colored papers simple geometrical designs based upon the square, when they study the cube; upon the circle, when they study the cylinder; and upon combinations of square and circle, when they have completed the study of both cube and cylinder.

Drawing of these designs upon slate, both in free-hand and by tracing around cardboard squares and circles.

SECOND YEAR.

Divisions of Sphere, Cube, and Cylinder.

FORM.	DIVISIONS.	NEW FORMS OBTAINED.
Sphere . .	Into two equal parts . .	Hemispheres.
Cube . . .	" " " " . .	Plinths.
	" " " " . .	Triangular prisms.
	" four " " . .	Oblong blocks.
	" " " " . .	Triangular prisms.
	" eight " " . .	Cubes (not new forms).
	" " " " . .	Square prisms.

Cylinder . .
{
Into two equal parts . . Cylinders (not new).

" " " " . . Half-cylinders, having two
semicircular faces.

" " " " . . Half-cylinders, having an
ellipse for one face.
}

The study of each of the new forms obtained by division should be carried on in the same order, and as thoroughly as the study of the sphere, cube, and cylinder during the first year.

LAST PART OF SECOND YEAR, OR FIRST PART OF THIRD YEAR.

Oblate and prolate spheroids, quadrangular, triangular, and hexangular pyramids, and the cone.

This series of lessons to be taken in the same way as the two preceding series have been.

THIRD YEAR.

Divisions of Spheroids, Pyramids, and Cone.

Each of the spheroids may be divided into two equal similar parts in three ways; but as the new forms obtained by these divisions are not specific geometric forms, and as they present no new surfaces for the child's investigation, it seems wise to spend considerably less time upon these forms than upon those which precede or follow them.

FORM.		DIVISIONS.	NEW FORMS OBTAINED.
Quadrangular Pyramid.	Into two parts		Frustum of pyramid.
	" " "		Truncated and oblique pyramids.
	Into two equal parts	{ from apex through diameter of base }	Rectangular pyramid.
	" " " "	{ from apex through diagonal of base }	Triangular pyramid.
Triangular Pyramid.	Into two parts		Frustum of pyramid.
	" " "		Truncated and oblique pyramids.
	" " " .	{ from apex through centre of base }	Oblique triangular pyramid.

Hexangular Pyramid.	Into two parts	Frustum of pyramid.
	" " "	Truncated and oblique pyramids.
	Into two equal parts	Trapezoidal pyramid.
	" " " "	Pentagonal pyramid.
Cone.	Into two parts	Frustum.
	" " " "	Truncated and oblique cone.

FOURTH YEAR.

1. A review of previous work.

2. A study of surfaces, lines, and angles.

Here, as in all the preceding work, the things to be studied are to be presented to the child, and he is *to learn from his own observation*, and is *to make his own definitions.*

Several illustrations of the special subject of study should be presented to the child, and the name given by the teacher.

The child notes the common characteristics, and gives a description.

An exact and concise definition is gradually drawn from him.

He gives other illustrations of the same surface, line, or angle.

1. Surfaces, lines, and angles derived from the *sphere* and *its divisions.*

(1) Curved surface.

Spherical surface (convex surface, concave surface).

(2) Plane surface.

Circle : circumference (arc), chord, segment, diameter, semicircle, semicircumference, greater arc, lesser arc, degree, radius, sector, quadrant, sextant, octant, angle (vertex), right angle, oblique angle (acute angle, obtuse angle).

The child should discover the number of right angles which can be made with their vertices at the centre of a circle ; also the number of acute and obtuse angles which can be placed in the same way.

2. Surfaces and lines derived from cube and its divisions.

Square: parallel sides, perpendicular sides, diameter, oblong, diagonal, triangle (vertex, base, altitude), right angles (isosceles, scalene), trapezoid, trapezium.

3. Surfaces of cylinder.

Cylindrical, ellipse (focus, centre, diameter, major axis, minor axis).

4. Surfaces of spheroids.

Spheroidal surface.

5. Surfaces of pyramids.

Equilateral triangle, hexagon, pentagon.

6. Surfaces of cone.

Conical surface.

7. Lines.

(1) From divisions of sphere.

Curved (circular), straight.

(2) From cube.

Parallel straight lines, perpendicular lines, horizontal lines, vertical lines, inclined or oblique lines.

(3) From cylinder.

Elliptical lines.

FIFTH YEAR.

The pupil begins his work in inventional geometry, following Spencer's text-book on the subject.

Hitherto nearly all his descriptions and definitions have been oral; from this point they should be written in a blank-book devoted to the purpose.

The problems should be solved by the pupil, and not by the teacher. So far as possible the pupil should give reasons for the successive steps in his work.

Work in inventional geometry should be continued in the grammar school until the last year.

During the last year there should be a thorough, scientific analysis and classification of all the geometrical knowledge which the pupil has acquired during the entire course. Correct conceptions of the geometric solid, surface, line, and point should be acquired at this time.

Industrial Drawing. — The order followed in the primary form lessons is to be continued in all of the subsequent work in drawing. From models and other objects knowledge is first gained, and afterwards is expressed by drawing. Following this, the knowledge acquired is combined in new forms by invention and design. Whatever books are used, therefore, the pupils should not be allowed to draw from "flat copy" without previous instruction.

Materials. — Some of the materials used for drawing should be provided, and kept for use at all times. Other materials may be gathered or made from time to time by the pupils themselves. The following materials will be found necessary for good work : geometric forms, and other forms for observation, such as boxes, leaves, flowers, etc.; sticks and paper (white and colored), lead-pencils (hard and soft), rulers, compasses, rubber erasers, drawing-paper and tracing-paper.

Preparation of Lesson. — To accomplish good results in drawing, it will be necessary for the teacher to carefully prepare each lesson. The plan and purpose of the books in use should be understood; and, if a teacher's edition is provided, the directions for giving each lesson should be carefully studied. The correct position of book, hand, and body in drawing, the use of eraser and ruler, and all other specific directions given in the books, should be well understood and observed by the pupils under the guidance of the teacher.

The following hints in regard to the kind of work to be done are not intended to take the place of what will be found in the books prescribed, but are given to assist the teacher in seeing the purpose of drawing, and in suggesting valuable supplementary work.

Working Drawings. — A working drawing is one by means of which an object of a definite form and size may be made. As soon as pupils have had some practice in drawing the faces of geometric forms, let them draw some plane surfaces to scale. The surface of a book may be drawn, reducing the dimensions one-half. The floor of the schoolroom may be drawn, one inch for every foot, etc. Say to the pupils that you want a box made of certain dimensions, and ask them to draw hasty working views of the top, side, and end, such as they would give a carpenter. After practice of this kind, draw upon the board free-hand working views of an object, and ask the pupils to draw with instruments accurate working views.

All of this work is of the most practical kind, for, besides training the hand and eye, it will enable one to give proper directions for the manufacture of any article.

Construction of Objects. — The modelling of objects in clay is carried on in the primary grades, and may be continued to some extent in the grammar grades. This work will be especially useful in connection with working views. Small cubes, cylinders, cones, etc., may also be made with paper or cardboard from drawings previously made. The work may be further pursued by encouraging the pupils to make articles at home from drawings, such as boxes, brackets, and picture-frames.

Perspective. — The *facts* of objects are represented by working drawings; the *appearance*, by perspective drawings. In making a working drawing, the eye is supposed to be opposite each part drawn; in making a perspective drawing, the eye is supposed to be kept in one position. The perspective view of a surface placed squarely in front of and near the eye may not be unlike the working view in form. Carry the object further away, or turn it from a square position, and the surface appears smaller. The free-hand drawing of this reduced appearance should be begun early in the grammar school course, and be continued throughout the course. Objects having plane surfaces may be first drawn, and afterwards other objects, as an apple, an orange, a bell, a hat, etc. Not until the later years of the grammar school should rules and problems, or instrumental perspective, be taught.

Invention. — Invention and design, begun in stick and paper laying, in the primary grades, should be continued throughout the course, both in drawing and applied work. With the units of design given (geometric and plant forms), and by the judicious direction and assistance of the teacher, the work in design will be at once the most practical and enjoyable part of the course. The rules of arrangement may be found in any good series of drawing-books, and will not be difficult to understand.

Home work in making brackets, shades, lamp mats, tidies, etc., will not be the least valuable part of the lessons in design.

Outline of Study. — Teachers may be guided by the following outline of an eight years' course of instruction for primary and grammar schools used at the Massachusetts Normal Art School, and in State work under direction of the Massachusetts Board of Education, by Charles M. Carter.

INDUSTRIAL DRAWING.[1]

NOTES.

Industrial drawing as herein presented is regarded by many educators as *the foundation of industrial training.*

It gives skill in the use of hand and eye, good habits of thought, and appreciation of the beautiful.

Drawing and designing are here combined with the *construction* of objects.

Where workshop instruction is introduced, the drawings and constructed work may be of practical examples, referring to courses in manual training. This plan shows how the natural tendency of children to occupy themselves in making objects at home can be made fruitful by intelligent direction.

It may be used either with or without text-books. Using it as a basis, teachers can determine whether to omit or add to the exercises of the book.

All work may refer to the following or their combinations: —
1. Working drawings. 2. Perspective drawings. 3. Invention or design. 4. Constructed objects.

OUTLINE OF EACH YEAR.

Ideas of form come from *observation*, they lead to *expression*, and may be combined into new forms by *invention* or *design*.

FIRST YEAR. — *Ten minutes daily, using slates and blackboard.*

Observation of the forms of objects in each year, by eye and hand.

Expression, employing construction, drawing, and language.

General form of objects: sphere, cube, cylinder, square prism, triangular prism. Teach objectively as wholes. Construct each of clay.

Observation and expression further developed by moulding simple objects based on them, as an orange, dice, stick of candy, etc. From the objects first used teach the common qualities of form, viz., surface (plane and curved), line, and point.

[1] Copyright, 1885, by C. M. Carter.

Commence teaching and representing the details of these qualities from models and objects : —

1. Points: position (centre, above, below, right, left).
2. Lines: direction (straight, curved); position (vertical, horizontal, oblique); relation (parallel, perpendicular, inclined); color
(light, dark). Dividing into halves and fourths.
3. Angles: right, acute, obtuse.

Objects and figures containing the above should be drawn.

Invention. Optional. If taught, to be similar to that of the
second primary year.

SECOND YEAR. — *Fifteen minutes daily, using slates, paper,
and blackboard.*

Review work of the first primary year, including moulding.

Expression, employing construction, drawing, and language.

From the following models, — triangular prism, square prism,
pyramids, etc., — teach : —

4. Triangle: right-angled, isosceles, equilateral.
5. Square: diagonals, diameters.
6. Oblong: judging, measuring, dividing, and ruling distances.

Draw single free-hand working views of models, objects, and
ornament illustrating the above plane figures. Construct them of
clay, paper, wood, etc.

Substitute paper for the slate during the last half of the year.

Invention. Principles: symmetry, repetition, and alternation.
Materials: sticks, colored paper triangles, squares, etc.

Teach pupils to arrange the materials so as to express the principles. Subsequently replace the materials by lines. Tracing
around units allowed.

The materials may also be used to represent various objects, as
house, ship, etc. Teach the names of colors represented by the
sticks and papers, and cultivate a taste for beautiful combinations.

Continue at times in the same lesson, — form, drawing, invention, color, arithmetic, language, etc.

THIRD YEAR. — *Thirty minutes three times a week, using
paper and blackboard.*

The first exercises review the work of previous grades, in order
that special attention may be given to the proper use of paper and
pencil.

Expression, employing construction, drawing, and language.
From models and objects teach : —
7. Circle : semicircle, quadrant, circumference, diameter, radius.
8. Ellipse : long diameter, short diameter, foci.
9. Oval.

Draw single free-hand working views of models, objects, and ornament illustrating the above plane figures. Construct them from drawings, using wood, paper, etc. Compare the beauty of curvature illustrated by different forms.

Invention and Design. Principles : symmetry, repetition, and alternation. Materials : colored paper geometric forms, both simple and varied. When pupils create the variations of units, the arrangements are called designs.

Ruling allowed. In all grades teachers should be familiar with the principles of growth, contrast, repose, etc.

FOURTH YEAR. — *Thirty minutes three times a week, using paper and blackboard.*

Review the circle, ellipse, and oval.
Expression, employing construction, drawing, and language.
From models and objects teach : —
10. Compound curves ; reversed curves.
11. Hexagon.   13. Octagon.
12. Pentagon.   14. Spiral.

Draw single free-hand working views of models, objects, and ornament illustrating the above plane figures. Construct the plane figures, and objects based on them, of paper, wood, etc.

Design. Principles : symmetry, repetition, and alternation. Materials : conventionalized leaves, flowers, and buds.

Ruling allowed. In all work strive for beauty of form.

FIFTH YEAR. — *Thirty minutes three times a week, using paper and blackboard.*

Expression, employing construction, drawing, and language.
From models and objects teach and draw : —
Free-hand working views, single and combined, illustrating plans and elevations. Construct the models of paper, first making

simple developments. These models will be useful in teaching free-hand perspective.

Perspective views (free-hand). The effects of foreshortening and distance explained in connection with drawing spherical objects, circles, cones, cylinders, and objects based on them. Explain that in a working view the eye is supposed to be opposite each part of the view represented. In perspective drawing the eye remains in one position.

Design. Principles: symmetry, repetition, alternation. Making arrangements on given main lines introduced. Materials: conventionalized plant form. Use ruler and tracing-paper.

Designs may be applied to objects, as pen-wipers, book-marks, etc., constructed by pupils. In this and the following years have pupils take "main lines" from good examples, and clothe them with different material. Cultivate taste by comparing examples of good and bad design.

SIXTH YEAR. — *Thirty minutes three times a week, using paper and blackboard.*

Expression, employing construction, drawing, and language.

From models and objects teach and draw : —

Working views, free-hand and instrumental, single and combined. Two views given to find a third. Marking dimensions; simple sections. Construct simple objects from working views, especially models useful in free-hand perspective.

Geometric problems, and their applications.

Perspective views (free-hand). The convergence of parallel lines; drawings made from the cube, oblong block, etc., and objects based on them.

Design. Principles: symmetry, repetition, and alternation. · Materials: conventionalized plant form.

Use rulers, compasses, tracing-paper, and geometric problems. Make more elaborate bisymmetrical arrangements, with and without outlines. Exercises may be planned in which designs are applied to objects constructed by pupils. Historic ornament or naturalistic views of plant form occasionally. Use them as a means of cultivating taste.

SEVENTH YEAR. — *Thirty minutes three times a week, using paper and blackboard.*

Expression, employing construction, drawing, and language. From models and objects teach and draw : —

Working views: free-hand and instrumental, single and combined ; marking dimensions ; advanced developments ; simple intersections. From measurement make full-sized, and scale drawings; also encourage home construction from drawings of such objects as lamp-shades, picture-frames, foot-stools, etc.

Geometric problems completed.

Perspective views (free-hand). General review. Prisms, pyramids, plinths, and objects based on them. Groups, tinting.

Design. Principles: symmetry, repetition, alternation, and balance. Materials: conventionalized plant form and details of historic ornament. Use instruments, tracing-paper, and geometric problems. Designs may be applied to objects constructed by children, such as lamp-mats, pin-cushions, match-boxes, etc.

Historic ornament or naturalistic views of plant form, occasionally. In all exercises cultivate appreciation of the beautiful.

EIGHTH YEAR. — *Thirty minutes three times a week, using paper.*

Expression, employing construction, drawing, and language. From models and objects teach and draw : —

Working drawings (free-hand and instrumental). Instrumental work to employ the T-square, scale, triangles, and drawing-board. Practical illustrations of drawing applied in industrial pursuits, sections, intersections, and developments. Continue to encourage home construction from drawings of useful objects, such as boxes, bird-houses, tool-boxes, brackets, trays, etc.

Perspective views (free-hand). Frames, crosses, and objects based on them. Leaning objects, groups, tinting.

Design. Optional. Principles previously studied combined with those of applied design. Materials: conventionalized plant form, historic ornament, nature.

Design wall-paper, inkstand, paper-weight, hinge, etc. Occasionally have objects designed that may be constructed by needle-work, etc. Miscellaneous ornament illustrating the highest forms of beauty.

Use drawing freely each year in illustrating other studies.

SINGING.

OF the value of singing as a regular exercise in school, it is unnecessary to speak. Neither should there be any question as to whether it should be regularly taught as other subjects are taught. The fact that teachers cannot sing, or do not know how to read music, should not .deter them from introducing the subject in their schools. However useful it may be for teachers to give good tones as a model for their pupils, it is true that many of the most successful teachers of singing are those who do not sing. The various school singing-books and charts now in use will furnish suggestions as to the order and amount of work to be done, and methods of teaching.

The following illustrative lessons, prepared by Mr. L. W. Mason, of Boston, will assist the regular teachers, especially teachers of ungraded schools: —

I. FINDING OUT HOW MANY KNOW THE SCALE.

Teacher. All listen to me, and tell me what I sing. (*Teacher sings.*)

| Do | Re | Mi | Fa | Sol | La | Si | Do |

Pupils. You sang the scale.
Teacher. All may sing as I did.

[Eight or ten of the class sing correctly, *and the teacher should be very careful to let the whole class share the credit.*]

Teacher. That was very well. Singing as you have just done, from the lowest sound, upwards, is called the ascending scale. You may commence with the highest sound and sing the scale downwards.

[The same pupils sing correctly.]

Teacher. This is called the descending scale.

DIAGRAM OF THE SCALE.

Teacher. I am glad that so many of you can sing the scale up and down. I have drawn a picture of the scale, or Music-Ladder, and have written the scale-names, 1, 2, 3, etc., upon each step; also the syllables which are used in singing the scale. You should know the sounds of the scale, so you can sing them in order or skipping about any way.

[Teacher draws this on the blackboard.]		
8	Do
7	Si
6	La
5	Sol
4	Fa
3	Mi
2	Re
1	Do

II. DEVELOPING THE IDEA OF TWO-PART MEASURE IN CONNECTION WITH SINGING THE SCALE, ASCENDING AND DESCENDING.

Teacher. All listen to me, and tell me what I do.

[Teacher sings with marked accent.]

Do Do Re Re Mi Mi Fa Fa Sol Sol La La Si Si Do Do

Teacher. What did I do?

Pupils. You sang two of each of the sounds of the scale.

Teacher. You may sing as I did.

[It is done correctly.]

Teacher. That was well done. You may sing the scale downward, beginning with 8, in the same way as you sang it upward.

[The pupils do it correctly.]

Natural Rhythm. — *Teacher.* Singing two of each of the sounds of the scale up and down, as you did just now, you sang the first of each pair louder than the second.

You did this *naturally;* that is, without thinking about it. When the time in music arranges itself into groups of *twos*, one loud and one soft, each pair is called a two-part measure. The loud part of the measure is called *accented ;* and the soft part, *unaccented.*

Beating Two-Part Measure, or Double-Time. — *Teacher.* To realize more fully, while singing, the accented and unaccented parts of measures in Double-Time, as music in two-part measure is called, certain motions of the hand are used. This is called *beating time.*

Directions for Beating Time. — *Teacher.* 1. Stand erect, poising a little forward.

2. Place the left hand directly in front of the body, as high as the waist, palm upwards, elbow against the side of the body.

3. Place the right hand in the left, so that the middle finger falls into the centre of the palm of the left hand. (*Teacher gives the example.*)

4. Raise the hand, *from the wrist only,* about 45 degrees. Strike down, and say *Down. Hold the hand down!* Strike up, *from the wrist only,* and say *Up. Hold the hand up !*

These are the motions in beating Double-Time. They should be as regular as the tick of a clock, and should be made as quickly as possible; and the hand should be held perfectly still during the time from one beat to another.

Teacher. We will now proceed to sing the last exercise; that is, two sounds of each of the scale, ascending and descending, while beating the time.

[Done correctly.]

Teacher. I fear you will become tired if you sing all the time; so I will form the class in two divisions, in order that one division may rest while the other sings.

Those on my right we will call the First Division ; and those on my left, the Second Division.

I wish you to sing the scale up and down in this way; namely, the First Division to sing the first measure, and the Second Division to sing the second measure, and so on.

You must continue to beat the time, whether you sing or not. In this way each division will rest during every other measure.

Now! all ready, and see if you understand what I want you to do.

[Enough of the pupils in each division understand so as to do it very well.]

Teacher. You have done that much better than I thought you could.

III. DEVELOPMENT OF THREE-PART MEASURE.

Teacher. Who can tell what I sing now, that is different from anything I have sung before?

[Teacher sings.]

| Do | Do | Do | Re | Re | Re | Mi | Mi | Mi | Fa | Fa | Fa |

| Sol | Sol | Sol | La | La | La | Si | Si | Si | Do | Do | Do |

Pupils. You sang three of every sound of the scale.

Teacher. Yes. I will sing the same again, and you may tell me which one of the three I sing loud.

[Teacher sings.]

Pupils. You sang the first of the three loud, and the other two soft.

Teacher. Yes. You may sing as I did.

[Pupils sing correctly.]

Teacher. That is right. This kind of measure, with three parts, — one loud and two soft, — is called a three-part measure.

Teacher. You see that this is another way in which sounds fall into groups naturally; that is, by *threes*, the first of which is accented, and the second and third unaccented.

Special Drill in Beating Triple-Time. — *Teacher.* In three-part measure there are three different motions of the hand. The first beat is the same as in two-part measure. The second beat is made by bringing the hand smartly to the left, so as to touch the body. The third beat brings the hand into position for the down-beat of the following measure.

[The pupils are to practise this kind of measure, saying, while beating, Down, Left, Up, till the class can do it perfectly, accenting the down-beat. When this is accomplished, they will be able to do the following dictation exercises.]

EXERCISES IN THE SCALE, ASCENDING AND DESCENDING, WITH TRIPLE-TIME.

Teacher. I will sing the last exercise while beating; then I want you to do it.

[The teacher sings the exercise, and the pupils do the same, being careful to accent the down-beat.]

Teacher. That is very well. Now you may sing it by divisions, one measure at a time, up and down the scale.

[This is done correctly.]

IV. Four-Part Measure.

Teacher. You may sing four of each of the sounds of the scale, by the syllables.

[The pupils sing.]

Teacher. That is very well. You may sing the same exercise again, and accent the first and *third* sounds in each measure, the first a little louder than the third.

Do Do Do Do   Re Re Re Re   Mi Mi Mi Mi   Fa Fa Fa Fa

Sol Sol Sol Sol   La La La La   Si Si Si Si   Do Do Do Do

[The pupils sing the exercise very well. The leading singers show that they *feel the time,* or recurrence of the accent, — some by an extravagant nod of the head, some by throwing forward the whole body, and others by stamping their feet, — all quite unconsciously.]

Teacher. You observed the accented parts very well; but it was very funny to see the different motions you made as you became interested in keeping the time. Regular practice in beating the time will prevent these awkward motions of the body and stamping of feet.

[The pupils may now take position for beating four-part measure.]

Teacher. The four beats in Quadruple-Time are : Down, Left, Right, and Up.

The Down-beat is made the same as in double and triple time, by bringing the tip of the middle finger of the right hand into the centre of the palm of the left.

The Left-beat is made like that of triple time.

The Right-beat is made by bringing the fingers of the right hand from the body on to the *fingers* of the left hand.

The Up-beat is made by bringing the hand up again to the position for making the down-beat.

Now sing — by the syllables — the last exercise, beating the time.

[The pupils do as directed.]

Teacher. Now sing by divisions, up and down.

[The pupils do it correctly.]

Teacher. I am very glad you have become so much interested in learning how to sing the scale in the different kinds of time, that you have not asked for any songs. If you go on in this way, you will soon be able to read music well enough to learn songs by the notes, without having ever heard them sung before.

V. Singing from Figures.

Teacher. We can write exercises and tunes in figures. I will write a few exercises which you will sing without any difficulty.

You are to understand that a figure with a comma after it means a short sound ; and with a dash after it, means a long sound. Also a cipher with a comma after it means a short rest; and a dash, a long rest. (*To be sung without beating time.*)

The following may first be sung by the teacher and pupils, then by divisions, the first division singing the teacher's part.

PITCH IN *D* OR *E*.

I.

Teacher.	Pupils.	Teacher.	Pupils.
1, 2,	3– ||	1, 2,	3–		3, 2,	1– ||	3, 2,	1–	
1, 3,	2– ||	1, 3,	2–		2, 3,	1– ||	2, 3,	1– ||

II.

Teacher.	Pupils.	Teacher.	Pupils.
1, 3,	5– ||	1, 3,	5–		5, 3,	1– ||	5, 3,	1–	
1, 4,	6– ||	1, 4,	6–		6, 4,	1– ||	6, 4,	1– ||

III.

Teacher.	Pupils.
1, 3,	5, 5,	1, 3, 5– ||	1, 3,	5, 5,	1, 3,	5–	
5, 3,	1, 3,	5, 3, 1– ||	5, 3,	1, 3,	5, 3,	1– ||

IV.

5, 5, 4, 2, | 1– 3– | 5, 5, 4, 2, | 1– 0– | 2, 2, 4, 4, | 3– 5– |

2, 2, 4, 4, | 3– 0– | 5, 5, 4, 2, | 1– 3– | 5, 5, 4, 2, | 1– 0– ||

In speaking of the sounds of the scale as represented by figures, always use the names of numbers. In singing, always use the syllables at first, then La, or any other syllable.

PITCH IN *D*, *E*, OR *F*.

I.

1, 2, 3, 2, | 3, 4, 5– | 5, 4, 3, 4, | 3, 2, 1– ||

II.

1, 2, 3, 4, | 5, 6, 5– | 6, 5, 4, 3, | 2, 2, 1– ||

III.

3, 2, 1, 2, | 3, 4, 5- | 6, 5, 4, 3, | 4, 3, 2- |

2, 3, 4, 5, | 6, 6, 5- | 5, 4, 3, 4, | 3, 2, 1- ||

IV.

5, 4, 3, 1, | 2, 3, 2- | 5, 5, 3, 1, | 2, 2, 2- |

2, 3, 4, 5, | 6, 6, 6- | 5, 3, 1, 3, | 2, 2, 1- ||

V.

5, 3, 1, 3, | 2, 2, 2- | 4, 3, 2, 1, | 5, 5, 5- |

1, 3, 5, 3, | 4, 5, 6- | 5, 5, 3, 1, | 2, 2, 1- ||

PITCH IN *C* OR *D*.

VI.

1, 2, | 3, 2, | 3, 4, | 5- | 6, 7, | 8, 7, | 6, 7, | 8- ||

VII.

8, 7, | 6, 5, | 4, 3, | 2- | 3, 4, | 5, 4, | 3, 2, | 1- ||

Nos. VI. and VII. may be sung with beating the time, — Two-part Measure or Double-Time. Also the following: —

TWO-PART SINGING.

Divide the class into two equal parts, taking care to have a few of the leading voices on each part.

VIII.

FIRST DIVISION.	0, 0,	3, 3,	0, 0,	3, 3,	0, 0,	4, 3,	2, 2,	1-	
SECOND DIVISION.	1, 2,	0, 0,	1, 2,	0, 0,	4, 3,	0, 0,	2, 2,	1- ||

IX.

| FIRST DIVISION. | 3, 3, | 2, 2, | 0, 0, | 0– | 4, 4, | 3, 3, | 0, 0, | 0– |
| SECOND DIVISION. | 0, 0, | 0, 0, | 1, 1, | 1– | 0, 0, | 0, 0, | 2, 2, | 2– |

| | 3, 4, | 5, 4, | 0, 0, | 0, 0, | 0, 0, | 5, 4, | 3, 2, | 1– |
| | 0, 0, | 0, 0, | 3, 3, | 2– | 3, 4, | 0, 0, | 3, 2, | 1– |

X.

| FIRST DIVISION. | 0, 0, | 0, 0, | 5, 6, | 7, 8, | 0, 0, | 0, 0, | 4, 3, | 2, 1, |
| SECOND DIVISION. | 1, 2, | 3, 4, | 0, 0, | 7, 8, | 8, 7, | 6, 5, | 0, 0, | 2, 1, |

XI.

| FIRST DIVISION. | 0, 0, | 0, 0, | 1, 3, | 5– | 0, 0, | 0, 0, | 5, 3, | 1– |
| SECOND DIVISION. | 1, 1, | 3, 3, | 0, 0, | 0– | 5, 5, | 3, 3, | 0, 0, | 1– |

XII.

| FIRST DIVISION. | 8, 8, | 7, 7, | 0, 0, | 0– | 0, 0, | 0, 0, | 5, 3, | 2– |
| SECOND DIVISION. | 0, 0, | 0, 0, | 6, 6, | 5– | 5, 5, | 6, 5, | 0, 0, | 0– |

| | 0, 0, | 0, 0, | 3, 4, | 5– | 0, 0, | 0, 0, | 6, 7, | 8– |
| | 2, 3, | 4, 4, | 0, 0, | 0– | 5, 5, | 6, 5, | 6, 7, | 8– |

XIII.

| FIRST DIVISION. | 5, 3, | 6, 4, | 5, 3, | 6– | 0, 0, | 0, 0, | 0, 0, | 0– |
| SECOND DIVISION. | 0, 0, | 0, 0, | 0, 0, | 0– | 5, 3, | 6, 4, | 5, 3, | 6– |

| | 5, 3, | 0, 0, | 6, 4, | 0, 0, | 3, 6, | 5, 4, | 3, 2, | 1– |
| | 0, 0, | 5, 3, | 0, 0, | 6, 4, | 3, 6, | 5, 4, | 3, 2, | 1– |

VI. — REGULAR STAFF NOTATION.

If the pupils have mastered the foregoing lessons, it will be very easy to read from the regular notation.

8	$\bar{\bar{c}}$	Do
7	$\bar{b}$	Si
6	$\bar{a}$	La
5	$\bar{g}$	Sol
4	$\bar{f}$	Fa
3	$\bar{e}$	Mi
2	$\bar{d}$	Re
1	$\bar{c}$	Do

THE PITCH-NAMES OF THE SCALE, IN ADDITION TO THE SCALE-NAMES AND SYLLABLES.

The Letters and G-Clef. — 1. The pitch of sounds is named by the first seven letters of the alphabet: *a, b, c, d, e, f,* and *g.*

2. You see by the diagram, that the pitch of 1 is *c;* 2 is *d;* 3 is *e;* 4 is *f;* 5 is *g;* 6 is *a;* 7 is *b;* and 8 is *c.*

3. You will notice that *c* is used as the pitch for both 1 and 8. We distinguish the *c*'s by the number of marks over them. The pitch of 1 is called "once-marked *c*"; and of 8, "twice-marked *c*."

4. Upon the fifth degree of the scale you will observe this character, which is called the $\bar{g}$-Clef or Key, and always stands for that letter or pitch.

We have already sung exercises in three kinds of measures: Two-part measures, Three-part measures, and Four-part measures.

The Staff. — Music is written upon five lines and the spaces between the lines. The lines and spaces, called the Staff, are named from the lowest upwards; thus: —

Fifth line.	Fourth space.
Fourth line.	Third space.
Third line.	Second space.
Second line.	First space.
First line.	

Sometimes the spaces below and above the staff, and also short added lines, are used; thus: —

First added space above.   First added line above.

First added space below.   First added line below.

VII. Notes and Rests.

In the regular musical notation the different lengths of sounds are represented by characters, called Notes. Their shape and names are as follows : —

The Whole-note (◯), which may represent the whole time of a quadruple measure in one sound.

The Half-note (𝅗𝅥), two of which would be contained in one measure.

The Quarter-note (♩), four of which would fill one measure; and the Eighth-note (♪), eight of which would fill a measure; according to the following example : —

It is usual to take the note as a standard for reckoning the time, which corresponds to one beat. In the above example the quarter-note is the standard, four of which fill a measure; the figures at the beginning of the example, in the form of a fraction, read, *four quarter-notes in a measure*, or their value in other notes.

$\frac{2}{4}$ means *two* quarter-notes in a measure, or their value in other notes ; as,

$\frac{3}{4}$ means *three* quarter-notes in a measure ; thus,

Rests, or Marks of Silence. — Each note has its corresponding rest. They are of this form : —

Whole-rest. Half-rests.   Quarter-rests.   Eighth-rests.

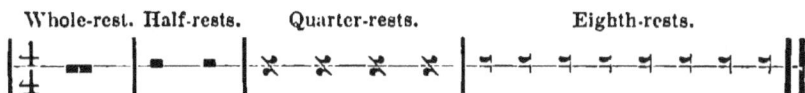

All these and other characters should be taken up, and their use demonstrated as they are needed.

From this stage of progress, we would recommend a choice from the many excellent text-books of recent publication.

The following synopsis indicates briefly the course which may be followed : —

1. A few exercises and songs within the compass of the scale in the key of C.

2. The extension of the scale upwards four sounds, and downwards five sounds, in the same key.

3. Instruction in time extended to two sounds of equal length in each part of the measure, in $\frac{2}{4}$, $\frac{3}{4}$, and $\frac{4}{4}$ time; also the dotted quarter ($\raisebox{0pt}{$\quad$}$) note.

4. The Chromatic scale, ascending by sharps and descending by flats.

5. The formation of the scale in the keys of G, D, A, E, F, B♭, E♭, and A♭.

6. The introduction of Triplets.

7. The introduction of $\frac{3}{8}$ time.

8. The formation of $\frac{6}{8}$ time, as made up of two measures of $\frac{3}{8}$ time.

9. Exercises and songs in Natural Harmonies, in all the above keys, avoiding difficult forms of Measure and unmusical Rhythms; that is, exercises with *five, seven,* and *eleven* measures, these being forbidden by the natural laws of rhythm.

If the time-names are used, they should not take the place of *beating time with the hand,* in developing the sense of measure.

MEMORY LESSONS.

FOR the purpose of cultivating the memory and at the same time of storing the mind with choice thoughts, there should be regular practice in memorizing and reciting what has been written by the best authors — both in poetry and in prose. To accomplish all that is desired to be accomplished, it will be necessary to give a definite time to the work, and to assign a given amount to be done in a given time. From five to ten lines a week should be committed to memory and recited by every pupil, and one hour a week of school time should be given to it. One or more books of good selections should be upon the table of every teacher, from which to copy what the pupils are to memorize. When the selection is placed upon the blackboard, all difficult words should be taught, and the selection be explained in such a way as to make it clearly understood by every pupil. It should then be memorized, and at the next memory-lesson hour it should be recited both in concert and by individual pupils. In all grades, a simple and natural expression of the author's thought is to be sought rather than attempts at oratorical display. Each week the selections of previous weeks should be recited. In the higher grades it may be well to have only one-fourth of the school recite or declaim each week, every pupil being expected to repeat from twenty to forty lines. The first part of the hour should be given to the recitation of pieces learned, and the latter part to teaching a new piece to the whole school, although only a fourth part of the school are expected to memorize it.

In addition to the regular memory lessons, birthdays of noted persons may be celebrated by giving sketches and anecdotes of their lives, and by reading and reciting what they have written. The pupils will greatly enjoy such exercises, by means of which a real interest in science, art, politics, and the best literature may be awakened. It is suggested that four birthday exercises be given every year in all grades above the primary, and that the parents and friends of the pupils be invited to attend them.

BUSY-WORK.

FEW habits acquired in school are more important than a habit of industry. The aim of the teacher should be to keep all pupils employed every moment of the day, except during times of recreation. But it is not enough that they be kept employed without reference to *what* they do, for their natural activity may lead them to do that. There should be in their employment an element of training, or something which will help to develop their faculties. How to provide such employment for pupils of all ages is indeed a difficult matter. It cannot be done if the natural capabilities of the pupils are not considered, — that is to say, if the work given is not adapted to the pupils' requirements and needs.

To keep the older pupils busy will not be very difficult. If their regular studies and teaching are what they should be, they will be pleasantly as well as profitably occupied in the preparation of lessons.

Younger pupils will need special attention and direction. It will not be enough to place in the hands of the children toys and pictures, and bid them amuse themselves as best they can. They must be directed how to use the things which are given them before they work with them independently and alone. Do not keep the children occupied too long upon any given work, but change the occupation as often as once in every fifteen minutes. The following kinds of busy-work may be suggestive : —

Every child should be provided with a good slate and a sharpened pencil, with which he will be occupied half of the time he is in school. At one time he may be copying words and sentences which are upon the cards or blackboard. At another time he may be doing number-work or drawing, alternating the slate-work with other exercises. Shoe-pegs and splints will afford occupation for a few minutes at a time in making designs in imitation of what is placed before him. With the pegs, also, the child may place in rows the number-work; as (letting each mark represent a peg), $|||+|| = |||||$. After covering the top of his desk with such work, he may represent upon the slate what he has done; as, $3 + 2 = 5$. Children can be profitably employed with colored pegs, sticks, splints, and papers, in making combinations taught in previous color and form lessons. Outlines of common objects, such as a ladder, fork, rake, or chair, may be drawn upon the blackboard for the children to imitate with the pegs or splints.

The kindergarten games are full of suggestion for primary teachers. Paper-folding, weaving, and stick-laying are especially useful for busy-work. It is not necessary to buy many materials, or to follow closely the order given in the kindergarten. Wooden toothpicks, splints, and different kinds of paper will constitute much of the needed material for these games. Pictures may be pasted upon cardboard which can be cut into pieces for the younger children to put together. The same may also be done with designs upon cardboard.

Forms of animals and other objects can be made of cardboard or pasteboard and given to the children for tracing. After the form is traced, the children should be encouraged to draw lines representing the various parts.

Second and third year pupils can be kept busy in language-work, copying from the reader, making sentences with given words, or making statements or stories from pictures placed before them.

Letters upon paper or cardboard for making words, and words for making sentences, will be found useful in keeping children busy. The letters and words can be bought in boxes, or they can be cut out and collected by the pupils and teacher. The older children of the primary and ungraded schools may be called upon at times to collect and distribute the cards, splints, etc., and they may sometimes assist the little ones in their slate-work.

It is not expected that the very youngest children will be in school during the whole of two sessions. They should be dismissed when the session is half through, or if the distance to their homes is too great for them to go alone, they should be allowed to go to the playground or anteroom to play.

PHYSICAL EXERCISE.

PLAY in the open air is undoubtedly the best exercise for children; but when large numbers of children are brought together on the playground, there are certain dangers which can only be avoided by the teacher's presence. To see that all are exercising, and that the exercise is not excessive, — not to mention still weightier reasons, — it is necessary for the teacher to oversee the games, and perhaps to participate in them. Whenever this cannot be done, or whenever the weather is cold or stormy, the recess should be omitted, and in its place there should be marching or other gymnastic exercises. It is not well to have the physical exercises immediately after recess or at the commencement of a session; neither should they be given just before dismissal. They should be given in the middle of a session when there is no recess; or if there is a recess, about three-quarters of an hour before they leave the room.

The exercise will be more enjoyable and the interest will be better maintained by having the movements made to music. If nothing better can be provided, a boy may mark the time with clappers, or the teacher may count. In the primary and kindergarten singing-books there can be found pretty motion songs, in which the children are led to combine motions with singing.

If the physical exercises are given merely as a diversion, the motions may be gently given; but if the exercises are meant to quicken the circulation and strengthen the muscles, the motions should be made with great rapidity and exactness. If, for example, the arm is to be raised to a horizontal position in front, much greater strength is required to raise it directly in front in a straight line very rapidly, and to stop it as soon as it has reached a horizontal position, than to raise it slowly and carelessly.

The following exercises have been used in some schools, and may be of assistance to teachers: —

I. Breathing Exercise.

(*Shoulders thrown back, hands on hips.*)

1. Draw in the breath slowly, and expel it slowly (indicated by motion of the teacher's hand).
2. Draw in the breath slowly, and expel it quickly.
3. Draw in the breath quickly, and expel it slowly.
4. Draw in the breath quickly, and expel it quickly.
5. Repeat each exercise, holding the breath a few seconds.

II. Breathing Exercise.

(*Good exercise for straightening the body.*)

1. Stand with arms folded behind, and one foot eight inches in front of the other.
2. Draw the head back, and tip it as far down behind as you can.
3. Hold the chin up high.
4. Rest there a moment, and then stand up straight again. Repeat the exercise six times.

Breathe deep, full breaths all the time, — slowly, and as large breaths as you can.

III. To enlarge the Chest.

1. Raise the chin as high up as you can, until your eyes look up at the ceiling right over your head.
2. Hold your chin this way a moment.
3. Take two or three full inspirations slowly. Repeat three times.
4. Put your hands upon your hips, fingers in front.
5. Draw your chin up; throw your head back.

6. Take one good, full inspiration, very slowly, and resume the erect position.

7. Repeat this exercise three times.

Whatever lifts the chin and throws the shoulders back, enlarges the chest and makes the lungs stronger.

IV. MOVEMENTS FOR YOUNG CHILDREN.

1. *Position.* — Sit erect; eyes steadily in front; shoulders thrown back; arms hanging by the side; feet in front; heels four inches apart; toes turning out, forming with each other an angle of twenty-five degrees.

2. Arms folded.

3. Hands clasped and resting on edge of desk.

4. Right hand thrown horizontally in front.

5. Left hand same as right in No. 4.

6. Strike hands together in front five times.

7. Right hand on head.

8. Both hands on head.

9. Strike hands together five times over head.

10. Fingers resting on top of shoulders.

11. Strike hands together five times in front.

12. Hands on top of head.

13. Strike hands together five times over head.

14. Hands twirling over head.

15. Hands brought suddenly to desk with noise.

16. Arms folded.

17. Fingers resting on top of shoulders.

18. Hands on top of head.

19. Strike hands together five times over head.

20. Fingers twirling rapidly over head.

21. Hands brought to desk, softly tapping with tips of fingers, in imitation of rain.

[*Remarks.* — The force of the storm may be graduated by signals from the teacher. The pupils may at the same time whistle in imitation of wind. Two or three of the pupils may be designated to strike heavily on their desks with the fists, at intervals, imitating thunder.]

22. Fold arms, sitting perfectly still.

V. Free Gymnastics. — Sitting.

(The counting is in measures from one to eight, each measure taken four times.)

A.

1. Hands on hips, fingers front.
2. Hands on shoulders (arms at side).
3. Hands on head.
4. Clap hands above head.
5. Hands on head.
6. Hands on shoulders (like 2).
7. Hands on hips (like 1).
8. Arms folded in front.

(Take four times.)

B.

(Two movements only.)

1. Hands on hips.
2. Clap hands in front.

Repeat to complete thirty-two counts.

C.

1. Strike left shoulder lightly with right hand.
2. Return right hand to right hip.
3. Strike right shoulder with left hand.
4. Return left hand to left hip.

Repeat to complete thirty-two counts.

D.

Position. — Hands on hips, fingers front.
1. Carry right hand to right shoulder (arm at side).
2. Carry left hand to left shoulder.
3. Return right hand to position.
4. Return left hand to position.

Repeat to complete thirty-two counts.

E.

1. Right hand on right shoulder.
2. Right hand up above head (arm straight).
3. Left hand on left shoulder.

4. Left hand up above head (arm straight).
5. Snap fingers of both hands.
6. Like 5.
7. Like 5.
8. Hands on hips.
Repeat to complete thirty-two counts.

VI. FREE GYMNASTICS. — STANDING.

Position. — Heels together; toes out, so that the feet may form a right angle; shoulders and hips drawn back; hands naturally at sides, unless otherwise specified; hands firmly clenched; all thrusts are from the chest, unless otherwise specified.

Time. — Each number extends through what may be called one strain of 4—4 music, or eight accented and eight unaccented beats. Time may be kept also by counting the numerals from one to eight for the heavy beats, and for the light beats, saying "and."

Hand Movements. — 1. Thrust R. H. down from chest twice; L. twice; alternate twice; simultaneous twice.

2. Repeat No. 1, thrusting out at side.

3. Repeat No. 1, thrusting up.

4. Repeat No. 1, thrusting in front.

5. R. H. down once; L. once; drum-beat (R. a little in advance of L.) once; simultaneous once; same out at sides.

6. Repeat No. 5, thrusting up and in front.

7. R. H. down once; L. once; clap hands; same out at sides.

8. Repeat No. 7, thrusting up and in front.

Foot Movements. — 9. Hands on hips; divide a circle about the body, with a radius of from two to three feet, into eight equal parts, by stepping forward, diagonal forward, at side, diagonal back, etc., with R. F. keeping L. knee straight and the feet at right angles, except last two steps, bending R. knee each step.

10. Repeat No. 9 with L. F.

11. Same movement, alternating R. and L. half around.

12. Complete the movement of No. 11.

13. Charge diagonal forward with R. F., advancing with three steps, bending R. knee, L. straight; same on the L. side; same diagonal back on R. side; same L.

14. Repeat No. 13.

Body Movements. — 15. Hands on hips; twist upper body half round to R., then to L., alternately, stopping in front on unaccented beats.

16. Bend upper body to R. and L.

17. Bend forward and back.

18. Bend body to R., back, L., front; then reverse, bending to L., back, R., front; repeat, becoming erect only on last beat.

Head Movements. — 19. Same as 15, except that the head alone is moved.

20. Same as 16, except that the head alone is moved.

21. Same as 17, except that the head alone is moved.

22. Same as 18, except that the head alone is moved.

Miscellaneous Movements. — 23. Arms extended in front, thumbs up, raise hands about a foot, and bring forcibly to shoulders.

24. Arms same as No. 23; raise R. H. to perpendicular over head twice; L. twice; alternate twice; and simultaneous twice.

25. Thrust hands down, out at sides, up, in front, twisting the arms at each thrust; repeat.

26. Repeat No. 25.

27. Thrust hands to floor, not bending knees; then over head, rising on toes, opening hands at each thrust. *

28. Hands at sides open; swing them over head, clapping them, at same time stepping R. F. to L., and L. F. to R., alternately.

29. Stamp L. F.; then R.; then charge diagonal forward with R.; bend and straighten R. knee, at same time throwing arms back from horizontal in front.

30. Repeat No. 29 on L. side.

* VII. BEAN-BAG EXERCISES.

These exercises are performed by couples, partners standing from six to ten feet apart, facing each other, unless otherwise specified.

The bag should be made of strong cloth, strongly sewed, and should be from eight to twelve inches square inside of seam; should be about two-thirds filled with beans, or other grain, and should be entirely free from dust.

1. Throw from chest with both hands.

2. Throw from chest with R. H.

3. Throw from chest with L. II.
4. Bag behind the head, throw over the head with both hands.
5. Same with R. II.
6. Same with L. II.
7. Partners standing R. side toward R., throw with both hands.
8. Same with R. II.
9. Same with L. II.
10. L. to L., throw with both hands.
11. Same with R. II.
12. Same with L. II.
13. Bag behind the back, throw over head with both hands.
14. Same with R. II.
15. Same with L. II.
16. Throw with R. II. behind the back, grasping R. elbow.
17. Same, throwing with L.
18. Back to back, throw over head with both hands, catching in same position.
19. Throw bag from R. elbow; catch with both hands.
20. Same from L. elbow.
21. Throw bag with feet; catch with both hands.
22. Two bags; throw at same time with R.; catch with L.
23. Same, except throwing with L. and catching with R.
24. Throw with both hands at the same time; catch with both.
25. Three bags; throw with R., catch with L.
26. Three bags; throw with L., catch with R.

Part III.

ORGANIZATION, MORAL TRAINING, AND SCHOOL GOVERNMENT.

———∘∘⟩⊶⟨∘∘———

ORGANIZATION.

School Buildings. — *Locality.* — The first consideration in fixing the locality of a schoolhouse is healthful-
ness. The ground upon which it is placed should be
high, and the soil sandy, so as to allow good drainage.
It should be located with reference to the convenience
of the pupils attending the school, and so retired that
the school will not be disturbed by noises from without.

Privies. — Privies should, if possible, be separated
from the schoolhouse, and have a separate apartment
and approach for each sex. Dry earth should be placed
daily in the vaults, which should be frequently cleaned
out. Great care should be taken in the construction of
water-closets located in the schoolhouse, and constant
attention should be given to the matter of cleansing and
disinfecting. The closets should be placed as far from
the furnace as possible, and should be thoroughly ven-
tilated by means of pipes and windows.

Size of School-rooms. — The size of schoolrooms

should depend upon the present and prospective number of pupils. There should be sufficient room for the seats and desks of pupils, recitation-seats, platform and desk of teacher, and apparatus. In determining the size of rooms reference should be had also to proper ventilation and heating, and to ease of speaking.

A school of thirty or forty pupils can be well accommodated in a room twenty-six feet by thirty, the teacher's desk being placed at the end of the room. If the number of pupils is fifty, or is likely to be fifty, the size of the room should be twenty-eight or thirty feet by thirty-six. For the sake of good order the gathering of a large number of pupils into one room should be avoided so far as possible. At least should the number of recitation-rooms belonging to a school be limited to one, located, if possible, on the same floor as the large room.

Lighting. — Windows should be placed if possible at the left and behind the desks of pupils. The window surface of a room should be from one-eighth to one-fifth of its floor surface. The amount of light admitted may be regulated by curtains or inside blinds. Windows should not be in front of pupils as they sit in their seats.

Ventilation and Heating. — Two things are to be accomplished in ventilation: first, to get rid of the bad air; and secondly, to introduce fresh air. To accomplish the first-named object there should be one large or, what is better, two small ducts connecting the room with the outer air. These ducts should extend from floor to ceiling, and should have openings in the upper and lower parts. To make strong and constant the out-going current, the ducts should be heated in some way. In buildings heated by steam, the ducts can be heated by means of pipes running through them. In other buildings the ducts can be constructed next to the chimney or smoke-stack, or they can be warmed by lamps or a kerosene stove. One of the best means of carrying away impurities is the open fireplace found in a few schoolrooms. At a comparatively slight expense this excellent means of ventilation can be provided in most of our country schoolhouses.

Having provided means of getting rid of the impure air, the next thing is to introduce pure air to take its place. To get a proper supply of fresh air, it is generally found necessary to open the windows, thereby exposing the pupils to draughts of cold air. This may be obviated in some degree by placing a strip of board five or six inches wide under the lower window-sash, so as to allow a current of air to pass upwards between the upper and lower sash. But it is neither economical nor healthful to bring into circulation air which is not first warmed. In rooms heated by stoves it is easy and entirely practicable to introduce a supply of warm fresh air. A covering may be made to encase the stove so as to form a hot-air chamber communicating with the outer air by a cold-air box. This is done in some places, and found to be of great service in ventilation.

The hot-air furnace is supposed to furnish a constant supply of warm fresh air. Great care, however, must be taken that poisonous gases do not enter the room. Constant attention must be given to the ventilation of the basement, to the cold-air boxes, to evaporation, and to the draughts of the furnace. Steam-heating by direct radiation is not uncommon, even in new and costly buildings, but it is little better than heating by stoves, so far as ventilation is concerned. There may be a saving of money, but not of health, by heating a building in this way. Some of the dangers may be avoided by constructing hot-air chambers about the radiators, to which fresh air can be introduced from without through cold-air boxes. Steam-heating by indirect radiation furnishes a constant supply of warm pure air, and is therefore the best method of heating schoolrooms. With properly arranged ducts for taking away the impure air, there need be little difficulty in securing good ventilation in rooms heated in this way.

If it is found necessary to heat the schoolroom by stove, two stoves will be found better than one. With two stoves a more equable temperature may be maintained than with one, and there will be less danger from an overheated surface, which burns the surrounding air. A dish of water should be placed upon the stoves for evaporation.

The temperature of the room should be kept as near as possible at 68° Fahrenheit.

Furniture and Furnishings. — Single desks for the pupils should be placed in rows two feet apart. The seats and desks should be constructed with special reference to the health and convenience of pupils. They should be of such a height and be placed at such a distance from the desk as to enable the pupils to take a comfortable position, with the feet upon the floor. The desks should be of sufficient size to allow the books to be placed inside, and to allow the pupils to take a good position in writing.

Ink-wells with covers should be placed in all desks designed for pupils who write with pen and ink.

Besides desks and seats for pupils, the following articles are necessary in every schoolroom: desk for teacher, chairs for teacher and visitors, crayons, erasers, pointers, clock, bell, thermometer, broom, ink-filler, dustpan, dusters, closet or bookcase, and table for number-work.

In addition to the above-named articles many school-rooms have the following: waste-basket, sponge-pail, wall-ornaments, toilet appliances, moulding-table, and piano or organ.

Blackboards. — Blackboards of natural slate or some well-tried artificial preparation should be placed entirely around the room, wherever spaces are left between windows and doors. They should be at least four feet in width and sufficiently near the floor to enable the pupils to reach them easily. If the liquid slate is used, care should be taken to have the foundation firm and smooth.

Apparatus. — The kind and amount of apparatus used in teaching indicate in no small degree the character of the work done. Therefore, the question so often asked, What apparatus is needed in the schoolroom? becomes a serious one. It is not always desirable to purchase apparatus which is the most costly. Indeed, much of the most valuable apparatus used may be made or gathered by the teachers and pupils — especially that which is needed in the Observation Lessons. Charts of any kind can be made of thick Manilla paper, marked with artist's crayon, or with a rubber pen. The following list comprises the *minimum* amount which should be

found in every schoolroom, or at least, which should
be accessible to every teacher.   Blocks, splints, and
shoe-pegs for number and "busy-work"; measures
(dry, liquid, linear, metric); balance, toy money, globe,
wall maps; charts for number, reading, writing, anatomy,
and music; numeral frame, drawing models and compasses, toys and other objects for reading; forms for
mensuration; pictures for language, geography, history, etc.; cardboard for number, language, etc.; colored
worsted, colored cardboard for form and color; plants,
minerals, mounted insects; appliances for busy-work;[1]
pen-holders and pens, slates and pencils, sponges or
slate-cloths, lead-pencils, paper (white and brown),
blank-books, ruler; coarse files for sharpening pencils
when pencil-sharpeners are not provided.

It will be seen that the above list does not comprise
some of the means of teaching physiology and other
observation lessons, which may be gathered from day to
day, such as flowers, leaves, and plants, which are of
temporary use only, and the parts of animals obtained
from the butcher's. Neither does the list include the
little contrivances used for illustrating mensuration of
boxes, walls, etc.

Reference-Books. — In addition to the text-books
regularly used there should be within easy access books
of all kinds for both teachers and pupils. For the
higher grades an encyclopædia, a gazetteer, a large dictionary, and several small dictionaries will be found
useful in connection with the geography, history, and
reading lessons. Histories, biographies, illustrated
books of travel, and other supplementary reading-books

[1] See page 280.

should be used for silent and sight reading daily; such reading will greatly increase the interest of the pupils in their regular studies.

The following list contains the names of a few books which will be found useful for reference. Among the books named, those marked with a star should be used by the teachers exclusively. Titles printed in italics name books which are specially adapted to primary grades; all others are adapted to the higher or to all grades.

ARITHMETIC.

Arithmetical Problems. *Fish.* I., B., T., & Co.
Arithmetic for Primary Grades. Fisher. N. E. Pub. Co.
Book-Keeping for Grammar Schools. *Meservey.* T., B., & Co.
Bradbury-Eaton Series. Thompson, Brown, & Co.
Common School Book-Keeping. *Bryant & Stratton.* I., B., T., & Co.
Crittenden Commercial. Eldredge & Co.
Exercises in Arithmetic. *Wentworth & Hill.* Ginn & Co.
Franklin Series. Wm. Ware & Co.
First Steps in Number. *Wentworth & Reed.* Ginn & Co.
Grammar School Arithmetic. *Wentworth.* Ginn & Co.
* *Grant's Arithmetic for Young Children.* Ed. by *Small.* L. & S.
Greenleaf (New Series). Leach, Shewell, & Sanborn.
Hagar's Series. Cowperthwait & Co.
Harper's Graded Arithmetics. Harper & Bros.
Intellectual Arithmetic. *Colburn.* Houghton, Mifflin, & Co,
MacVicar Series. Taintor Bros., Merrill, & Co.
Numbers Applied. *Rickoff.* D. Appleton & Co.
Numbers Illustrated. D. Appleton & Co.
Number Lessons for Supplementary Work. L., S., & S.
Walton's Arithmetical Tables. Wm. Ware & Co.
White's Graded School Series. Wilson, Hinkle, & Co.

GEOGRAPHY AND TRAVELS.

Arctic Explorations. *Kane.*
Aunt Martha's Corner Cupboard. Kirby.

Common School and Primary Geographies. *Appleton's, Guyot's, Harper's, Maury's, McNally's, Our World, Swinton's.*
Compendium of Geography and Travels ; 6 vols., Illus. Stanford.
Each and All. *Andrews.* Lee & Shepard.
Earth and Man. *Guyot.*
*Geography for Young Children. *Grant.*
Geographical Reader. C. Scribner's Sons.
Geographical Reader Series. G. Philip & Son.
Geographical Reader. *Johonnot.*
Little Lucy's Wonderful Globe. *Yonge.* MacMillan & Co.
Man and Nature. *March.*
* Methods of Teaching Geography. *Crocker.* Bos. Sch. Sup. Co.
* Physical Geographies. *Geike's, Guyot's, Johnston's, Mrs. Somerville's, Maury's.*
* Physiography. *Huxley.*
Pronouncing Gazetteer of the World. Lippincott & Co.
Seven Little Sisters. *Andrews.* Lee & Shepard.
Statesman's Year-Book.
World at Home. Six nos. T. Nelson & Sons.
World by the Fireside. *Kirby.* T. Nelson & Sons.

HISTORY AND BIOGRAPHY.

Abbott's Series of Biographies. Harper & Bros.
American Biography. *Sparks.*
American Statesmen Series. Houghton, Mifflin, & Co.
Aunt Charlotte's Stories of American History. D. Appleton & Co.
Bodley Books.
Boys of '76. *Coffin.* Harper & Bros.
Boys of '61. *Coffin.* Harper & Bros.
Child's History of England. *Dickens.*
Child's History of England. *Yonge.*
Discoveries and Inventions of the 19th Century. *Routledge.* H. & B.
First History of Greece. *Sewell.* D. Appleton & Co.
First History of Rome. *Sewell.* D. Appleton & Co.
History of American Politics. *Johnston.* Holt & Co.
History of America. *Bryant.*
History of the United States. *Scudder.* J. H. Butler & Co.

History of the United States. *Eliot.*
History of Our Country. *Richardson.* Houghton, Mifflin, & Co.
North American Indians. *Catlin.*
Old Times in the Colonies. *Coffin.* Harper & Bros.
*Methods of Teaching and Studying History. Ed. by *Hall.* D. C. Heath & Co.
Pictorial History of the Revolution. *Lossing.*
Story of Our Country. *Monroe.* Lee & Shepard.
Ten Boys who lived on the Road from Long Ago to Now. L. & S.
Young Folks' Heroes of History. *Towle.* Lee & Shepard.
Young Folks' History of America. *Butterworth.* Estes & Lauriat.
Young Folks' History of the United States. *Higginson.* L. & S.

INFORMATION LESSONS.

Child's Book of Nature. Three parts. *Hooker.*
Civil Government. *Martin.* Barnes & Co.
Childhood of the World. *Clodd.*
Commercial Law. *Clark.* Clark, Maynard, & Co.
Government Class-Book. *Young.* Clark, Maynard, & Co.
Homes without Hands. *Wood.*
Household Economy. Ivison, Blakeman, Taylor, & Co.
How we are Governed. *Dawes.* Int. Pub. Co.
Information Cards. Cambridge Series. Lee & Shepard.
Lessons on Manners. *Wiggin.* Lee & Shepard.
Lessons on Practical Subjects. Little, Brown, & Co.
Little Folks in Feathers and Fur. *Miller.* Dutton & Co.
Little People of Asia. *Miller.*
Manual of Commerce. *Browne.*
Natural History Series of Readers. D. Appleton & Co.
Natural History Series of Readers. *Wood.* Bos. Sch. Sup. Co.
Natural History Stories. *Prang.*
Our Government. *Macy.* Ginn & Co.
Politics for Young Americans. *Nordhoff.* Harper & Co.
Popular Science Reader. *Monteith.* Barnes & Co.
Quizzism and its Key. *Southwick.*
Silver Wings and Golden Scales. Cassell.

Talks with my Boys. *Mowry.*
The Citizen and Neighbor. *Dole.*
Young Folks' Catechism of Common Things. *Champlin.* H. & Co.

LANGUAGE.

INCLUDING WRITING, SPELLING, COMPOSITION, AND GRAMMAR.

Child's Book of Language. *Stickney.* D. Appleton & Co.
Elementary Lessons in English. Parts I. and II. *Knox.* Ginn & Co.
Essentials of English Grammar. *Whitney.* Ginn & Co.
Graded Instruction in English. *Bright.* D. Appleton & Co.
Graded Spelling Book. *Harrington.* Harper & Bros.
*Grammar Land. *Nesbitt.* Holt & Co.
Grammar for Common Schools. *Tweed.* Lee & Shepard.
Handbook of Punctuation. *Bigelow.* Lee & Shepard.
How to Talk. *Powell.* Cowperthwait & Co.
How to Write. *Powell.* Cowperthwait & Co.
*How to Write Clearly. *Abbott.* Roberts Bros.
New Word Analysis. *Swinton.* I., B., T., & Co.
School Composition. *Swinton.* Harper & Bros.
Selected Words for Spelling and Language Lessons. A. Lovell & Co.
Some Topics in English Grammar. *Hinds.*
*Study of Words. *French.*
Thought and Expression. *Greene.* Cowperthwait & Co.
*Treatise on Punctuation. *Wilson.* Potter, Ainsworth, & Co.
Word Lessons. *Reed.* Clark & Maynard.

MEMORY LESSONS.

Ballads and Lyrics. Sel. by *Lodge.* Houghton, Mifflin, & Co.
Five-Minute Declamations. Ar. by *Fobes.* Lee & Shepard.
Five-Minute Recitations. Ar. by *Fobes.* Lee & Shepard.
Golden Treasury for Children. *Palgrave.*
Graded Selections. Ed. by *Peaslee.* Van Antwerp, Bragg, & Co.
Little Gems of Literature. Potter, Ainsworth, & Co.
Memory Gems, in prose and verse. Ed. by *Lambert.* Ginn & Co.
Memory Gems. 3 vols. *Northend.* Lee & Shepard.
One Hundred Choice Selections. Several vols. P. Garrett & Co.
Pieces to Speak. *Ballard.* D. Appleton & Co.

Poetry for Children. *Eliot.* Houghton, Mifflin, & Co.
Select Poetry for School and Home. Ed. by *Campbell.* L. & S.
Simple Poems and Easy Rhymes. Ed. by *Campbell.* L. & S.

OBSERVATION LESSONS.

Astronomy by Observation. *Bower.* D. Appleton & Co.
Ants, Bees, and Wasps. *Lubbock.*
Botany for Beginners. *Masters.*
Boys and Girls in Biology. *Stevenson.* D. Appleton & Co.
Butterflies. *Scudder.*
Easy Experiments in Physical Science. *Cooley.* Scrib., Arm., & Co.
Elementary Lessons in Botany. *Oliver.*
*Exercises for the Improvement of the Senses. *Grant.* L. & S.
Elements of Physics. *Gage.* Ginn & Co.
Fairy Land of Science. *Buckley.* D. Appleton & Co.
First Book of Botany. *Youmans.* D. Appleton & Co.
First Book in Geology. *Shaler.*
First Book of Zoölogy. *Morse.* D. Appleton & Co.
First Principles of Natural Philosophy. Sheldon & Co.
Geological Excursions. *Winchell.* Griggs & Co.
Geological Story briefly Told. *Dana.*
*Guides for Science Teaching. D. C. Heath & Co.
Guide to the Study of Insects. *Packard.*
How Plants Behave. *Gray.* Ivison & Co.
How Plants Grow. *Gray.* Ivison & Co.
How to find the Stars. *Clarke.* Lockwood, Brooks, & Co.
Insects, How to Catch, etc., for Cabinet. *Manton.* L. & S.
Improvement of the Senses. Grant. Ed. by Small. Lee & Shepard.
Insects Injurious to Vegetation. *Harris.*
Lessons on Color, with Color and Form Cards. Interstate Pub. Co.
Life and her Children. *Buckley.* D. Appleton & Co.
*Manual of Mineralogy. *Dana.* Wiley & Sons.
Natural History of Animals. *Tenny.* Scribners.
Natural Philosophy. *Cooley.* Scribners.
Object Lessons of Botany. *Wood.*
Physics. *Hotze.* Central Publishing Co.
Primary Object Lessons. Calkins. Harpers.

Science Primers. D. Appleton & Cô.
Short Course in Astronomy. *Kiddle.* Ivison & Co.
Tenants of an Old Orchard. *McCook.*
The Earth in Space. D. C. Heath & Co.
Winners in Life's Race. *Buckley.* D. Appleton & Co.
Young Folks' Astronomy. *Champlin.* H. Holt & Co.
Zoölogy. *Colton.* D. C. Heath & Co.
Zoölogy. *Packard.*

PHYSIOLOGY AND HYGIENE.

Blaisdell's (Lee & Shepard); *Brand's* (Leach, Shewell, & Sanborn); *Dalton's* (Harper & Bros.); *Hooker's* (Sheldon); *Dunglison's* (Porter & Coates); *Hutchison's* (Clark, Maynard, & Co.); *Huxley's* (MacMillan & Co.); *Martin's* (Holt & Co.); *Smith's* (Ivison, Blakeman, Taylor, & Co.).
* Foundation of Death. *Gustafson.* D. C. Heath & Co.
Health Notes for Students. *Wilder.* Putnam & Sons.
History of a Mouthful of Bread. *Macé.*
How to get Strong. *Blaikie.*
* School Hygiene. Ginn & Co.
Sound Bodies for Boys and Girls. *Blaikie.*
Servants of the Stomach. *Macé.*
* Skeleton Lessons in Physiology and Hygiene. *Guernsey.* Inter-
state Publishing Co.
Temperance Physiology. A. S. Barnes & Co.
The Tobacco Problem. *Lander.* Cupples, Upham, & Co.

SUPPLEMENTARY READING.

[Titles of other books suitable for sight-reading will be found under
"Geography and Travels," "History and Biography," and "Information
Lessons."]

Age of Fable. *Bulfinch.*
A. B. C. Reader. For first half-year. Lowell & Co.
Appleton's Series of Readers. D. Appleton & Co.·
Barnes's New National Readers.
Book of Fables. Ed. by *Scudder.* Houghton, Mifflin, & Co.
Butler's Series of Readers.

Classics for Children. Several books for all grades. Ginn & Co.
Edward's Analytical Readers. T., B., M., & Co.
Franklin New Readers. Wm. Ware & Co.
From Blackboard to Books. *Calkins.* I., B., T., & Co.
Grandfather's Chair. *Hawthorne.*
Harpers' New Readers. Harper & Bros.
McGuffy's Eclectic Readers. Van Antwerp, Bragg, & Co.
Modern Classics. 33 vols. Houghton, Mifflin, & Co.
Monroe's New Readers. Cowperthwait & Co.
Sheldon's Readers. Sheldon & Co.
Supplementary Reading. Ed. by *Tweed.* Lee & Shepard.
Supplementary Reading. *Parker & Marvel.* L., S., & S.
Swinton's Series of Readers. I., B., T., & Co.
Tales from Shakespeare. *Lamb.*
Tanglewood Tales. *Hawthorne.*
Wonder Book. *Hawthorne.*

GENERAL AND MISCELLANEOUS.

Book of Days. Chambers.
Calisthenic Songs. *Parsons.* Ivison, Blakeman, Taylor, & Co.
Cyclopædias. *Appleton's* (16 vols.); *Chambers's* (10 vols. or 5
    vols.) ; *Johnson's* (8 vols. or 2 vols.).
Cyclopædia of English Literature. Chambers.
Dictionaries. *Webster's* and *Worcester's.*
English Synonyms. *Soule.* Little, Brown, & Co.
First Weeks in School. *Stickney & Peabody.* Ginn & Co.
First and Second Lessons in Geometry. *Hill.*
Model and Object Drawing. *Baker.* I., B., T., & Co.
National Music Course. *Mason.* Ginn & Co.
Normal Music Course. *Tufts & Holt.* Wilson, Winkle, & Co.
* Power and Authority of School Officers.
Industrial Education in Public Schools. *Straight.* Ginn & Co.
Inventional Geometry. *Spencer.* D. Appleton & Co.
Learning to Draw. *Le Duc.* Putnam & Co.
* Manuals and Teachers' Guides for Drawing-Books.
Political Economy. *Walker.*
School Amusements. *Root.*

School Studies in Words. *Gilbert.* Leach, Shewell, & Sanborn.
Statutes of the State.
Theory and Design. *Baker.* Ivison, Blakeman, Taylor, & Co.
Three Thousand Words. Handbook of Pronunciation. L. & S.

PROFESSIONAL BOOKS FOR TEACHERS.

Application of Psychology to Teaching. *Hailmann.* Small.
Art of School Management. *Baldwin.* D. Appleton & Co.
Common School Education. *Currie.*
Education. *Herbert Spencer.*
Educational Reformers. *Quick.*
Form Discipline. *Sedgwick.*
History of Education. *Painter.* D. Appleton & Co.
History of Pedagogy. *Compayré.* D. C. Heath & Co.
Infant School Education. Currie.
John Amos Comenius. *Laurie.*
Lectures on Teaching. *Fitch.*
Lectures on Science and Art of Teaching. *Payne.*
Life and Work of Pestalozzi. *Krüsi.* Wilson, Hinkle, & Co.
Manuals for Teachers. Five vols. Eldridge Bros.
Methods of Instruction. *Wickersham.*
On Teaching. *Calderwood.*
Outline Study of Man. *Hopkins.*
Philosophy of Education. *Tate.*
Principles and Practice of Teaching. *Johonnot.* D. C. Heath & Co.
Record of a School. *Peabody.*
Reminiscences of Fröbel. *Von Bulow.* Lee & Shepard.
School at Hofwyl.
School Management. *Landon.*
Some Thoughts on Education. *Locke.*
Teachers' Handbook of Psychology. *Sully.*
The Kindergarten and the School. Milton Bradley & Co.
Theory and Practice of Teaching. *Page.*
True Order of Studies. *Hill.*

PROFESSIONAL PERIODICALS FOR TEACHERS.

American Journal of Education. St. Louis, Mo.
American Teacher. Monthly. Boston, Mass.
Carolina Teacher. Monthly. Columbia, S. C.
Colorado School Journal. Denver, Col.
Central School Journal. Monthly. Keokuk, Iowa.
Education. Monthly. Boston, Mass.
Educational Courant. Monthly. Louisville, Ky.
Educational Journal. Monthly. Richmond, Va.
Educational Monthly. Toronto, Canada.
Educational Weekly. Toronto, Canada.
Illinois School Journal. Bloomington, Ill.
Indiana School Journal. Monthly. Indianapolis, Ind.
Intelligence. Monthly. Chicago, Ill.
Journal of Education. Monthly. Madison, Wis.
National Normal Exponent. Monthly. Cincinnati, O.
New England Journal of Education. Weekly. Boston, Mass.
New Orleans School Journal. New Orleans, La.
Normal Monthly. Iowa.
North Carolina School Journal. Raleigh, N. C.
Ohio Educational Monthly. Akron, O.
Our Country and Village Schools. Monthly. Illinois.
Popular Educator. Monthly. Boston, Mass.
School Bulletin. Monthly. Syracuse, N. Y.
School Education. Monthly. Minnesota.
School Herald. Chicago, Ill.
School Journal. Weekly. New York.
School Journal. Monthly. California.
School Journal. Monthly. Lancaster, Pa.
School Journal. Semi-monthly. Missouri.
School Moderator. Semi-monthly. Lansing, Mich.
Southwest Journal of Education. Nashville, Tenn.
Teacher. Monthly. Philadelphia.
Teacher's Institute. Monthly. New York.
Texas School Journal. Dallas, Texas.
Western School Journal. Monthly. Kansas.
Wisconsin School Journal. Madison, Wis.

CLASSIFICATION.

The importance of bringing together pupils of nearly equal attainments into one class, in each of the subjects taught, is recognized by all. The practical question for teachers to consider is, How shall the classification be made so as to secure the greatest good to the greatest number, and at the same time encourage to the greatest extent, or rather discourage to the least extent, the natural propensities and activities of each individual?

To accomplish these ends, it is evident that those only who know the needs, capacities, and acquirements of the pupils should make the classification. The result of a single examination, or of any number of examinations, alone should not determine the class into which pupils shall go. The age, health, habits, and purposes of the pupil should be considered in determining his place, the only question being, Where can the pupil do most for himself?

Graded Schools. — A close classification would make all the pupils of a school recite in the same classes in all studies. There are certainly advantages in this plan; but it is a question whether it may not be well sometimes to allow pupils to recite in a higher or lower class in one or two studies. For example, a boy is by nature or by extra study farther advanced in arithmetic than in reading and geography. If he has but a limited time to attend school, it would seem to be right to have him recite with one class in reading and geography, and with another class in arithmetic.

Again, there are occasionally pupils who, by reason

of weakness or ill health, cannot take all the studies taught in the school. Such pupils should be allowed to omit one or more of the regular studies, and even be excused from school attendance, except when their classes are reciting.

There is of course danger in such irregularity of classification, and the number of cases must be limited; but there are instances when it is not only justifiable, but necessary for the best interests of the pupils.

Basis of Classification. — The rights of active and bright-minded pupils should be protected, no less than those of the weak and dull. Inequalities both in the abilities of pupils, and in the amount accomplished, should be recognized in classifying, as well as in arranging the course of studies and conducting the recitation. The average abilities and attainments, therefore, should be the basis of classification, so far as the amount of work required is concerned. Where close classification is required, as it should be required generally in graded schools, it is customary to take reading as the basis in the primary schools, and arithmetic in the higher grades.

Size of Classes. — The mistake should not be made of making the classes too large. The number should be sufficiently small for the teacher to reach every individual member, at least to the extent of knowing the peculiarities of each pupil, and of adapting the teaching and instruction to the needs of each. Thirty pupils in primary grades, and forty in grammar grades, are quite as many as one teacher can be expected to teach, and teach well. A less number would doubtless be better for individual pupils, while more would tend to force the teacher into mechanical ways of teaching, making one pupil do the same work as every other one, and in precisely the same way.

Divisions. — If there is but one grade in a room, it should be divided into two divisions, so as to allow time for one division to study while the other is reciting. There are several reasons why a school of thirty or forty should not recite together in arithmetic, reading, or geography. First, as has been intimated, the wants of individual pupils are not attended to as they should be. Secondly, the time for independent study and reflection is exceedingly limited, and even the brief time for study is frequently interrupted by remarks and explanations from the teacher.

Intervals between Classes. — In most graded schools at the present time, the classes are one year apart; that is, the gradation is so made as to render a readjustment, or "promotion," necessary only once a year. This plan of grading may be necessary in some places and under some circumstances, but where there is a sufficient number of pupils, the intervals should be shorter and the promotions more frequent. The aim should be to have the work adjusted as nearly as possible to the wants and capacity of each pupil. If this aim is a true one, it is manifest that the shorter the interval between the classes, the better, provided of course the transfer of pupils from one grade to another does not cause too great interruption. An interval of only ten weeks, or one-fourth of a year, has been tried with success in some places. In other places the interval is twenty weeks, or half of a year. This plan is entirely feasible in most

of our cities and large towns, and its adoption would do
much to overcome the faults of the system of yearly
promotions. In writing, drawing, and other general
exercises, all can work together; but in all other studies
the divisions will recite separately, one division studying
while the other is reciting. In this way one great fault
of too much help and recitation is avoided, and the
benefits of independent work assured. Concentration
and originality are gained when pupils are required to
work independently and alone a portion of the time, to
a degree far greater than when much time is spent in
recitation, and when too much assistance is given in
study. The advantage of semi-annual promotions is
most clearly seen in classifying new pupils or those who
have been absent a part of the year. It is a well-known
fact that, under the system of yearly promotions, pupils
are frequently obliged to go over once or twice work
which has been done before, and in some cases pupils,
notably those who work a part of the year in the factory,
do not get beyond the merest rudiments before they are
fourteen years of age. Under the other system, these
faults are largely overcome, and pupils are much better accommodated. Moreover, if a pupil is not well
enough to do the whole work of the class, he may do a
portion of it and lose but six months instead of a year,
— time which he may be able to gain later in the course.
Many a pupil under the system of annual promotions,
discouraged by the loss of several months, leaves school
long before he otherwise would.

But the feature of shorter intervals between classes
commends itself most strongly in the greater facility
with which the work of pupils may be adapted to

their capacity and strength. A system of classification which practically permits no difference in the amount of work to be done by pupils, but forces dull pupils beyond their strength and keeps back bright ones, is harmful alike to both classes. When only five months' work lies ahead of a bright and ambitious pupil, it may easily be overcome, especially when the plan of study is graded to the average capacity only of a class. Many pupils will be able to work into higher divisions, who otherwise would form habits of idleness and distaste of study in being obliged to do only the required work of less fortunate pupils. To avoid the danger of undue pressure, the parents in every case should be notified, and the child be given extra work only by their consent. The mistake of slighting important parts of the course is also avoided by having the pupil work into the higher division gradually, — an additional argument for having two divisions in a room.

Partially Graded Schools. — In some places the conditions require all the pupils of a neighborhood to be placed in two or three rooms. When this is the case, it is necessary to make the intervals between the classes one year or more, and to have three or four classes in each room. With such an arrangement of classes it is not difficult to follow the plan as outlined in the graded course, making a careful selection of work assigned for general exercises.

Ungraded Schools. — The classification of ungraded schools will depend much upon circumstances. If there are two teachers (as there should be if there are more than twenty-five pupils), more minute classification may be made than if there is only one. In some ungraded schools the older pupils predominate; in others, the younger. In some places the older pupils are taken from the ungraded district schools and placed in a central grammar or high school; in other places no higher school of any kind supplements the work of the ungraded school. No exact rule, therefore, for classifying ungraded schools can be laid down. But in general it may be said that no close classification should be attempted in ungraded schools, but that every pupil should recite in the class for which he is best fitted, whatever the subject may be. For instance, a pupil may be in the first class in arithmetic and the second in reading; while another pupil may be in the second class in arithmetic and the first in reading. Again, there should be as few classes as possible consistent with the good of all. The false pride of pupils and the ignorance of parents as to what is best for their children should not prevent the teacher from doing his duty in this regard. Too often the pupil and parent alike measure progress in education by the number of pages of the book that are "gone over." And too often, also, there is some disgrace attached to a pupil who is put into another class. All of these hindrances to good classification must be met and overcome in one way or another. The parents may be made to see that the older pupils should recite only two or three times a week in some studies, and that there may be a less minute classification in some studies than in others. In geography, for example, they may see that a knowledge of one country does not depend upon a knowledge of another, and that drill in one part of the spelling-book may be as useful as drill in another part. The following classification might be made in many ungraded schools, consisting of pupils from five to fifteen years of age: four classes in reading, including one class in the reading of history; five classes in arithmetic; two classes in geography, besides the class of younger pupils who are reciting orally lessons in home geography; four classes in spelling, two of which may be heard at the same time; one class in physiology, — the rest to be heard orally; one class in history; one class in English grammar; and one in language. The singing, drawing, and observation lessons may be taught as general exercises to all the pupils at once.

It may not be well for a new teacher to make such a classification at once, nor carry out all at once the plan of hearing the older pupils recite on alternate days. It might be better for him to adopt for a time the classification which he finds, in the hope that he may gradually change it for the better.

Daily Programme of Recitations and Study. — The good teacher always has, either in mind or on paper, a carefully prepared programme in which the times and subjects of recitation and study are well defined. Without a definite plan of work, there is danger of unequal attention being given to the subjects, and of disturbance in the preparation of lessons. To make a programme in which a proper share of time is given to recitation and to study, and in which the time allotted to each subject is commensurate with the importance of that subject, is no easy task. It is obvious that no one programme would be suited to all schools, or even to all schools of the same kind and grade, so widely dissimilar are the conditions in different schools, and even in the same school at different times. The following programmes, which were found in actual operation, may be suggestive to teachers: —

VI. GRAMMAR GRADE.— Two Divisions.

| TIME. | | RECITATION. | STUDY. | |
BEGIN.	LENGTH.		A DIVISION.	B DIVISION.
A.M. 9.00	MIN. 5	Devotional Exercise	. . . .	. . . .
9.05	15	Singing	. . . .	. . . .
9.20	20	General Exercise	. . . .	. . . .
9.40	20	Arithmetic. A.	. . . .	Arithmetic
10.00	10	Arithmetic. A. & B.	. . . .	. . . .
10.10	20	" B.	Reading	. . . .
10.30	15	*Recess.*	—	—
10.45	20	Reading. A.	. . . .	Reading
11.05	20	Reading. B.	Geography	. . . .
11.25	35	Language. A. & B.	—	—
12.00	—	*Intermission.*	—	—
P.M. 1.30	30	Writing or Drawing. A.&B.	—	—
2.00	30	Geog. & Sight-Reading. A.	. . . .	Geography
2.30	30	Geog. & Sight-Reading. B.	Spelling	. . . .
3.00	15	*Recess.*	—	—
3.15	15	Spelling. A. & B.	. . . .	. . . .
3.30	30	Gen'l Exercise and Study	—	—
4.00	—	*Dismission.*	—	—

Friday. Physiology, Observation Lessons, Memory Lessons, etc.

PRIMARY SCHOOL. — Four Grades.

Thirty-nine pupils from six to twelve years of age.

TIME.		BUSY-WORK AND STUDY.				
BEGIN.	LENGTH.	RECITATION.	GRADE I. (Lowest.)	GRADE II.	GRADE III.	GRADE IV.
A.M.	MIN.					
9.00	5	Devotional Exer.	—	—	—	—
9.05	5	Mem. Gems (all)	—	—	—	—
9.10	5	Music (all)	—	—	—	—
9.15	15	Writing (all)	—	—	—	—
9.30	30	I. &. II. Reading	....	....	Number	Number
10.00	15	III. Number	Slate and Splints	Number	....	Number
10.15	15	I. Number	....	Number	Writing	Number
10.30	15	Recess.	—	—	—	—
10.45	10	General Exercise	—	—	—	—
10.55	15	IV. Number	Slate-w'k	Number	Reading	....
11.10	10	II. Number	Slate-w'k	....	Reading	Language
11.20	15	III. Reading	Copying	Language	....	—
11.35	15	IV. Geography	Designs	Language	Language	....
11.50	10	IV. Sp. & Lang.	Splints	Language	Language	....
12.00	—	Intermission.	—	—	—	—
P.M.						
1.30	15	Music (all)	—	—	—	—
1.45	15	I. Reading	....	Reading	Reading	Reading
2.00	10	II. Reading	Busy-w'k	....	Reading	Reading
2.10	15	III. Sp. & Lang.	Busy-w'k	Busy-w'k	....	Geogr'y
2.25	5	Recess.	—	—	—	—
2.30	15	IV. Reading	Busy-w'k	Busy-w'k	Language	....
2.45	15	IV. Drawing	Busy-w'k	Busy-w'k	Language	....
3.00	30	Obs. L.&L'g.(all)	—	—	—	—
3.30	—	Dismission.	—	—	—	—

Tuesday A.M. 11–12. Sewing Teacher.
Monday. Once in two weeks. 9.30–10. Music Teacher.
Friday P.M. 3–3.30. Good time.

PRIMARY AND INTERMEDIATE SCHOOL.

Twenty-five pupils, ranging from six to twelve years of age. The youngest pupils are beginners, and the most advanced pupils are studying Fractions and reading in the Fourth Reader. There are four classes in most subjects.

TIME.		RECITATION.	BUSY-WORK AND STUDY.			
BEGIN.	LENGTH.		GRADE I. (Lowest.)	GRADE II.	GRADE III.	GRADE IV.
A.M.	MIN.					
9.00	15	Dev.Ex.& Singing	....	....	.....ᴛ...	....
9.15	20	Writing (all)	....	....	....	....
9.35	10	I. Reading	....	Arithme'c	Arithme'c	Language
9.45	15	II. Read. & Spell.	Copying	....	Arithme'c	Arithme'c
10.00	20	III. Arithmetic	Splints & Pegs	Arithme'c	....	Arithme'c
10.20	15	*Recess.*	—	—	—	—
10.35	20	IV. Arithmetic	Cop'g,etc.	Language	Geogra'y	....
10.55	15	I.& II. Arithmetic	....	....	Geogra'y	Geogra'y
11.10	10	Gymnastics	*Dismissed*	....	....	....
10.20	20	III. Geography	—	Language	....	Geogra'y
10.40	20	IV. Geography	—	R'g & Sp'g	Language	....
12.00	60	*Intermission.*	—	—	—	—
P.M.						
1.00	20	I. Read. & Numb.	....	R'g& Lan.	Language	Language
1.20	20	II. Read. & Lang.	Busy-w'k	....	R'g &Sp'g	Language
1.40	25	III. & IV. Lang.	Busy-w'k	Copying	....	....
2.05	5	Gymnastics	—	—	—	—
2.10	10	Ment.Arith. (all)	....	....	....	....
2.20	15	I. & II. Obs. Less.	....	....	R'g &Sp'g	R'g &Sp'g
2.35	10	*Recess.*	*Dismissed*	—	—	—
2.45	25	III. Read. & Spell.	—	Language	....	R'g &Sp'g
3.10	25	IV. Read. & Spell.	—	Reading	Arithme'c	....
3.35	15	Obs. Less. (all)	—	....	....	....
3.50	10	Gen. Exer. (all)	—	....	....	....

UNGRADED SCHOOL.

Thirty-five pupils from five to sixteen years of age.

[One afternoon each week given to general exercises.]

TIME. — Min.

5. Devotional Exercise.
10. Singing.
15. First Reader and Number.
15. Second Reader.
20. I. Arithmetic.
15. IV. Arithmetic.
15. Recess or Gymnastics.
15. III. Arithmetic.
15. II. Arithmetic.
15. I. and II. Spelling.
20. Primary and Intermediate Language.
20. General Exercise (Observation Lesson).

INTERMISSION.

15. Grammar.
15. First Reader and Number.
15. Second Reader.
20. Third Reader.
25. Writing or Drawing.
15. Recess or Gymnastics.
15. I. Geography or History.
15. II. Geography.
20. Fourth Reader.
25. General Exercise.

Records and Reports. — The time and strength of the teacher should be given to no work which does not directly or indirectly conduce to the welfare of the school. No records for mere show should be kept, nor reports and averages be made out which appeal to the pride of any one, or which serve as an artificial stimulant to study.

Statistics of the age and attendance of pupils in accordance with the requirements of the State should be kept, and such records as will enable the teacher to note the progress of his pupils and to aid him in placing them where they will do the most for themselves.

For the purpose of informing the parents of the character of their children's work and of securing their co-operation, blanks should be filled out either periodically or when occasion requires. It is well for parents to receive a report as often as once a month. This report should indicate in a general way how the pupil is doing in each branch of study and what his conduct is. It should not contain the standing of the pupil with reference to others in his class, nor is it necessary to indicate fine distinctions, such as would be made by per cent marks. All that it is necessary to give in the report is what the teacher would give in reply to the parents' questions: How is my child doing in each branch of study? What is his behavior? What is his attendance? The following report for grammar-school pupils is suggested. It should be upon a card six or seven inches long and four or five inches wide. The months can be indicated to suit the circumstances.

PUBLIC SCHOOLS.

————•◦•————

Report of --

------------------------------*School.* ------------------*Class.*

For the Month of	Reading.	Spelling.	Arithmetic.	Language.	Writing.	Drawing.	Geography.	History.	Conduct.	Days absent.	Times tardy.	Signature of Parent or Guardian.
SEPT.												
OCT.												
NOV.												
DEC.												
JAN.												

To the Parent or Guardian:

A means Excellent; B, Good; C, Fair; D, Poor; E, Very Poor.

If the Scholarship or Deportment continues to be poor, will you please call at the schoolroom for further particulars, especially if poor health or any other circumstance prevents h.... from doing more work. Irregularity of attendance greatly interferes with the progress of the pupil, and may oblige h.... to repeat the work of a term or year. You are cordially invited to visit the school at any time.

Please sign and return as soon as possible.

------------------------------*Teacher.*

--*School,*

-------------,---------------------- *188___.*

M_____

You will see by _____
Monthly Report that _____ is not doing thoroughly
the work of the School. Thus far this term neither
the written examination nor daily work indicate
that it will be best for _____ to go into a higher
division next _____, but that it may be
necessary to review the present studies another term.
If, however, you think it possible or best for _____
to do more work, will you please call here at the
Schoolroom, or drop me a note, so that we can have
a better understanding of _____ needs and capacity,
and arrange the work with reference to them.

Respectfully,

----------------------------*Teacher.*

Please sign and return this.

[Place for signing.]_____

_____*School,*

_____,_____ *188*___.

*M*_____

_____*deportment*

at school is not satisfactory.

I think it best to inform you of the fact, that all influences may be brought to bear upon _____ *before any serious form of punishment is resorted to.*

_____

_____

_____

Respectfully,

_____*Teacher.*

To aid in maintaining good order, please sign and return this.

*[Place for signing.]*_____

[To be sent to the School Committee or Superintendent.]

REPORT OF THE PUNISHMENT

*of*_____[NAME] _____[AGE]

_____*Residence.*

*Date of Punishment,*_____*188*____.

THE TEACHER WILL PLEASE WRITE ANSWERS TO THE FOLLOWING:

1. In what manner was the above-named pupil punished?_____

_____

2. What was the offence?_____

_____

3. What was his general character?_____

_____

4. What do you know of the home influences surrounding him?_____

_____

5. What other means have you employed for his reform?_____

_____

6. Were his parents duly notified of his conduct before you resorted to corporal

   punishment?_____

   What was the response?_____

_____

7. Has he ever been referred to the Principal or Superintendent?_____

   How many times?_____

8. What was the result of the punishment?_____

_____

_____*Teacher.*

MORAL TRAINING AND SCHOOL GOVERNMENT.

If we ask ourselves seriously the question, What is education for? there will arise in our minds a train of reasoning which will lead to the conclusion that the building up of character is not only a great and important part of education, but that it is really the only end to be sought. To know how to buy and sell commodities, to be able to learn the ideas of others through the printed page, and to be able to express to others our ideas by writing, — all these acquirements are good and useful for us to have; but they are good and useful only so far as we put them to a good use in right living, — only so far as our actions are the expression and ultimation of a high and unselfish purpose of being useful to others.

Acknowledging that moral training for the young is necessary, we have first to inquire whether any part of that work belongs to the school. It is said by some that the function of the school is to cultivate the intellect alone, and that moral training belongs to the home. There is no question that the home should have a large share in the moral training of the child. It is a fact, however, patent to all, that there are many homes in almost all communities which do nothing to elevate the condition of the young, and if example counts for anything, as we know it does, there are thousands of children to-day who are becoming worse rather than better, by constant association with unprincipled parents. For the sake of these children and for the protection of the community some means must be provided to do what parents leave undone.

But it is said that moral training belongs to the church. An hour or two a week of counsel and instruction, however good the counsel and instruction may be, is not enough to counteract the bad influences constantly surrounding the child. And even if the church should do more than it now does, it cannot afford to scorn assistance which the school is able to give. Again, we are told that there is moral power gained by cultivating the intellect alone. This is undoubtedly true to a certain extent, but the elevating influence of mere mental training is much exaggerated in the minds of most people. Indeed, when we see the rapidly increasing amount of worse than useless literature which is being read by persons possessed of the rudiments of learning only, we may well wonder if a little learning or only learning is not a most dangerous thing. No ; it belongs to the school, and to the school mainly, to lead the young into habits of " complete living," which depends quite as much upon the cultivation of the sensibilities and will as upon the cultivation of the intellect or the acquisition of knowledge.

Regular Studies, Means, not Ends.—"But," says the overworked teacher, struggling with his crowded course of studies, " where is the time for all this ? " Here is implied the greatest mistake of our common-school system, — the notion that the branches of study are so many separate subjects to be taught and studied as ends rather than as means. The subjects which may be classed under the general head of " Morals," and which should be taught in school, may perhaps take no set time for presentation; yet there should be no time of the school in which they are not in the mind of the teacher, ready for use whenever an opportunity presents itself. The instruction need not be by formal lectures, though these are by no means as objectionable as many would have us believe, especially if they are given in the form of familiar illustrations or stories. But the spirit of these virtues should so pervade the atmosphere of the schoolroom as to give to the child every hour of the day newer and higher ideas of his relation to others. Even in the regular studies must the teacher keep in mind their ethical side.

In reading, the children should be brought into close contact with all that is good, true, and beautiful in human life. By means of the printed page the best examples of practical wisdom and goodness are set before them. While they are learning these lessons, they are learning to look for goodness in others, and they are also learning to incorporate it in themselves. Continuous practice in reading will make such employment easy and pleasant; and if the reading is rightly directed, the habits thus formed will lead the children to seek the best literature after they leave school. And this direction should not be merely general and occasional: it must be particular and constant. Instead of talking about good reading, such reading should be brought into the schoolroom and read there. School libraries should be formed in every grammar and high school building, and the books from these libraries and from the public library should be used under the direct supervision and encouragement of the teacher. Let us not for a moment lose sight of the dangers which threaten our young people in the bad and unwholesome literature with which the shelves of our shops are loaded. That it is to-day poisoning the intellectual and moral life-blood of our people, no one who keeps his eyes open to what is going on about him can deny. As teachers we cannot expect to bring into healthy life these diseased minds. But we can and should do much to counteract the evil influences of our time by making the poison bitter or nauseous to the taste, and by creating a desire and love for the best literature.

What is true of reading is true of every branch of study taught in the schools. The end to be reached is not to cultivate the intellect of the pupils alone, nor to help them to gather facts together merely for the sake of possession; but it is to prepare them for the duties of life — to ennoble and to make more effective the employments upon which they are to enter. Therefore, in every subject taught, whether it be language, or history, or mathematics, or science, the one great end of education, "complete living," should be kept constantly in mind by the teacher.

The direct influence of good methods of teaching upon the behavior of children can scarcely be over-estimated. When subjects are presented in the right way, the interest in study and in the subjects studied is so great that the inclination to wrong-doing is prevented; and if the child has evil tendencies or has formed bad habits, they can be corrected much more easily if he has acquired a good method of doing, and a love of doing, some useful work.

Influence of Example. — We must recognize the fact that a child is guided in his early years more by his feelings than by any intellectual perception of right and wrong. We must remember, also, that he is by nature imitative in all his acts, and that the influence of example is especially powerful in these early years. Whatever is wrong in the conduct of the parent or teacher will be, we may be sure, incorporated to some degree in the child's life. The personal surroundings of the child, therefore, come to be an important factor of his education. Reverence, truthfulness, sincerity, and unselfishness make their first and strongest impressions upon the child when they are practised in the lives of those who are about him, and especially of those in whose charge he is and to whom he naturally looks for guidance.

The principle that the teacher should be all he would have his pupils be is a most important one, and exacts from him more than at first appears. Both in school and out he must be watchful, lest by the slightest word or act he swerves from the path in which he would lead his pupils. This high standard of living is demanded of the teacher not only for its direct influence upon the young, but also for the added power which his words of counsel will have.

MORAL INSTRUCTION.

Can anything more be done in school than is done in the regular studies to accomplish the highest ends of education? Two direct ways present themselves — ways that are at once practicable and effective. The first of these ways is instruction.

Regular Talks. — The use of regular talks with pupils upon subjects connected with morals has been spoken of. It is true that these exercises are deprecated by many teachers. But a little observation may convince us that those who deprecate most strongly the practice of giving regular talks to their pupils, seldom resort to other and better methods. Of course it would not be necessary or well to give set discourses upon the various virtues to young children. But if — say upon every Monday morning — the teacher should direct the attention of his pupils to some one subject, such as honesty, forgiveness, temperance, justice, kindness to animals, and the like, by giving appropriate illustrations and anecdotes, who can say that some seed may not be sown upon good ground? The stories may be of incidents in the lives of illustrious men and women, or they may be of incidents which have actually occurred within the observation of the teacher.

Incidental Instruction. — But useful as such exercises are, they should not take the place of what may be called incidental instruction. In every school events are constantly happening in connection with which some good lesson may be given at the time of their occurrence. A boy has, perhaps, found a knife and not restored it to the owner; or a pupil has copied a lesson or an examination from a classmate's paper; or the boys have been found playing marbles "for keeps": these and a hundred other incidents of school life may furnish the very best text for a talk with the pupils, when the wrong or injury done is fresh in their minds.

Devotional Exercise. — There is another exercise of the school which should have an elevating influence upon the children, and that is the devotional exercise. As commonly conducted, this exercise has little or no good moral influence; indeed, when conducted, as it too often is, in a cold, careless, or perfunctory way, there may be more harm than good done by it. Indifference on the part of the teacher induces indifference and disorder on the part of the pupils, and when disorder accompanies the devotional exercise, there is encouraged in the children a spirit of disregard and contempt for serious things which may affect the whole future of their lives. The devotional exercise must be marked by a devotional spirit on the part of the teacher. More will depend upon that than upon what is done. When the hands of the clock indicate that the time for opening has come, let every pupil be in his seat; and when there is absolute stillness in the room, — not before, — let the teacher take the Bible reverently in his hands and read slowly a few verses. Then let him repeat slowly and devoutly the prayer with which all are familiar, and to conclude let the children sing two stanzas of some familiar hymn. It may take less than five minutes for all this; but if it is done as it should be, in a subdued and devout spirit, it will have an effect upon all the subsequent work of the day. Moreover, it will lead the children to respect and venerate all the counsels that the teacher may give, for they see better than any one else that such counsels come from a Christian spirit of love.

Memorizing Gems. — Akin to this exercise in its effect is the recitation by the children of gems, — noble sentiments in prose and poetry. A stated number of lines weekly — say from five to ten — should be memorized and written correctly in books prepared for the purpose. For this purpose two or three of the best books of selections should be upon the table of every teacher. These and the ordinary reading-books will furnish material with which the children's minds may be elevated and enriched.

The second direct means of teaching morals is the regulation of conduct in the

GOVERNMENT OF THE SCHOOL.

Morals, as defined by Webster, is "the doctrine or practice of the duties of life, — manners, conduct, behavior." It is not necessary to discuss here the relation of morals as thus defined, to the morals which belong to religion; nor that other question which is constantly forced upon us, namely, whether we are not trenching upon ground which properly belongs to the church when we depart from purely intellectual training. Suffice it to say, that the morals which it is incumbent upon us to teach relate to the outward conduct of the individual in his relations with others, and that the character thus formed is the basis of the religious experience and life which follow. This idea by no means precludes the necessity of giving close attention to motives in older children. Indeed, without such attention the child may be led to believe that outward order or correctness of living is the only end to be sought independent of the governing motive. In this way hypocrisy — the most insidious of evils — unconsciously creeps into the life hidden behind a kind of "smartness," which is too often regarded as the highest virtue to be sought.

Toward what, then, shall we direct the steps of our children? To do contentedly and happily some useful work in the world; to resist temptations to do wrong, independent of external restraints; and in all the relations of life to treat others as he himself would be treated, — these are the characteristics of the life of a good man, and they are the ends toward which we should work in school. These can best be secured in the government of the school, by which is meant everything pertaining to the school life of the child.

There is nothing in the life of the good man or woman that cannot find its counterpart, or at least its image, in the schoolroom. The conditions of life in the school and in the world are much the same, and he is a wise teacher who makes the experience of the one a direct preparation for the experience of the other.

Formation of Habits. — We all know the tendency of repetition which the child has. If he does pleasurably or easily an act at any time, the presumption may be, that he will repeat the act at a convenient opportunity, and again repeat it, until a habit is formed. If the habit thus formed is a good one, as, for example, the habit of attention or of truthfulness, it will be a powerful means of mental or moral growth; but if it be a bad habit, as the habit of inattention or of deception, it will stand in the way of progress until by hard experience it is removed. The formation of a habit, therefore, is everywhere recognized as a powerful agent for good or ill in the child's education. Indeed, the usefulness of the school consists mainly in the formation of good habits. The habits of observation, of attention, and of industry, for example, are much more to the child than all the information he acquires; while in matters of conduct, the habits he forms in school are worth to him more than all other things combined.

We desire first of all to get the child into the habit
of doing just what we hope to have him do in after
life. We desire to have the good habits so fixed that he
will involuntarily act from them during the first few
years of childhood, and that afterwards they will be a
bulwark of defence against temptations, and will be
followed from a free and happy choice.

Obedience. — The habit of obedience stands first
among the best habits of childhood. In his earlier
years the child obeys implicitly, without asking for reasons; that is, he thus obeys if we have not been careless, inconsistent, and vacillating in the exercise of our
authority. Our will is his will in these early years, and
he is satisfied to have us regulate his conduct. Later,
he begins to desire to exercise his will, and demands
more frequently than before reasons for our denials of
his requests. All this may be a sign of development,
and his growing independence should be respected, and
even anticipated. We must not assume that the child
is always obstinate or wilful when he demurs or hesi-
tates. The fault may be partly our own. If we give a
thoughtful consideration to every request before our
decision is made, and then uniformly adhere to the
decision when it is made; if all our judgments are for
the best interests of the child, and we take pains to
make them appear so to him; if, in a word, the child
has confidence in our wisdom, there will be little or no
opposition on his part to our judgments as they are
given. But if we give our decisions in a hasty way,
considering them after they are given rather than before, or if our decisions are arbitrary, with no apparent
justice in them even to the child himself, there will be

much opposition on his part, not only to our unjust
decisions, but to all decisions we may give.

It cannot be denied that even with the greatest care
from the first, our will and the will of the child may
sometimes come into collision. Adverse conditions may
exist over which we have no control. The child's mind
or our own may be in an unhealthy state through sick-
ness of the body; frequent change of masters may be
made whose methods do not agree; or the child may
inherit a quick temper, which sometimes shows itself
very early in life. All these conditions or any one of
them may prevent prompt and willing obedience. But
generally it may be said that, if proper care is taken,
there will be little need of an active exercise of authority on our part, and that we shall never need to do
what some parents and teachers regard as necessary,
namely, break the will of the child by severe punishment. Sternness, and even severity, may be at times
necessary, but they should be exercised — and be seen
to be so exercised — in love and sorrow, rather than
in a hasty or angry manner, as too many commands
and punishments seem to be.

Truthfulness. — There are few qualities of childhood
more full of grace, and at the same time more full of
promise for the future, than that of open-hearted, sincere
truthfulness. How to secure it is indeed a difficult
task, all the more difficult from the fact that the earliest
forms of untruthfulness are likely to escape our notice
because they are so hidden. Sly evasions both in word
and deed, unfulfilled promises, exaggerated descriptions
of what has been seen, one-sided and colored accounts
of wrong done, — all these and many other forms of

untruthfulness need most careful management. It is surprising how careless we become in some matters which may have little effect upon our characters, but which have great influence upon children. It is a comparatively small thing, for instance, to tinge the description of an event or thing in such a way as to give a wrong impression to others. We may even encourage the children to do this, by manifesting interest or surprise in their descriptions when we know that they are not strictly accurate. Success or non-hindrance in equivocating leads the child still further on, until, before we are aware of it, deception and falsehood have fastened themselves upon his acts and words. The remedy lies in our vigilance in detecting the fault, and in our patience in correcting it every time it is seen. How this may be done will be spoken of in another place.

Industry. — The influence of the good school is in no way more plainly manifest than in the formation of the habit of industry. When the child first enters school, he should be given employment of a suitable kind; by frequent change he should be kept profitably and pleasantly occupied all the time he is in school. Generally, it may be said that idleness on the part of pupils indicates an improper kind or insufficient amount of work required. It is true that many pupils who are irregular in attendance find it difficult to apply their minds to the same kind of work as is given other pupils; and it is also true that, to do justice to all, the teacher cannot spend much extra time on these irregular pupils. But to as great an extent as possible, the requirements should be made to suit the state and capacity of every pupil, to the end of keeping all pupils at all times properly employed.

Order and Neatness. — To inculcate proper habits of order, the teacher finds it necessary to attend to little things which to an outsider may seem trivial. Such trifling offences as littering the floor with paper, or throwing the books in a heap together in the desk, or not returning a book to its proper place, must be corrected constantly; and it can be done in no better way than by having the child do properly what is left undone. The same may be said of carelessness and untidiness. No punishment is so good for the prevention of these faults as the prompt and unvarying correction of them by the pupil himself. It is well sometimes to appoint for each week a committee of two whose duty it is to inspect the desks and other parts of the room, and report to the teacher daily their condition as to order, etc.

It is desirable to have toilet appliances constantly at hand for the use of pupils who need them.

Politeness. — The duties of politeness, and a regard for the feelings of others, should be taught objectively in the every-day life of the school. Constant attention to these things will do much to fix a good habit, and make the common acts of courtesy in after life less irksome and difficult. No rudeness like laughing at the mistakes of others, or annoying them in any way, should ever be allowed. For every favor received proper acknowledgments should always be made. and for everything done which disturbs or incommodes others excuses should be given or an apology be offered. Who has not seen the marked effect of such a course of training given by some faithful teacher, and who can doubt that the improved manners of the children react in stimulating a better feeling toward others?

Contamination. — One of the most common charges against the public schools is that there is danger of contamination. It is a serious charge, and one to which we should give great heed. Wink at it as we may, there is real danger, where so many children are thrown together, that the better and more sensitive children will suffer by contact with others at recess and before and after school. Is it too much, under such circumstances, that the parents of such children ask, nay, demand, from us all the protection that we can give? To add to the teacher's burden of care, which is already great, seems almost unreasonable; but knowing as much as you do of the bad influence which some of your pupils may exert over others, what would you wish done, if you were a parent? Would you not prefer that your child should have no education if, in getting that education, he must be exposed to the degrading influence of vicious companions? But it must not be forgotten that while you are protecting the innocent and good, you are at the same time correcting the habits of the bad. The longer you keep a boy from the use of bad words, the less likely will he be to form the habit of using them. These are the principal reasons why you, or some teacher, should be within sight or hearing of your pupils at recess. There are other reasons. By directing and sympathizing with the children in their play, you will find that your hold upon them will be stronger in the schoolroom, and that you can lead them better there. Besides, you will find the fresh air and exercise as good and necessary for your bodily health as they are for your pupils. For all of these reasons we see that it is not only well, but necessary, for a teacher to be with his pupils *all* the time they are committed to his care.

The Condition of the School Premises. — It is not necessary to allude to the degrading effects of the improper words and pictures that are found on too many of our buildings. There is absolute demoralization and degradation not only to the authors of these markings, but to all the young and innocent children who see them, — evil effects which can never be effaced. Where defilement and symbols of impurity exist, it is *absolutely necessary for somebody to do something to remedy the evil.* The teachers who do not report to the school committee the bad condition of the buildings, and the committees who do not remedy it, are guilty of a most grievous wrong. When the objectionable markings are removed, and the buildings are restored, there should be constant vigilance on the part of the teachers. The doors of all buildings should be locked, and a system of inspection be inaugurated that will prevent a repetition of the evil.

We are inclined to place all these things outside of what we call the government of the school, whereas they are an important part of it. The truth of the "ounce of prevention" adage is nowhere more apparent than in the precautions which have been mentioned. But of all the precautions that can be taken by the teacher, none are more powerful in preventing disorder and cultivating the will than that of leading pupils to govern themselves.

Punishment. — Few schools can be conducted for any length of time without punishments of some form; and the success or failure of a teacher frequently depends upon the manner in which the punishments are administered. It becomes a matter of some importance, therefore, to know how to punish judiciously. The statement of a few principles and cautions may be helpful to some teachers.

1. Kindness, firmness, and justice should characterize every punishment. Punishments which tend only to irritate or degrade the offender should be avoided, such as pulling the hair or ears, confining pupils in a dark room, putting pepper upon the tongue, compelling pupils to wear a dunce-cap, using ridicule or sarcasm.

2. Punishments should never be arbitrary, but should as nearly as possible naturally follow the offence. Extra tasks, for example, should never be given pupils for misconduct, not only because there is no connection between the offence and punishment, but because such a course tends to make pupils dislike study.

3. Penalties should be consistent and uniform; that is, an offence should not be punished at one time, which is passed over in silence at another time. Never threaten, or at least never promise what cannot be carried out to the letter. Inconsistency and vacillation in the matter of punishment have caused more failures in discipline than anything else.

4. While the power to punish corporeally should not be denied teachers, such punishment should be given but seldom. A teacher who teaches well, and who is able to keep his pupils constantly employed, one who is quick to detect the signs of disorder, and who is skil-

ful in preventing it, is likely never to have a case of corporal punishment. Others, through want of experience and tact, may be obliged to resort to corporal punishment to maintain their authority. If such punishment is unavoidable, let it be clearly known what it is for, and let it be dispassionately given. It might be well, to avoid any danger of passion, to keep the instrument used for punishment in a place not easily reached. An hour at least should intervene between the offence and the punishment. The punishment should be upon the hand, and with a light rattan. It should not be so slight as to excite contempt, nor so severe as to do injury to the mind or body of the offender. As a rule, it should not be administered in the presence of other pupils. As a safeguard against mistakes, a report of every case of corporal punishment should be sent to the school committee or superintendent. A blank for such a report is given on page 320.

Conditions of Good Government. — The most frequent and at the same time the gravest fault of discipline, is the encouragement of deception. The offence, in the eyes of the pupils, is generally " *being found out,*" not the wrong done. A good disciplinarian is, in the estimation of many, not only one who is strong enough to punish his pupils vigorously, but one who is sharp enough to catch them at their tricks. Too many schools are governed on the assumption that the governor and the governed naturally pull in opposite directions; that the children are necessarily the sworn enemies of the teacher, and he of them. The essential elements of good government are, first, a friendly public sentiment in favor of law and order; and, secondly, a disposition on the part of the larger portion of the governed to do right, not merely because they are commanded by law to do so, but because it is right. Without these conditions no government can long continue, and without them society can scarcely be called civilized. Without these conditions, also, no school can be said to be civilized, or at least civilizing in its influence. It is a wrong estimate to make upon the moral strength of older boys and girls, to assume that they need to be tended like babies, on the one hand, or watched like criminals, on the other, — an assumption which tends to deprive them of the opportunity of exercising their freedom of choice between right and wrong.

Self-Control. — With the young child this principle is kept out of sight to a great degree; but as he advances in age he is led to depend less and less upon others and more upon himself. It is for us, therefore, to place before him higher and higher motives of action. At least, we should not appeal, as many do, to the low motives; such as the fear of punishment and the desire for high per cent marks.

We should encourage, so far as we can and so soon as we can, the performance of duties based upon the principle that the doer is to exercise self-control and self-denial, because it is best for him to do so. The school is a miniature world, and there are few trials, perplexities, privileges, and enjoyments of active life in the world which are not experienced to a greater or less degree in the schoolroom. Who are the best citizens? They who govern themselves. Who are the most useful members of society? They who look to the welfare and comfort of others. Who are best prepared to meet the difficulties which contact with the world is sure to bring? Plainly, they who have met and mastered similar ones while they were young. Self-government and a sacred regard for the welfare of others should, therefore, be the guiding principles in the government of the school.

Illustrative Example. — To see more clearly how children may be led into habits of truthfulness and self-control, let us go somewhat into details. You are, it may be, before a new class or school. What is your first duty? Plainly, not to read a lecture upon the importance of being good; nor to expound a long set of rules. Let your manner, on entering the school, give them assurance that you are the friend of the pupils and glad to be with them. If you say anything, simply say that you have come to help them, and that you hope they will let you. Nothing need be said of order. Let the assumption be at the outset that there will be no disorder. Set the school to work as soon as possible, and endeavor to make the work pleasant and agreeable. Upon the first violation of good order, say to the offender and to the school that that particular offence, and everything like it, ought never to be committed, and then tell them *the reason why.* Be sure that this is not omitted, for you must remember that your first purpose is to bring your pupils over to your side, and you can best do this by establishing a reputation for kindness and fairness at the start. Soon there is, perhaps, more disorder of a similar kind. Now comes your first really practical lesson in self-control. Your question is, " Did you know that I do not want

that done?" or, "Would you have done that if I had •
been looking?" If the pupil says that he did not know
that you do not want it done, tell him plainly again,
and the reason for the prohibition, as before. It is
neither right nor politic for the teacher to assume,
as many do, that every offence comes from malicious
intent. Then may be given what will have to be
repeated hundreds of times, in one form or another, the
Golden Rule of the schoolroom, "*Do nothing that you
would not do if the eye of the teacher were upon you.*"
Either the words or spirit of this rule must be kept
constantly in mind and uniformly followed.

So far you have imposed few restraints. Let this
course be continued as long as possible, and whenever
the liberty of pupils is abridged, see to it that they
have a good reason for it. Also impress upon them
by practice the fact that the rules which govern their
behavior are practically made by themselves, and that
to abuse any privilege they may have, ought of course
to deprive them of the privilege.

But to go back to the first day with our new class.
By your kindness and evident fairness, you have won
the respect of the better part of your class. This will
be a powerful help to you in leading the more wilful
and refractory part of your school. You go on with
the work of the school, showing that you trust every
member of it. At length there is disturbance in the
room from one or more, or it may be that you leave
the room for a moment and find upon your return
evidences of disorder. Stop the work, and ask the
attention of the school for a moment. Say to them
that you are sorry to know that there is any one who

is willing to do wrong because he is not watched. Show how weak such a boy or girl must be. Compare him with those unfortunate and weak men and women who have to dodge the policeman for fear he will see them; show the injustice that is done others in making you suspect some who are really innocent, and who are trying to do their best. Now is the time to get them to agree with you that it is much better, and entirely within the power of every pupil, to govern his own conduct. Then it will be an easy matter for you to exact a pledge from every boy and girl under your charge that an effort will be made in this direction. Do not require too much at this point. They have made a reasonable promise, one they are able to keep, when they promise to *try* to take care of themselves. If they promise no more than this, you will have a far greater hold upon them than if you made them promise that they *would* govern themselves. You know, and they will discover after a time, that they would break such a promise; but you know, and they know, that they can and ought to keep the promise to try.

Sooner or later you come to the time, in the natural order of events, when one or more of your pupils have not done as they promised to do. That is, you have found them dodging you, or doing something disorderly behind your back, or in your absence from the room. *The first case* of this kind demands your prompt attention. It is a most trying time for you. The pupils' estimate of their teacher's wisdom and justice is in suspense. Upon your action at this time may depend the success or failure of your plan. The punishment must not be too slight, nor must it be too severe. Above all, it must not be arbitrary ; but this, as every punishment, must naturally follow the offence. What is the offence? Deception. Doing a thing because you were not looking. Plainly, then, the punishment for him should be that he must be watched, — he of all the school ; no one else. It is a notoriety that he does not like ; but he sees, and all his mates see, that it is just. Let him understand, however, that he will be trusted as he proves his sincerity in really trying to govern himself.

By this time your pupils are thoroughly convinced that you are in earnest (that is, if you *are* in earnest) in discouraging something wrong. What is it? Deception in every form. They learn, too, that you are in earnest in encouraging something good and right. What is it? Obedience to authority and self-control.

You may have occasion to resort to various appeals before you can bring your pupils to do right in all things because it is best. One means of encouragement may be the " roll of honor," consisting of all who are not in the least deceptive, but who are open and honorable in all their actions. They are trusted fully and entirely by you, and they will be found to assist in everything pertaining to the welfare of the school. Again, there may be others, — a very small number if the right methods are pursued, — who do not control their own conduct, and who are not making an effort to do so. These pupils demand your serious attention. They are afflicted with a moral disease, and they should be most carefully treated. They should be labored with, both in and out of school. The help of their parents and of the other pupils should be sought, and every inducement placed before them to change their course. When punishment is resorted to, it should be in a kind and just spirit, and as near as possible a direct consequence of the offence. In extreme cases all social privileges may be taken away from the offending pupil while he is in or near the schoolhouse, he not being allowed the privilege of playing with or speaking to his mates. He is to be kept entirely apart from the rest of the school, on the principle that his influence is dangerous and harmful.

Thus you will go on from day to day, following out patiently this or some other well-defined plan, until success crowns your efforts; not the fullest and most complete success, perhaps, but such a degree as encourages you to believe that every one of your pupils is affected by a desire and purpose to do right, — not from fear of any external consequence, but from choice.

Sympathy. — But whatever you do for your pupils, whether it is by example or precept, whether it is to enlarge their understandings or to elevate and strengthen their purposes, do not forget that crowning grace of the teacher — sympathy. It is a bond between the teacher and his pupils by means of which his influence will be felt, and without which the highest results of his work cannot be realized.

The example of the wisest teachers may well be followed by us. Shall we ever forget the pictures drawn for us in "Schooldays at Rugby," where the old doctor is seen at all times as a sympathizing friend and companion to the boys? Can we wonder at the influence of Pestalozzi which has extended throughout the world, and which is felt to-day by us all, as we call to mind the patience with which he worked among those beggar children at Stanz, gaining their love by the power of his love and sympathy? Do we not recall with gratitude the devotion with which the founder of the kindergarten studied the games and plays of little children, to know how best he could enter into their states and lead them? It is for us to imitate the noble example of these great teachers, and, so far as we can, work with and for the children who are placed in our care. Whether we have to do with the child of poverty or the child of wealth, whether the child is bright or dull, whether good or bad, we must remember that the destiny and happiness of a human being are partly in our hands, and that only as we perceive the states and feel the needs of the child are we instrumental in guiding him into a higher manhood.

THE

NATIONAL MUSIC COURSE.

BY

LUTHER WHITING MASON, formerly Supervisor of Music, Boston, and recently Director of Music, Japan; **JULIUS EICHBERG,** Director of Music, Boston; and **J. B. SHARLAND,** Supervisor of Music, Boston.

~~~~~~~~~~

FIRST AWARDS AT THE UNIVERSAL EXPOSITIONS OF

VIENNA, 1873.   PARIS, 1878

PHILADELPHIA, 1876.   NEW ORLEANS, 1885.

More than any other *endorsed by wide use and satisfactory results.*
More than any other *approved by musical authorities here and abroad.*
More than any other *recommended on a careful examination of its merits.*
More than any other *enjoyed by the teachers who teach and the children who study it.*

~~~~~~~~~~

THE NEW SERIES IS NOW READY:

New First Reader, New Second Reader, New Third Reader, Independent Reader, Abridged Fourth Reader, New High School Reader.

New First, New Second, and New Third Series of Charts.

The new books and charts retain the best features of the old, and add the fruits of farther experience and study.

WENTWORTH & REED'S

FIRST STEPS IN NUMBER.

TEACHERS' EDITION.

VI + 474 pp. Retail Price, $1.25. Also issued in
Three Parts, at 40 cents each, retail.
Special terms to Agents.

PHILADELPHIA, Pa. — These books are in exact accord with the methods of teaching primary arithmetic now required in the Philadelphia schools. JAMES MacALISTER, *Superintendent.*

PROVIDENCE, R.I. — It is admirable in plan, and thoroughly worked out in its details. It deserves an immense success.

H. S. TARBELL, *Superintendent.*

NEW HAVEN, Conn. — We have recently placed "First Steps in Number" in the hands of all our primary teachers, and it is proving a most valuable aid to their work. S. T. DUTTON, *Superintendent.*

CHICAGO, Ill. — It is unique. There is no other book of the kind to be compared with it. O. T. BRIGHT, *Prin. Douglas School.*

GRAND RAPIDS, Mich. — I regard it as the best primary arithmetic that I have ever seen — an inspiration to a good teacher, and an invaluable aid to a poor one. I. N. MITCHELL, *Superintendent.*

FREE TO TEACHERS:

◁ "HOW TO TEACH NUMBER," ▷

An Outline of the Method of this Book.

FIRST STEPS IN NUMBER. — PUPILS' EDITION. Introduction Price, 30 cents; allowance for old book, 12 cents.

WENTWORTH'S GRAMMAR SCHOOL ARITHMETIC. Introduction Price, 75 cents; allowance for old book, 30 cents.

——————*A Complete Two-Book Course.*——————

SAMPLE COPIES POSTPAID ON RECEIPT OF THE INTRODUCTION PRICE.

GINN & COMPANY, Publishers,

BOSTON, NEW YORK, AND CHICAGO.

CLASSICS FOR CHILDREN.

Choice Literature; Full Notes; Large Type; Firm Binding; Low Prices.

Each of the volumes is printed in large type, on good paper, and firmly bound. Each is complete; or abridged, where cutting has been necessary, by a skilful hand, without impairment of style or story. Illustrations, when desirable, are freely used. Illustrated books are indicated by stars. The prices have been made as low as possible. An edition has been bound in cloth, omitting the headline "Classics for Children." The books may be had in sets, boxed.

Hans Andersen's Fairy Tales.
    *First Series: Supplementary to the Third Reader.
    *Second Series: Supplementary to the Fourth Reader.

*Æsop's Fables, with selections from Krilof and La Fontaine.

*Kingsley's Water-Babies: A Story for a Land Baby.

*Ruskin's King of the Golden River: A Legend of Stiria.

*The Swiss Family Robinson. Abridged.

Robinson Crusoe. Concluding with his departure from the island.

*Kingsley's Greek Heroes.

Lamb's Tales from Shakespeare. " Meas. for Meas." omitted.

Scott's Tales of a Grandfather.

*Martineau's Peasant and Prince.

Scott's Lady of the Lake.

Lamb's Adventures of Ulysses.

Church's Stories of the Old World.

Scott's Talisman. Complete.

Scott's Quentin Durward. Slightly abridged.

Irving's Sketch Book. Six Selections, including " Rip Van Winkle."

Shakespeare's Merchant of Venice.

Scott's Guy Mannering. Complete.

Scott's Ivanhoe. Complete.

Johnson's Rasselas: Prince of Abyssinia.

Gulliver's Travels. The Voyages to Lilliput and Brobdingnag.

*Plutarch's Lives. From Clough's translation.

OTHERS ARE IN PREPARATION. SEND FOR FULL CIRCULAR.

GINN & COMPANY, Publishers,

Boston, New York, and Chicago.

ELEMENTARY LESSONS

IN ENGLISH.

These admirable books harmonize and utilize to a surprising degree most, if not all, of the practical advantages of conflicting theories.

— Dr. G. STANLEY HALL, *Johns Hopkins University.*

Their universal use would raise many schoolmasters to the rank of *teachers.*

— *State Supt.* M. A. NEWELL, *Md.*

Need only their presence to recommend them.

— F. W. PARKER, *Prin. Cook Co. Normal School, Ill.*

The brightest and most practical book on the subject yet published.

— *Supt.* J. O. WILSON, *Washington, D.C.*

None more suggestive and helpful to the young teacher.

— *Supt.* GEO. HOWLAND, *Chicago, Ill.*

Better than any other.

— *Supt.* JOHN B. PEASLEE, *Cincinnati.*

The *only* books that meet the wants of our elementary schools.

— E. V. DE GRAFF, *Institute Conductor.*

GINN & COMPANY, Publishers,
BOSTON, NEW YORK, AND CHICAGO.

This book is what the schools have been waiting for.
It has had no predecessors, and it has
no rivals.

— ALBERT SHAW, *Ed. Minneapolis Tribune.*

———◆———

Our Government:

HOW IT GREW; WHAT IT DOES; AND HOW IT DOES IT.

By JESSE MACY,

Professor of History and Political Science in Iowa College.

---

250 pp. Cloth. Mailing Price, 88 cts.; for Introduction, 80 cts.

---

*Everything in it is intelligible to school children,
and important for them to know.* — A. D. MORSE, *Prof. of
Hist. and Polit. Econ., Amherst College.*

*It is certainly very philosophical, and at the same
time very simple.* — A. B. WATKINS, *Asst. Secy., University of
New York.*

*It ought to be introduced in every high school and
academy.* — A. D. WHARTON, *Prin. of High School, Nashville, Tenn.*

*The idea of Prof. Macy is a clear-cut one, and it
seems to me to be an inspiration.* — EDWARD TAYLOR, *Supt.
of Schools, Vincennes, Ind.*

*It is certainly the best book of the kind that has
been prepared for use in our schools.* — L. C. HULL, *Prin.
of High School, Detroit.*

It is a delightful book. It is just what we want. —
J. M. SWETT, *Prin. of Girls' High and Normal Schools, San Francisco.*

COMBINED
NUMBER AND LANGUAGE LESSONS.

Designed for the Second Year of School (Second Grade of Primary).

BY F. B. GINN AND IDA A. COADY.

TEACHERS' MANUAL.

Retail and Mailing Price, **60 cents;** *for Introduction,* **50 cents.**

This book contains an oral and also a written lesson in number, and also a lesson in language for each school day in the year, together with full directions for the teacher. By this arrangement all the pupils in the same grade are required to do the same work at the same time, and in a similar manner. Such uniformity of work is very important in a graded school, where transfers must frequently be made, and pupils go from several rooms to form a class in a higher grade. The school work is also better graduated by these lessons than it can be where the teacher prepares lessons for her class from day to day.

LESSONS FOR SEAT-WORK.

These lessons are bound in four blocks, or tablets, each of which contains ninety-four lessons, covering ten weeks. Forty-seven are number lessons, and forty-seven are language lessons. Directions for the work are printed in script at the top of the page. The rest of each of the odd pages is single-ruled for number work. When the number work is done, the sheet is torn off, and on the other side of it is a script language lesson, with a double-ruled page. By this arrangement the page is clean and new each day; and, when finished, the sheet may be taken home to show what has been done in school.

The price for each tablet is, at retail, **10 cents;** *for introduction,* **8 cents.**

GINN & COMPANY, Publishers,
BOSTON, NEW YORK, AND CHICAGO.

www.ingramcontent.com/pod-product-compliance
Lightning Source LLC
Chambersburg PA
CBHW021105270326
41929CB00009B/745